AQA GCSE
FRENCH
Foundation

Séverine Capjon
Amandine Moores
Paul Shannon
Consultant: Christophe Fico

OXFORD
UNIVERSITY PRESS

Great Clarendon Street, Oxford, OX2 6DP, United Kingdom

Oxford University Press is a department of the University of Oxford. It furthers the University's objective of excellence in research, scholarship, and education by publishing worldwide. Oxford is a registered trade mark of Oxford University Press in the UK and in certain other countries.

© Oxford University Press 2024

The moral rights of the authors have been asserted

First published in 2024

All rights reserved. No part of this publication may be reproduced, stored in a retrieval system, or transmitted, used for text and data mining, or used for training artificial intelligence, in any form or by any means, without the prior permission in writing of Oxford University Press, or as expressly permitted by law, by licence or under terms agreed with the appropriate reprographics rights organization. Enquiries concerning reproduction outside the scope of the above should be sent to the Rights Department, Oxford University Press, at the address above.

You must not circulate this work in any other form and you must impose this same condition on any acquirer

British Library Cataloguing in Publication Data
Data available

978-1-38-204573-5

978-0-19-830892-8 (ebook)

10 9 8 7 6 5 4 3 2 1

The manufacturing process conforms to the environmental regulations of the country of origin.

Printed in Great Britain by Bell and Bain Ltd., Glasgow

This textbook has been approved by AQA for use with our qualification. This means that we have checked that it broadly covers the specification and we are satisfied with the overall quality. Full details of our approval process can be found on our website.

We approve textbooks because we know how important it is for teachers and students to have the right resources to support their teaching and learning. However, the publisher is ultimately responsible for the editorial control and quality of this book.

Please note that when teaching the AQA GCSE French course, you must refer to AQA's specification as your definitive source of information. While this book has been written to match the specification, it cannot provide complete coverage of every aspect of the course.

A wide range of other useful resources can be found on the relevant subject pages of our website: aqa.org.uk

Contents

Introduction	7–9
Useful language	10–11
Sound–spelling links	12–13

Theme 1 People and lifestyle — 14

Introduction: Identity and relationships with others; Healthy living and lifestyle	14
Introduction: Education and work	16

Unit 1 – Identity and relationships with others — 18

Spread title	Verb focus	Grammar focus	Pronunciation focus	Page
1.1G Qui suis-je?	The present tense of regular -er verbs	The position of adjectives		18
1.1F Ma personnalité	The present tense of regular -re verbs	Adjective agreement	Silent final -e and final consonants	20
1.2G Voici ma famille	Reflexive verbs in the present tense	qui		22
1.2F Les familles de nos jours	The present tense of regular -ir verbs	Comparative adjectives	-aill- / -ail and -ill- / -ille	24

Unit 2 – Healthy living and lifestyle — 26

Spread title	Verb focus	Grammar focus	Pronunciation focus	Page
2.1G On mange!	Negative sentences	The position of adverbs		26
2.1F Aïe aïe aïe!	The near future tense	Plural nouns		28
2.2G Mon mode de vie	Imperatives in the tu form	Interrogative adjective: quel	qu	30
2.2F Hier, j'ai…	The perfect tense of regular verbs with avoir	Indirect object pronouns		32

Unit 3 – Education and work — 34

Spread title	Verb focus	Grammar focus	Pronunciation focus	Page
3.1G Les règles scolaires	pouvoir and devoir	Ordinal numbers		34
3.1F Lycée et université?	Negative constructions	Nouns ending in -ation	-tion	36
3.2G Quel métier pour toi?	il faut + infinitive	Feminine person nouns		38
3.2F Mon métier créatif	il y a and il y aura	Indefinite adjectives	c and ç; s, qu and th	40

trois

Contents

Culture: Mon métier francophone		42
Grammar practice		44
Vocabulary		48
Test and revise	Listening	52
	Speaking	54
	Reading	56
	Writing	58

Theme 2 Popular culture — 60

Introduction: Free-time activities — 60

Introduction: Customs, festivals and celebrations; celebrity culture — 62

Unit 4 – Free-time activities

Spread title	Verb focus	Grammar focus	Pronunciation focus	Page
4.1G Qu'est-ce que tu aimais faire?	The imperfect tense of regular verbs	Adverbs ending in -ment		64
4.1F Le week-end dernier	The perfect tense with *avoir*: irregular past participles	Emphatic pronouns (*moi, toi*)	*u* and *ou*; *oi* and *oy*	66
4.2G Sport ou musique?	Revising the near future tense	Partitive articles (*du, de la, de l', des*)	-tion, -sion, -ssion	68
4.2F En voyage!	The perfect tense with *être*	*en* and *à* with places	*e* and *eu*; *é, er* and *ez*	70

Unit 5 – Customs, festivals and celebrations

Spread title	Verb focus	Grammar focus	Pronunciation focus	Page
5.1G Les journées spéciales	*C'est* and *il y a*	Question words and subject–verb inversion		72
5.1F Bon anniversaire!	The present tense of common irregular verbs	Direct object pronouns (*me, te, vous, le, la*)	-eur / -œur and *r*	74
5.2G On a fait la fête!	Revising the perfect tense with *avoir* and *être*	Forming irregular plural nouns	Liaison	76
5.2F Les fêtes dans le passé et à l'avenir	Two tenses together (past and near future)	Functions of definite and indefinite articles		78

quatre

Contents

Unit 6 – Celebrity culture

Spread title	Verb focus	Grammar focus	Pronunciation focus	Page
6.1G J'ai eu du succès!	The perfect tense of *avoir*, *être*, *faire* and *prendre*	*de* to show possession		80
6.1F Vous voulez être célèbre?	The imperative (*tu* and *vous* forms)	Infinitives used as nouns	*i*, *y* and *-ien*	82
6.2G Je sais réussir!	*Savoir* + infinitive	Demonstrative adjectives (*ce*, *cet*, *cette*, *ces*)	*è*, *ê*, *ai* and *c'est*, *ces*, *sais*	84
6.2F La vie de célébrité	The present tense of *avoir*, *etre*, *faire* and *aller*	Possessive adjectives	*j*, *g*, *ch* and *gn*	86

Culture: Les Jeux de la Francophonie		88
Grammar practice		90
Vocabulary		94

Test and revise		
	Listening	98
	Speaking	100
	Reading	102
	Writing	104

Theme 3 Communication and the world around us — 106

Introduction: Travel and tourism; media and technology	106
Introduction: The environment and where people live	108

Unit 7 – Travel and tourism, including places of interest

Spread title	Verb focus	Grammar focus	Pronunciation focus	Page
7.1G Le temps pendant les vacances	Weather expressions	Adjectives ending in *-able*		110
7.1F Les îles francophones	The imperfect tense of *être*, *avoir* and *faire*	Revising adjective agreement	*è*, *ê*, *ai* and *a*	112
7.2G Mes visites de touriste	Revising the perfect tense	Prepositions for countries and modes of transport		114
7.2F Vacances de rêve	Two tenses together: perfect and imperfect	*pour* and *sans* + infinitive	Open *o*	116

cinq 5

Contents

Unit 8 – Media and technology

Spread title	Verb focus	Grammar focus	Pronunciation focus	Page
8.1G Les médias	Revising regular verbs in the present tense	Revising infinitive verbs		118
8.1F Le monde avant et après Internet	Present and past tenses together	Opinion / modal verbs + infinitive	*au*, *eau*, closed *o* and *ô*	120
8.2G Ton portable, ta vie	Revising *être*, *avoir*, *faire* and *aller* in the present tense	*avant de* + infinitive		122
8.2F J'utilise la technologie!	Three time frames	Adjectives beginning with *in-* or *im-*	*en* / *an* / *em* / *am*, *on* / *om*, *ain* / *in* / *aim* / *im* and *un*	124

Unit 9 – The environment and where people live

Spread title	Verb focus	Grammar focus	Pronunciation focus	Page
9.1G Tu es écolo?	Verbs + *à* / *de* + infinitive	*a* and *à*	*a* and *à*	126
9.1F Sauvons la planète!	*je voudrais*	Infinitives used as nouns		128
9.2G Une visite chez mon ami	Revising the perfect tense with *avoir* and *être*	*de* after a negative or expression of quantity		130
9.2F Un guide de ma ville	Modal verbs in the present tense	*si* and *quand*	*h*	132

		Page
Culture: Cannes, la ville des médias		134
Grammar practice		136
Vocabulary		140
Test and revise	Listening	144
	Speaking	146
	Reading	148
	Writing	150
Test and revise: all themes	Listening	152
	Speaking	154
	Reading	156
	Writing	158
Reference	Grammar	160
	Verb tables	174
	Glossary	180

Introducing AQA GCSE French

| Learning vocabulary | Sound–spelling links | Translation skills | Writing | Reading & reading aloud |

| Dictation | Speaking | Culture | Grammar knowledge | Listening |

Understanding how the specification works

The AQA GCSE French specification is divided into three main subject areas, called Themes. This book is divided up in the same way, with colour-coding to help you know where you are.

Theme 1 People and lifestyle

Theme 2 Popular culture

Theme 3 Communication and the world around us

Each theme is divided into three Topics, making a total of nine Topics to study during the course. The exam is divided up according to the four Language Skills: Listening, Speaking, Reading and Writing. Each one of these has its own separate exam, in the form of an end-of-course paper.

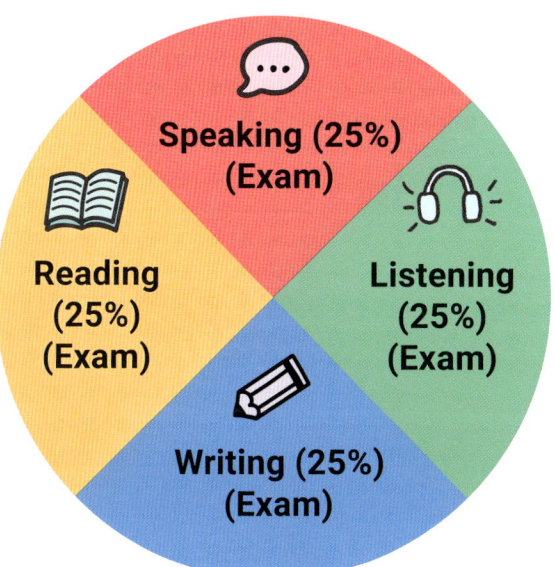

sept 7

Introduction

Useful language
The section on pages 10–11 provides useful key vocabulary and phrases which are commonly used in real-life, everyday situations.

🎙️ Phonics and sound–spelling links

- The section on pages 12–13 groups together all the sounds included in the *Phonétique* boxes and provides tips on how to pronounce widely used words and phrases to speak French confidently and clearly. Your knowledge of how spelling represents sounds will be tested through dictation and a read-aloud task in the exam.
- The *Phonétique* boxes cover all the common sounds in the French language and the sound–spelling links included in the specification, and include pronunciation tips.

> **Phonétique** 🎙️
>
> **Silent final -*e* and final consonants**
> In French, the final -*e* on a word is not pronounced:
> drôl**e**   timid**e**   frèr**e**   catastroph**e**

Themes and topics
Each Theme is divided into three Topics. Each Theme starts with two introductory double-page spreads introducing key themes, core vocabulary and structures that you may have covered at Key Stage 3. These pages provide an opportunity to recap and practise important language and/or lay the foundations for further learning.

The three Topics are then each covered over four double-page spreads, two at Groundwork level and two at Foundation level. Each spread introduces specification vocabulary and features a verb focus and a grammar focus. All the key skills required in the specification are also covered, including phonics and cultural knowledge.

Learning vocabulary
Vocabulary support is provided in various ways throughout the book and on Kerboodle:

- Vocabulary lists – the introductory double-page spreads at the start of each Theme include lists of key words and phrases practised in the texts and on the page. Vocabulary from each of the core spreads and the culture pages is listed in the vocabulary pages at the end of each Theme. Items highlighted in grey are words that are useful but do not appear in the specification. It is important that you learn the specification vocabulary.
- Vocabulary tasks – these help to build the vocabulary required in each topic of the specification.
- Interactive activities – the vocabulary builders on Kerboodle provide activities with instant feedback.*
- Glossary – the glossary at the back of the book combines the vocabulary from the Themes' vocabulary pages.

> ## Features
>
> ### 📖 Reading
> The Student Book contains plenty of French reading material on the Themes and Topics included within the specification. The activities that follow the reading passages help develop your comprehension skills so that you can access unfamiliar texts in the future.
>
> ### 🎧 Listening
> Activities with a listening icon next to them help you to improve listening comprehension skills. The audio can be accessed through Kerboodle.
>
> ### 💬 Speaking
> The speaking activities are designed to build your confidence in speaking French and to practise using the vocabulary you've learnt in the unit or Theme. There are also practice role plays and photo card activities throughout the book.
>
> ### ✏️ Writing
> The writing icon indicates an activity that will help you to use the language you've learnt to build sentences and paragraphs of written French.
>
> ### 🔀 Translation
> Translation activities throughout the book develop your ability to tackle translation tasks.

Introduction

Language support in speaking and writing

Examples of language to be used or language structure boxes are provided for some speaking and writing tasks. These can be used as models to build your own sentences.

Mon frère	est	plus	drôle(s) / sympa(s)	que…
Ma sœur		moins	timide(s) / strict(e)(s)	
Mon cousin		aussi	amusant(e)(s)	
Mes parents	sont		intelligent(e)(s)	

8 💬 In pairs, take turns to say what you would do in order to become famous.
Example: Pour devenir célèbre, je chercherais / je participerais à /

Building grammar knowledge

- Understanding grammar is key to understanding French and building your own phrases. *AQA GCSE French* helps you to consolidate and deepen your grammar knowledge in a logical way with no assumption of prior learning.
- Grammar boxes outline key grammar points, with accompanying activities on the same page to put theory into practice.

Grammaire

Using negative constructions

To make a sentence negative, use *ne … pas* around the verb:

- Additional grammar practice is also provided in two double-page spreads at the end of each Theme.
- Interactive activities on Kerboodle provide further consolidation with instant feedback.*
- There is a grammar section at the back of the Student Book to refer to whenever you need to.

Verbs

Specific emphasis is given to the formation of verbs and tenses, and how they are used.

Les verbes

The present tense of -re verbs

To form the present tense of regular -re verbs, remove -re from the infinitive and add the endings:

Culture

- Culture boxes throughout the book highlight aspects of Francophone culture relevant to each topic.

Culture

In France, students aged 11 to 15 go to *le collège* and at the end, they take exams called *le brevet*, equivalent

- There is a *Culture* double-page spread at the end of each Theme showcasing aspects of Francophone history, literature and contemporary culture.

Language tips

These boxes give extra support and information about what to look out for or how to do a particular activity.

Conseil

Use your knowledge of grammar, especially verbs and tenses, to choose the correct answer. Adverbs of time

Test and revise

There are regular revision and practice opportunities throughout the book in the four test and revise sections (one test per Theme and a cross-Theme test at the end of the book). Each test offers exam-style activities in the four skill areas.

Kerboodle

Kerboodle for *AQA GCSE French* provides resources focused on developing key grammar, vocabulary, phonics and all the language-learning and exam skills required at GCSE. This includes auto-marked interactive activities and tests, worksheets, listening activities with downloadable transcripts, practice questions and assessments, and comprehensive teacher support.

Interactive activities can be completed on tablets or mobile devices.

Kerboodle Books

Kerboodle Books are digital versions of the Student Books, which can be accessed on a range of devices and tablets.

Activities and audio can be launched directly from the page and individual users have their own digital notebook for use within their Kerboodle Book, in which they can use various tools and annotate pages to create their own personalised copy.

*These resources are not part of the AQA approval process.

neuf 9

Useful language

Numbers

French numbers can seem like a challenge, so it's best to revise and learn them in stages.

- Start with the numbers 1–16.

1 un	5 cinq	9 neuf	13 treize
2 deux	6 six	10 dix	14 quatorze
3 trois	7 sept	11 onze	15 quinze
4 quatre	8 huit	12 douze	16 seize

- Then you can combine the numbers you know to make others.

17	= 10 + 7	dix-sept
18	= 10 + 8	dix-huit
19	= 10 + 9	dix-neuf

Remember to link the two numbers with a hyphen, when you write them out as words.

- The next stage is to learn the multiples of 10 up to 60, and continue combining numbers as shown.

20	vingt
30	trente
40	quarante
50	cinquante
60	soixante

21 vingt et un, 22 vingt-deux,
27 vingt-sept, 31 trente et un,
35 trente-cinq, 49 quarante-neuf,
51 cinquante et un, 66 soixante-six

- The most challenging stage is to learn the numbers above 69. Here, again, it's about combining smaller numbers to make larger ones.

Look at these examples.

70	= 60 + 10	soixante-dix
71	= 60 + 11	soixante et onze
75	= 60 + 15	soixante-quinze
80	= 4 × 20	quatre-vingts
81	= 4 × 20 + 1	quatre-vingt-un
88	= 4 × 20 + 8	quatre-vingt-huit
90	= 4 × 20 + 10	quatre-vingt-dix
91	= 4 × 20 + 11	quatre-vingt-onze
93	= 4 × 20 + 13	quatre-vingt-treize
96	= 4 × 20 + 16	quatre-vingt-seize
99	= 4 × 20 + 19	quatre-vingt-dix-neuf

(Watch out for the 's' which appears at the end of *quatre-vingts* only.)

- Finally, you need to know *cent* (100) and *mille* (1000).

102 (*cent deux*)

Note *deux-cents* (200) but *deux cent deux* (202).

Numbers are useful to state ages:
J'ai quinze ans. Mon père a cinquante ans.

You also need numbers for prices: 10€ (*dix euros*), 5,50€ (*cinq euros cinquante*), 8,99€ (*huit euros quatre-vingt-dix-neuf*), 100€ (*cent euros*). Notice that French uses a comma, not a full stop, for the decimal point in prices.

Days and dates

- Remember that the days of the week are written with small letters in French.

  lundi, mardi, mercredi, jeudi, vendredi, samedi, dimanche

- The same is true of the months.

  janvier, février, mars, avril, mai, juin, juillet, août, septembre, octobre, novembre, décembre

- To say the date, simply use *le* + number + month.

  le quatorze février, le six mai

  Use *le premier* for '1st'.
  le premier septembre, le premier juin

Useful language

Time

There are two ways of telling the time in French: the traditional 12-hour clock method and the 24-hour clock method, which is often used in French, particularly to discuss travel times.

To say what time it is using the traditional 12-hour clock, start with *Il est ...*

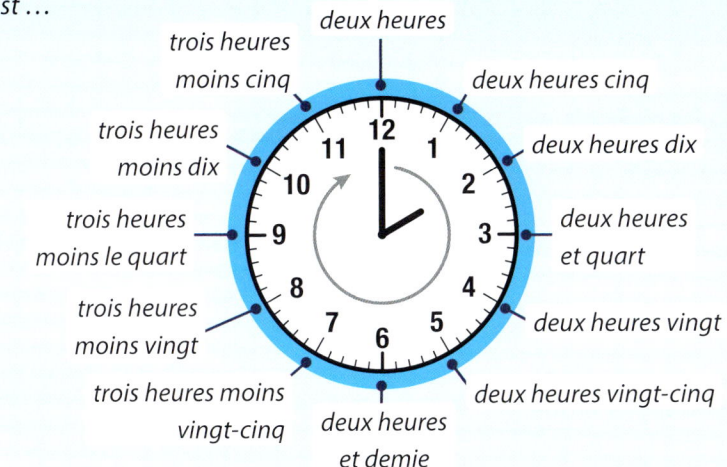

Il est deux heures dix. It's ten past two.
Il est trois heures moins le quart. It's quarter to three.
une heure 1 o'clock, *minuit* midnight, *midi* midday

To say 'half past twelve', use *midi et demi* or *minuit et demi* depending on whether you are referring to midday or midnight.

The 24-hour clock is very straightforward to use, as long as you know the numbers: keep counting from 12 to 24 for the pm times: 11.00, 12.00, 13.00 (1pm), 14.00 (2pm) ... 23.00 (11pm).

- For whole hours, simply say the number and *heures*:
  13.00 → **treize** heures (1pm)

- Where minutes are given too, say:
  the first number + *heures* (where the dot appears) + the second number.
  17.27 → *dix-sept heures vingt-sept*
  21.30 → *vingt-et-une heures trente*

Interrogatives

Qui?	Who?
Quand?	When?
Comment?	How? / What ... like?
Où?	Where?
Pourquoi?	Why?
Combien?	How much? / How many?
Quel ...? Quelle ...? Quels ...? Quelles ...?	Which ...?
Que ...? Qu'est-ce que ...?	What ...?

Greetings and ages

bonjour!	hello! / good morning!
salut!	hello! / hi!
au revoir!	goodbye!
à tout à l'heure!	see you later!
bonne nuit!	good night!
(comment) ça va?	how are you?
bien, merci	fine, thanks
pas mal	not bad
comme ci comme ça	not too bad
Quel âge as-tu / avez-vous?	How old are you?
J'ai seize ans.	I'm sixteen.
Et toi / vous?	And you?

Conjunctions

et	and
mais	but
ou	or
parce que / qu'	because
où	where
quand	when

Intensifiers

assez	quite
plus	more
très	very
moins	less
trop	too

Adverbs of frequency

jamais	never
rarement	rarely
de temps en temps	from time to time
normalement	normally
parfois / quelquefois	sometimes
souvent	often
toujours	always

onze 11

Sound–spelling links

The new GCSE exam involves a reading-aloud task and a dictation task to test your knowledge and understanding of sound–symbol correspondences. Learning how spelling represents sounds and using clear pronunciation when speaking French are key skills at GCSE. It is important that you are confident with pronunciation and know how to pronounce words correctly to help you speak French confidently.

Sound	Example	Page
silent final e	drôl**e**, timid**e**, frèr**e**, catastroph**e**	20
silent final consonant	amusan**t**, bavar**d**, jamai**s**, ennuyeu**x**	20
-aill- / ail	trav**aill**eur, je trav**aille**, a t**aille**, le trav**ail**	25
-ill- / -ille	ju**ill**et, me**ill**eur, la fam**ille**, la f**ille**	25
qu	**qu**el, **qu**and, **qu**i, **qu**'est-ce **qu**e	31, 41
-tion, -sion, -ssion	nata**tion**, equita**tion**, ac**tion**, Atten**tion**!, télévi**sion**, déci**sion**, occa**sion**, émi**ssion**	37, 69
ç, soft c	**ç**a, **c**'est **c**arrière **c**onnue **c**oncert	41
-s-	mai**s**on, plu**s**ieurs, cui**s**ine	41
th	**th**ème, biblio**th**èque	41
u	j'ai b**u**, j'ai v**u**, t**u** as l**u**	67
ou	n**ou**s, v**ou**s c**ou**rses, p**ou**r, c**ou**ru	67
oi / oy	s**oi**r, m**oi**, hist**oi**re v**oy**ager, env**oy**er, empl**oy**é	67
e	j**e**, l**e**, d**e**	70
eu	d**eu**x, un p**eu**, le j**eu**	70
é (-er, -ez)	all**er**, je suis all**é**, vous all**ez**	71
open eu / œu	l**eu**r, plusi**eu**rs, c**œu**r, s**œu**r	75
r	j'ado**r**e, annive**r**saire, pa**r**ents, décemb**r**e, **r**aison, aut**r**es, ch**r**étien, **r**ecevoi**r**	75
s-liaison	Nou**s** **a**vons acheté des livres. Vou**s** **a**vez rencontré des amis.	77
t-liaison	J'ai vu mo**n** **o**ncle.	77
n-liaison	On a découvert de nouveau**x** **e**ndroits.	77
x-liaison	Mon frère es**t** **a**rrivé ce matin.	77
i / y	s**y**stème, ph**y**sique, les P**y**rénées fac**i**le, l**i**sez, **i**l **y** aura	83
-ien	b**ien**, v**ien**s, ch**ien**, entret**ien**	83
è / ê / ai	tr**è**s, pr**è**s, routi**è**re, ch**è**re f**ê**te, t**ê**te, arr**ê**ter, vous **ê**tes vr**ai**, j'**ai**, j'**ai**mais, vr**ai**ment	85, 112
c'est / ces / sais	tr**è**s, c**é**l**è**bre, r**ê**ve, f**ê**te j'**ai**, fran**ç**a**i**s **c'est**, **ces**, je **sais**	85

Sound-spelling links

Sound	Example	Page
j / g	je, j'ai, je protège les girafes	86
ch	j'ai de la chance j'ai choisi	86
-gn-	gagner, espagnol, montagne	86
a / à	la capitale, il y avait, j'habitais, canadienne Il voyage à vélo. Il a voyagé à vélo.	112, 127
open o	dormi, logement, Portugal	117
au / eau / closed o / ô	aujourd'hui, aussi beaucoup, nouveau vidéo, trop hôtel, drôle	121
en / an / em / am	prendre, avant, temps, chambre	125
on / om	salon, contre, comme, tomber	125
ain / in / aim / im	prochain, injuste, faim, impossible	125
un	lundi, emprunter	125
h	hôtel, à l'hôtel historique, j'habite	133

Phonétique

en / an
Together, these letters make a sound like 'on' in English (but very nasal, high in the nose, and you can't hear the 'n').
Examples: **en**, Fr**an**ce

in
These letters also make a nasal sound, but sound slightly different, more like 'an' in English (as in 'hand').
Examples: c**in**q, **in**juste

Tip box

Reading aloud in French poses challenges when you come across new words, or sometimes words can just come out wrong when you read them out.
- Try to read and understand the sentence before you start.
- Work with a partner and seek their advice once you have finished.
- Practise reading aloud regularly.
- Record yourself and listen to it with a critical ear.

Phonétique

u
The letter 'u' makes a sound a bit like 'oo' in English (but say it with pursed lips, further forward in the mouth).
Examples: *j'ai bu, j'ai vu, tu as lu*

Tip box

Intonation
To sound as fluent as possible in French, it is important to think not just about *what* you say, but also *how* you say it. You also need to think about 'stress' (where the emphasis is placed within words), 'rhythm' (the beat and flow of the language in sentences) and 'pitch' (varying the tone of your language). Listen to as much authentic French as possible and imitate as best as you can.

Phonétique

gn
Together, these letters make a 'nyuh' sound, like in 'onion.'
Examples: *ga**gn**er, espa**gn**ol, monta**gn**e*

Theme 1
People and lifestyle

Identity and relationships with others

1 📖 **Read the email from Pierre and find the name (in bold) of each person in the photo (a–f).**

✉ papapierre82@monmail.fr

Bonjour! Je m'appelle **Pierre** et j'habite en Suisse avec ma famille. Voici une photo de nous. Je suis à gauche. Je suis le père de deux enfants: un garçon et une fille.

Mon fils s'appelle **Lucas** et il a les cheveux bruns et courts. Sa petite sœur, ma fille, c'est **Alicia**. Elle a les cheveux un peu longs.

Ma femme, leur belle-mère, s'appelle **Nadine** et sur la photo elle porte un t-shirt blanc. La grand-mère de Lucas et Alicia s'appelle **Valérie**. Elle a les cheveux blancs. Leur grand-père, c'est **Antoine**. Il sourit car il est toujours content.

2 📖 **Read the email again and answer the questions.**

a Who is Lucas?
b What is Lucas's hair like? (Give **two** details.)
c What relation is Nadine to Lucas and Alicia?
d Who is Valérie?
e What does Pierre say about Valérie's appearance?
f Why does Antoine smile?

3 📖 **Copy and complete the sentences with the correct word for a member of the family.**

a C'est la fille de mon oncle, c'est ma ___.
b C'est le mari de ma mère, c'est mon ___.
c C'est la femme de mon oncle, c'est ma ___.
d C'est le père de mon cousin, c'est mon ___.

la famille	family
le père	father
le beau-père	stepfather, father-in-law
la mère	mother
la belle-mère	stepmother, mother-in-law
le mari	husband
la femme	wife
le frère	brother
la sœur	sister
l'oncle	uncle
la tante	aunt
le cousin	male cousin
la cousine	female cousin
le fils	son
la fille	daughter
le grand-père	grandfather
la grand-mère	grandmother
mon, ma, mes	my
ton, ta, tes	your
son, sa, ses	his / her
leur, leurs	their

4 🎧 **Listen (1–6). Write down each family member Noémie mentions and if her opinion is positive (P), negative (N) or both (P+N).**

je m'entends bien avec	I get on well with
j'adore	I love
j'aime	I like
je n'aime pas	I don't like
content(e)	happy
sympa	nice
gentil(le)	kind
méchant(e)	nasty
strict(e)	strict
sportif / sportive	sporty

Theme 1 — People and lifestyle

Healthy living and lifestyle

1 📖 **Choose the correct word from the box to match the food and drink items (a–j).**

du pain	du fromage	du poisson	de la viande
des frites	des fruits	des légumes	du gâteau
de la glace	du thé	du café	du lait	du vin	de l'eau

2 📖 **Work out the English for the remaining words in the box (activity 1).**

3 🎧 **Listen (1–4) and choose *two* correct statements for each person.**

a I don't do sport.
b I never ride my bike.
c I swim three times a week.
d I love sport.
e I eat too much meat.
f I drink lots of water.
g I eat healthily.
h I eat lots of fruit and vegetables.

je bois	I drink
je mange	I eat
je fais	I do
la natation	swimming
le vélo	bike, bicycle
sain(e)	healthy
du, de la, des, de l'	some

4 📖 **Read the blog post and answer the questions.**

> **Thao**
>
> Je m'appelle Thao et j'habite au Vietnam. Je suis très actif et j'adore le sport. Je joue au football deux fois par semaine pour l'équipe de ma ville et on gagne souvent des matchs.
>
> Au collège, je fais de la natation car on a une piscine et le samedi, je fais du vélo. C'est très intéressant.
>
> En général, je ne bois pas assez d'eau mais je mange équilibré. Mes parents et moi, on mange du riz, du poisson, un peu de viande et beaucoup de légumes.
>
> Mon ami Dan ne mange jamais de fruits et légumes et en plus il ne fait pas de sport!

actif / active	active
le sport	sport
le football	football
une équipe	a team
la piscine	swimming pool
faire du vélo	to go cycling
le riz	rice

a How often does Thao play football?
b What sport does he do at school?
c What does he do on Saturdays?
d What is Thao not doing enough of?
e Name **three** types of food that he eats regularly.
f What does he say about his friend Dan? Give **two** details.

quinze 15

Theme 1 — People and lifestyle

Education

1 ✏️ Copy and complete the table for yourself, in French.

Subjects I do this year	Subjects I don't do this year
le français	

2 📖 Put the sentences (a–h) in the correct order to describe Christelle's school day.

Christelle

a Après, vers dix heures, j'ai une récréation de 20 minutes.
b L'école commence à huit heures du matin.
c Ensuite, c'est le déjeuner. Je mange et puis je vais à la bibliothèque.
d En premier, j'ai deux heures de maths.
e L'après-midi, je rentre à la maison à cinq heures.
f Après la récréation, j'ai une heure de musique et une heure de français.
g Après le déjeuner, je fais une heure de sciences.
h Mon dernier cours, c'est la géographie.

le français	French
l'anglais	English
l'espagnol	Spanish
l'allemand	German
les maths	maths
les sciences	sciences
l'informatique	IT, computer science
la technologie	D&T
la géographie	geography
l'histoire	history
la musique	music
le théâtre	drama

j'ai	I have
je fais	I do
je vais	I go
je suis	I am
je rentre	I return home
le matin	(in) the morning
l'après-midi	(in) the afternoon
la récréation	break
le déjeuner	lunch
la bibliothèque	library
après	after
ensuite	next
puis	then
en premier	first
un, une	a
le, la, les, l'	the

3 🎧 Listen (1–8). Write the letter (a–h) of the subject Mathis mentions and whether he has a positive (P) or negative (N) opinion of it.

4 🎧 Listen again (1–8). Write in English *two* details for each subject.

la matière	subject
le prof(esseur)	teacher (m)
la prof(esseure)	teacher (f)
amusant(e)	fun
facile	easy
génial(e)	great
difficile	difficult
ennuyeux / ennuyeuse	boring
nul	rubbish
je déteste	I hate

People and lifestyle — Theme 1

Work

1 📖 Read the sentences. Choose a job for each person and write the job name in French.

a J'aime travailler avec des enfants dans une école.
b Je travaille dans plusieurs villages. J'apporte les lettres aux personnes.
c Je travaille au théâtre ou dans des studios pour faire des films.
d Je travaille dans un café ou dans un restaurant.
e J'écris mes chansons et je fais des concerts.
f Je fais la sécurité dans les rues.

acteur / actrice

chanteur / chanteuse

policier / policière

professeur(e)

facteur / factrice

serveur / serveuse

2 🎧 Listen (1–6) and choose the sector (a–f) each person would like to work in.

a

b

c

d

e

f

travailler	to work
les enfants	children
les chansons	songs
la sécurité	safety, security
les rues	streets
le gouvernement	government
la politique	politics
la construction	construction
l'éducation	education
l'informatique	IT
la mode	fashion

3 📖 Match the statements (1–6) with the hopes for the future (a–f).

1 L'important pour moi, c'est d'avoir un bon salaire.
2 Je veux un travail où je peux voyager.
3 J'espère faire le métier de mes rêves: acteur!
4 Moi, je veux avoir du succès et devenir célèbre.
5 Je veux un travail sûr: je ne veux pas être au chômage.
6 Je veux avoir beaucoup d'indépendance dans mon travail.

a to travel
b to do my dream job
c to have a good salary
d to have a lot of independence
e to become famous
f to have a stable job

au chômage	unemployed
le travail	work
le salaire	salary
espérer	to hope
le succès	success
célèbre	famous
voyager	to travel
le métier	job, occupation
sûr(e)	safe, sure, secure
devenir	to become

1.1G Qui suis-je?

OBJECTIVES
- Introducing yourself
- The position of adjectives
- The present tense of regular -er verbs

1 Match the French and the English adjectives.

1 jeune 2 amusant(e) 3 gentil(le) 4 bon/bonne
5 sympa 6 nouveau/nouvelle 7 vieux/vieille 8 beau/belle

a funny   e beautiful
b new   f good
c young   g kind
d nice   h old

2 Read the texts (1–4) and match them to the pictures (a–d).

1 Moi, je suis **Arnaud**. J'ai douze ans et j'habite à la montagne, en Suisse. J'ai les cheveux courts et les yeux verts. J'aime bien ma famille et mon petit chien blanc.

2 Bonjour, je m'appelle **Nour** et j'habite dans une grande ville en France. Je porte toujours de vieux vêtements comme mon pantalon noir. Je n'aime pas les couleurs comme le vert et le bleu.

3 Je suis **Patrick**. J'habite dans un petit village au Québec. J'habite avec mon frère, qui est plus jeune que moi, et mes grands-parents. J'aime faire la cuisine et chez moi, on mange toujours à table.

4 Moi, c'est **Alex**. J'habite dans une belle maison au Sénégal, avec mes parents. Je parle le français, le sénégalais et l'anglais. J'adore le sport et je joue tous les jours au foot.

3 Read the texts again. Copy and complete the statements.

a Arnaud has __ hair and __ eyes.
b Arnaud's dog is __ and __.
c Nour lives in a __ town.
d Nour wears __ clothes.
e Patrick lives with his __ brother and __.
f Patrick likes __.
g Alex's house in Senegal is __.
h Alex likes playing __.

4 Listen (1–3). Copy and complete the table.

	Name	Age	Physical appearance	Lives in (country)	Likes	Dislikes
1						

Identity and relationships with others 1.1G

5 Rewrite the sentences, putting the adjective in brackets in the correct position.

a Ma sœur aime avoir les cheveux. (*longs*)
b Je porte des vêtements. (*noirs*)
c Elle aime son frère. (*jeune*)
d J'ai un chien. (*petit*, *blanc*)
e Nous habitons dans une maison. (*grande*, *blanche*)

6 Choose the correct form of the verb to complete each sentence.

a J'**habite** / **habites** / **habitent** en France.
b On **préfères** / **préférons** / **préfère** le cinéma français.
c Tu **aimes** / **aime** / **aimer** les fruits?
d Nous **déteste** / **détestent** / **détestons** le football.
e Elles **portent** / **porter** / **porte** des vêtements rouges.
f Mon frère **joue** / **jouent** / **joues** à des jeux vidéo.

7 Translate the sentences into French.

a I like my dog.
b I live in a small village.
c I love sport.
d I speak French.
e I play football.
f I wear old trousers.

8 In pairs, take turns to choose a person from activity 2 and ask and answer the questions.

- Où habites-tu?
- Tu es comment?
- Qu'est-ce que tu aimes?
- Qu'est-ce que tu n'aimes pas?

9 Write a paragraph (50 words) in French. Mention:

- your name and age
- where you live
- what you like
- what you dislike
- what you like wearing.

Je suis / Je m'appelle… J'ai … ans.			
J'habite	en	Angleterre / Écosse / Irlande.	
	au	Pays de Galles / Royaume-Uni.	
	à	la montagne / la campagne / la mer. York / Swansea.	
	dans	un petit	village / appartement.
		une grande	ville / maison.
J'aime Je n'aime pas	ma famille / mes amie(e)s / mon chien. le sport / le football / la natation / la musique. les couleurs bleu et vert / les jeux vidéo.		
J'aime porter	un pantalon blanc / une robe rouge. des vêtements noirs / des chaussures bleues.		

Grammaire

The position of adjectives

In French, most adjectives **follow** the noun they describe.

*J'ai les cheveux **courts** et les yeux **verts**.*
I have **short** hair and **green** eyes.

However, some adjectives usually come **in front of** the noun. For example:

grand(e)	big, tall, large
petit(e)	small, short, little
bon, bonne	good
mauvais(e)	bad
jeune	young
joli(e)	pretty
beau, bel*, belle	beautiful
nouveau, nouvel*, nouvelle	new
vieux, vieil*, vieille	old

* in front of a vowel

*J'aime mon **nouveau** pantalon.* I like my new trousers.
*J'habite dans un **petit** village.* I live in a small town.

Les verbes

The present tense of regular -er verbs.

To form the present tense of regular -er verbs, remove -er from the infinitive and add the endings:

aimer (to like/love)	
j'aim**e**	nous aim**ons**
tu aim**es**	vous aim**ez**
il / elle / on aim**e**	ils / elles aim**ent**

*Je **joue** au foot.* I play / am playing football.
*Elle **aime** les chats.* She likes cats.

dix-neuf 19

1.1F Ma personnalité

OBJECTIVES
- Personality descriptions
- Adjective agreement
- The present tense of regular -re verbs
- Phonics: silent final -e and final consonants

1 📖 Read the texts and note down all the adjectives that describe personality.

Laure
Mes copines me trouvent assez sérieuse car je travaille bien à l'école. Je suis aussi une bonne amie, je pense! C'est vrai, je suis très sympa et amusante. Parfois, je suis embêtante, surtout avec mon petit frère, mais il peut être méchant aussi!

Cédric
Je suis très fier car je suis travailleur et j'aime avoir de bonnes notes. Je suis bavard aussi et jamais timide. Je suis très gentil, surtout avec mes copains. Ma sœur et moi, on est drôles. Elle est toujours heureuse et jamais triste, c'est génial.

Morgane
Mon cousin est drôle et gentil. Il n'est jamais ennuyeux mais il est très paresseux à l'école. C'est une catastrophe. Ses parents, qui sont assez travailleurs, trouvent ça très inquiétant.

2 🔀 Translate the adjectives (activity 1) into English.

3 📖 Read the texts again. Copy and complete the statements.
- a Laure's friends find her ___.
- b Laure's brother can be ___.
- c Cédric is ___ with his friends.
- d Cédric's sister is ___ sad.
- e Morgane's cousin is lazy at ___.
- f Her cousin's parents find this ___.

4 ⭐ Copy and complete the sentences, using the French for the adjective given in brackets.
- a Ma sœur est très ___. (chatty)
- b Mes copains sont toujours ___. (shy)
- c J'adore mon père mais il est ___. (lazy)
- d Ma petite sœur est très ___. (annoying)
- e Ma mère est souvent trop ___. (serious)
- f Mes profs de sport sont assez ___. (kind)

Attention
Remember to make the adjectives agree with the nouns in gender and number.

Grammaire

Adjective agreement
In French, adjectives must agree in gender and number (singular or plural) with the noun. For most adjectives, you add -e if the noun is feminine singular, -s if the noun is masculine plural, and -es if the noun is feminine plural.

Some adjectives follow different patterns:

Masculine		Feminine	
-e	timid**e**	-e	timid**e** (no change)
-x	sérieu**x**	-se	sérieu**se**
-f	neu**f**	-ve	neu**ve**
-er	fi**er**	-ère	fi**ère**

Phonétique

Silent final -e and final consonants
In French, the final -e on a word is not pronounced:

drôl**e**   timid**e**   frèr**e**   catastroph**e**

Most final consonants in French are not pronounced.

amusan**t**   bavar**d**   jamai**s**   ennuyeu**x**

However, the consonants c, r, f and l are often pronounced at the end of a word. Use the English word CaReFuL to help you remember them.

un par**c**   fie**r**   neu**f**   génia**l**

vingt

Identity and relationships with others — 1.1F

5 Read and listen to the dialogue between two spies. Listen and write down the words you hear (1–12) to complete the speech bubbles.

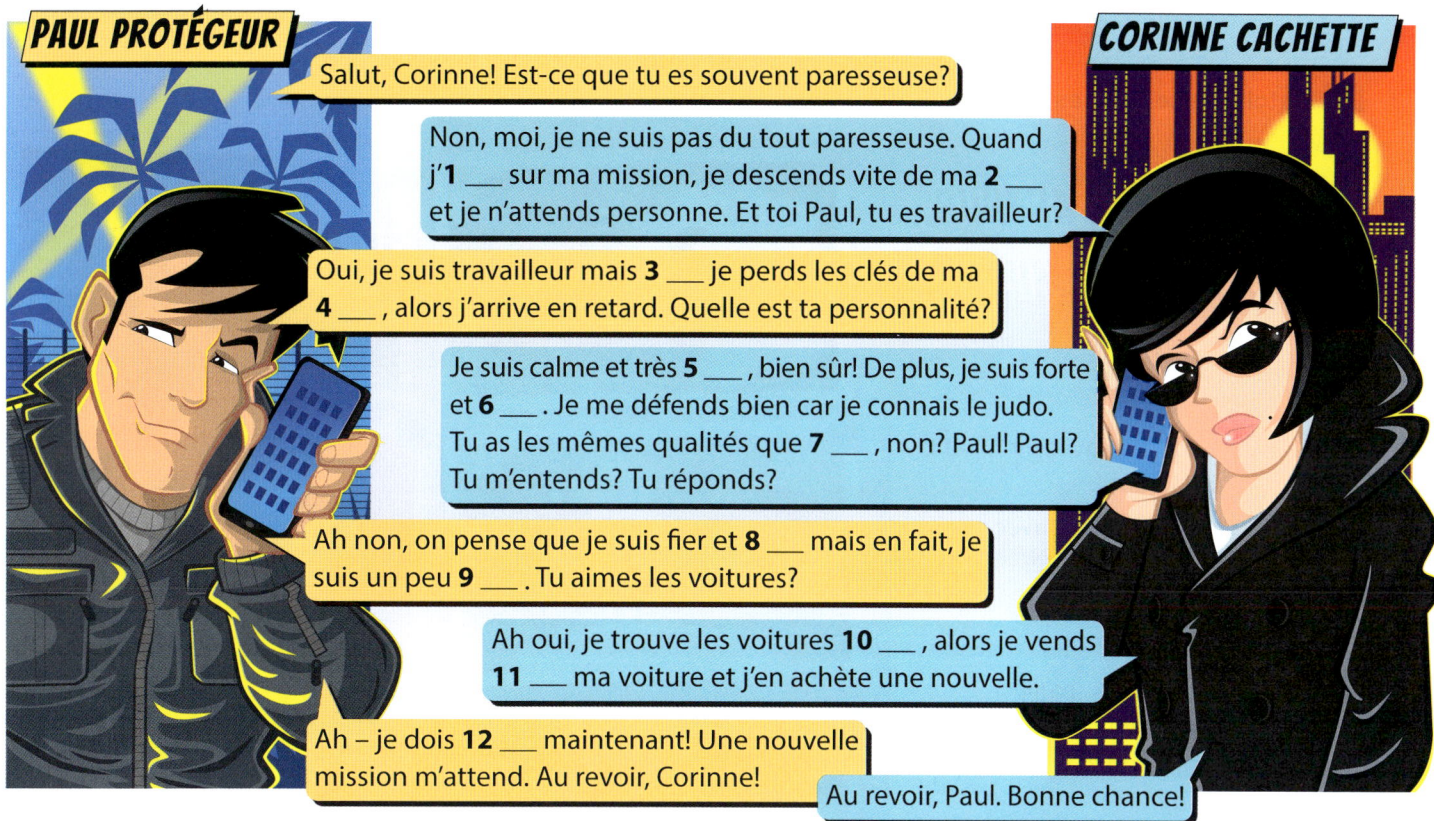

PAUL PROTÉGEUR: Salut, Corinne! Est-ce que tu es souvent paresseuse?

CORINNE CACHETTE: Non, moi, je ne suis pas du tout paresseuse. Quand j'**1** ___ sur ma mission, je descends vite de ma **2** ___ et je n'attends personne. Et toi Paul, tu es travailleur?

PAUL: Oui, je suis travailleur mais **3** ___ je perds les clés de ma **4** ___, alors j'arrive en retard. Quelle est ta personnalité?

CORINNE: Je suis calme et très **5** ___, bien sûr! De plus, je suis forte et **6** ___. Je me défends bien car je connais le judo. Tu as les mêmes qualités que **7** ___, non? Paul! Paul? Tu m'entends? Tu réponds?

PAUL: Ah non, on pense que je suis fier et **8** ___ mais en fait, je suis un peu **9** ___. Tu aimes les voitures?

CORINNE: Ah oui, je trouve les voitures **10** ___, alors je vends **11** ___ ma voiture et j'en achète une nouvelle.

PAUL: Ah – je dois **12** ___ maintenant! Une nouvelle mission m'attend. Au revoir, Corinne!

CORINNE: Au revoir, Paul. Bonne chance!

6 Read the dialogue again and answer the questions.

a Who sometimes arrives late?
b Who likes cars?
c Who is different from how other people see them?
d Who says they are not lazy?
e Who says they are clever?
f Who says they are shy?

7 Note down all the regular -re verbs in the dialogue.

8 Copy and complete the sentences with the present tense of the verb in brackets.

a J'___ toujours mes frères. (attendre)
b Nous ___ les enfants. (entendre)
c Mon copain ___ du train. (descendre)
d Je ___ souvent mes clés! (perdre)
e Tu ne ___ pas au téléphone? (répondre)
f Mes parents ___ des vêtements sur Internet. (vendre)

9 Translate the sentences from activity 8 into English.

Les verbes

The present tense of -re verbs

To form the present tense of regular -re verbs, remove -re from the infinitive and add the endings:

attendre (to wait)	
j'attend**s**	nous attend**ons**
tu attend**s**	vous attend**ez**
il/elle/on attend	ils/elles attend**ent**

10 Write a paragraph (50 words) about a famous person. Mention:
- their name
- positive traits
- negative traits
- what you think of them
- a reason for your opinion.

11 In pairs, take turns to read out your paragraph from activity 10.

12 In pairs, ask and answer the questions.
- Comment est ta personnalité?
- Et tes amis, ils sont comment?

vingt et un 21

1.2G Voici ma famille

OBJECTIVES
- Family relationships
- *qui*
- Reflexive verbs in the present tense

1 📖 Match the sentences to the pictures.

JE M'APPELLE ARTHUR. VOICI MA FAMILLE.

1 Je m'entends bien avec mon petit frère, qui est gentil.
2 Je me dispute souvent avec ma sœur, qui est embêtante.
3 Ma tante, qui est sportive, se sépare de mon oncle.
4 Ma cousine, qui est géniale, se marie cette année.
5 Ma mère, qui est trop stricte, s'excuse toujours.
6 Je m'entends bien avec mon père, qui est super sympa.

a
b
c
d
e
f

2 📖 Read the sentences in activity 1 again and answer the questions.

a Who does Arthur say is kind?
b Who is separating from their partner?
c Who is getting married?
d Who does Arthur find annoying?
e Why does Arthur get on well with his dad?

Les verbes

Reflexive verbs in the present tense

Reflexive verbs are useful to talk about your body, your state of mind, and relationships. They have an extra pronoun (shown here in bold) before the verb. This is called the reflexive pronoun.

je **me** dispute	I argue
tu **te** disputes	you argue
il / elle / on **se** dispute	he / she argues, we argue

3 🎯 Note down the phrases containing reflexive verbs in the texts in activity 1 and translate them into English.

Example: je m'entends bien – I get on well

4 🎯 Rewrite the sentences in the correct order.

a Je | mon frère | me dispute | avec .
b Elle | avec | sa sœur | s'entend bien .
c appelles | Marc | t' | Tu ?
d marie | se | à | son fiancé | Ma cousine .
e Ma mère | de mon père | sépare | se .

Identity and relationships with others — 1.2G

5 Listen (1–4). Copy and complete the table in English.

	Family member mentioned	Get on well? ✓ or ✗	Why (not)?
1			

6 Copy and combine the pairs of sentences, using *qui*.

Example: J'aime ma mère. Elle est sympa. → J'aime ma mère, qui est sympa.

a Je n'aime pas mon père. Il est méchant.
b Elle aime son frère. Il est drôle.
c Je me dispute avec ma sœur. Elle est terrible.
d Ma cousine se marie avec son petit copain. Il est génial.
e J'adore ma mère. Elle est gentille.

> **Grammaire**
>
> **qui**
> Use *qui* (who) to refer back to someone you have already mentioned in the sentence.
> *J'aime ma sœur, **qui** est gentille.*
> I like my sister **who** is kind.

7 In pairs, take turns to read the text aloud.

> J'ai un grand frère, qui s'appelle Arnaud.
> Je me dispute tout le temps avec mon frère.
> Je n'ai pas de sœur.
> Et toi, tu as des frères et sœurs?
> Tu t'entends bien avec ta famille?

8 Translate the text in activity 7 into English.

9 Imagine you are a member of a famous family. Write a paragraph saying who you you do or don't get on with, and why.

Je m'entends bien avec…	Il/Elle est…
Je ne m'entends pas bien avec…	strict(e)
Je me dispute avec…	méchant(e)
Je n'aime pas…	embêtant(e)
J'aime…	gentil/gentille
J'adore…	paresseux/paresseuse

1.2F Les familles de nos jours

OBJECTIVES
- Different types of families
- Comparative adjectives
- The present tense of regular -ir verbs
- Phonics: -aill- / -ail and -ill- / -ille

1 📖 Read the texts and match them to the pictures.

Comment est ta famille?

Chiara
J'habite avec ma sœur Zara et mes parents à Bruges, en Belgique. Mes grands-parents habitent en Côte d'Ivoire et on va souvent là-bas pour les vacances. À Noël, on se réunit avec mes cousins et on joue à des jeux vidéo – on réussit toujours à gagner car ils sont pires que nous!

Timéo
J'habite à Nice, en France, avec mon père. Le vendredi, quand il finit le travail, on fait les courses: on remplit le frigo pour la semaine. Le dimanche, on adore aller à la plage; c'est aussi amusant que regarder la télé.

Léa
Je suis canadienne et j'habite à Montréal. Mes parents sont séparés. En ce moment, je choisis de vivre avec mon père et mon beau-père car ils sont moins stricts que ma mère. J'adore ma demi-sœur et mon demi-frère et on rit tous les jours. On grandit tous ensemble, c'est génial!

Sébastien
Je suis adopté. Je suis né à Calais et maintenant j'habite à Toulouse. Je trouve que Toulouse est une meilleure ville que Calais car la ville est plus intéressante. Je n'ai pas encore de frères et sœurs, mais mes parents attendent un enfant pour le mois de septembre.

1

2

3

4

2 📖 Read the texts again and answer the questions.

a Why do Chiara and her sister always beat their cousins at video games?
b What do Timéo and his dad do after work on Fridays?
c What do they like doing at the weekend?
d Why does Léa prefer living with her dad and stepdad at the moment?
e Why does Sébastien prefer Toulouse to Calais?
f How many brothers and sisters does he have?

3 ⭐ Translate the sentences into French.

a The beach is as fun as the cinema.
b My dad is less strict than my mum.
c Sport is more interesting than video games.
d Cinema is better than TV.
e My sister is worse than my brother.

Grammaire

Comparative adjectives

Use comparative adjectives to make comparisons:

plus … que   more … than / …er than
moins … que   less … than
aussi … que   as … as

*Angelin est **plus amusant que** Nicole.*
Angelin is **funnier than** Nicole.

*Je suis **moins gentil que** ma sœur.*
I am **less kind than** my sister.

*Elle est **aussi sympa que** moi.* She is **as nice as** me.

Remember to make the adjective agree with the subject of the sentence.

Bon and *mauvais* have irregular comparatives, *meilleur(e)* and *pire*:

*La musique est **meilleure que** la lecture.*
Music is better than reading.

*La télévision est **pire que** la lecture.*
Television is worse than reading.

Identity and relationships with others 1.2F

4 Listen (1–4). Write P for a positive opinion of the person, N for a negative opinion, and P+N if the opinion is both positive and negative.

| 1 brother | 2 grandparents | 3 cousin | 4 friend |

Les verbes

The present tense of regular -ir verbs

To form the present tense of regular –ir verbs, remove -ir from the infinitive and add the endings:

finir (to finish)	
je fin**is**	nous fin**issons**
tu fin**is**	vous fin**issez**
il / elle / on fin**it**	ils / elles fin**issent**

Je **choisis** un film. I choose / am choosing a film.
Ils **finissent** leurs devoirs. They finish / are finishing their homework.

5 Copy and complete the sentences with the present tense of the verb in brackets.

a Il ___ ses devoirs. (*finir*)
b Je ___ toujours les devoirs de maths. (*réussir*)
c Elle ___ son sac de fruits et légumes. (*remplir*)
d Tu ___ quelle émission? (*choisir*)
e Nous ___ notre jeu après le déjeuner. (*finir*)

6 Look at the picture. In pairs, take turns to ask a question and answer as if this were your family. Use comparative adjectives.

Comment est…?
- ton frère
- ta sœur
- ton cousin
- tes parents

Mon frère Ma sœur Mon cousin	est	plus moins aussi	drôle(s) / sympa(s) timide(s) / strict(e)(s) amusant(e)(s) intelligent(e)(s) gentil(s) / gentille(s) travailleur(s) / travailleuse(s) paresseux / paresseuse(s)	que…
Mes parents	sont			
			pire(s) / meilleur(e)(s)	

7 Use the picture in activity 6 to write a paragraph (90 words) describing your family (using verbs in the present tense). Mention:
- the personality of each person
- who you do / don't get on with
- comparisons between yourself and some of the family members.

Phonétique

-aill- / -ail and *-ill- / -ille*

| trav**aill**eur | je trav**aill**e | la t**aille** | le trav**ail** |
| ju**ill**et | m**eill**eur | la fam**ille** | la f**ille** |

vingt-cinq 25

2.1G On mange!

OBJECTIVES • Food preferences • Negative sentences • The position of adverbs

1 📖 Match the words and phrases (1–12) to the pictures (a–l).

1 J'ai faim.
2 J'ai soif.
3 les fruits
4 les légumes
5 le poisson
6 la viande
7 le pain
8 le fromage
9 le gâteau
10 la glace
11 la boisson
12 le fast-food

2 📖 Read the online forum and answer the questions.

Mehdi
Moi, je suis végan, alors je ne mange pas de viande ou de poisson. Je mange des fruits et des légumes. Je bois beaucoup d'eau et parfois du thé, mais pas de lait.

Stéphanie
Je mange souvent du fast-food, mais seulement le poisson-frites! Ma belle-mère a une super recette de poisson-frites. Je ne mange jamais de hamburger – je n'aime pas ça du tout.

Oscar
Normalement, je prends trois repas par jour: le petit-déjeuner, le déjeuner et le dîner. Je mange des produits comme le fromage et le lait pour me donner de l'énergie. Je ne bois pas de café ou de thé.

Mariama
Moi, je ne mange rien entre les repas. J'habite dans une ferme, alors on mange tous les jours de la viande car on aime ça. Ma sœur boit toujours du lait au petit-déjeuner mais il n'y a personne d'autre qui boit du lait dans ma famille.

Who…?
a likes fish
b doesn't eat meat or fish
c finds milk gives them energy
d doesn't snack between meals
e drinks tea
f eats meat
g doesn't like burgers

Grammaire

The position of adverbs

Adverbs of time, manner, frequency and place usually go **after** the verb in French.

Je mange **souvent** des fruits.
I **often** eat fruit.

Je bois **parfois** du thé.
I **sometimes** drink tea.

3 ⭐ Find *five* adverbs of time, manner, frequency or place in the texts in activity 2. Translate them into English.

Healthy living and lifestyle 2.1G

4 Copy and complete the sentences, using the negative form in brackets.

a Je ___ aime ___ les fruits. (*not*)
b Il ___ va ___ au marché. (*never*)
c Elles ___ mangent ___. (*nothing*)
d Tu ___ prends ___ de glace? (*not*)
e Il ___ voit ___ au restaurant. (*no one*)

5 Listen (1–3). Copy and complete the sentences.

1 Benoît doesn't eat ___. He loves ___ but doesn't eat ___ after dinner.
2 Jamal often eats ___. He drinks ___ and ___ but not ___.
3 Chantal lives ___. She never ___ at home. Instead, she goes ___ every day.

6 In pairs, look at the photo and take turns to ask and answer the questions.

- Parle-moi de la photo.
- Qu'est-ce que tu manges normalement?
- Qu'est-ce que tu ne bois jamais? Pourquoi pas?
- Manges-tu souvent des légumes? Pourquoi (pas)?

Normalement…		
Je mange	un fruit / une glace.	
	du poisson / de la viande / des legumes.	
	beaucoup de fruits.	
	un peu de pain.	
Je bois	un thé / un café / de l'eau.	
Je ne mange	jamais	de viande / poisson.
	pas souvent	de lait / café.
	pas beaucoup	
… parce que	j'adore ça.	
	je n'aime pas ça.	

Les verbes

Negative sentences

To make a sentence negative, add *ne … pas* around the verb:
*Je **ne** mange **pas** de viande.* I **don't** eat meat.

Shorten *ne* to *n'* in front of a vowel or silent *h*:
*Je **n'aime pas** le lait.* I **don't** like milk.

In negative sentences, use *de* or *d'* instead of an indefinite article (*un, une, des*) or a partitive article (*du, de la, de l', des*):

*Je mange **de la** glace.* → *Je ne mange pas **de** glace.*

*J'ai **un** animal.* → *Je n'ai pas **d'**animal.*

ne … jamais, ne … rien and *ne … personne* follow the same pattern:

*Il **ne** boit **jamais** de café.* He **never** drinks coffee.
*Je **n'achète rien** au supermarché.* I **don't** buy **anything** in the supermarket.
*Je **ne** vois **personne**.* I **don't** see **anyone**. / I see **no one**.

7 Use the profile card to write a paragraph (50 words) describing your eating and drinking habits.

Example: Je mange… Je bois…

Attention

Try to use negatives and adverbs in your writing and give reasons.

Nom: Antoine **Âge:** 16 ans

beaucoup ✓ (glace)
souvent ✓ (café)
n'aime pas ✗ (légumes)
jamais ✗ (poisson)

vingt-sept 27

2.1F Aïe aïe aïe!

OBJECTIVES
- Health problems and addictions
- Plural nouns
- The near future tense

1 📖 **Read the patients' problems (1–3) and match them with the correct response (a–c).**

Problèmes

Réponses

1 J'ai mal à la tête, j'ai mal à la gorge. J'ai aussi mal aux oreilles. Je n'ai pas d'énergie. Je suis très fatigué et je ne mange pas beaucoup. Je suis malade!

2 Allô! C'est pour une urgence! Il y a un accident. Je vois une vieille dame qui a très mal au pied et à la jambe et elle est vraiment inquiète.

3 Aïe aïe aïe, j'ai mal au bras! Je veux jouer au tennis demain mais je ne peux lever le bras gauche et ça me fait vraiment mal.

a D'accord, je vais envoyer une ambulance. La dame va aller à l'hôpital et on va tout de suite l'examiner.

b Alors, donnez-moi votre numéro de téléphone. Le médecin va vous appeler et il va peut-être vous donner des médicaments. Il ne faut pas faire d'exercice!

c OK, je vais vous donner un rendez-vous chez le médecin. Il va vous voir cet après-midi… à 16 heures 10, d'accord? Maintenant, vous allez rester au lit. Il faut boire beaucoup d'eau et manger, si vous pouvez.

2 🎧 **Listen to the phone calls and check your answers.**

3 💬 **In pairs, read aloud the matching problems and responses.**

4 📖 **Find in the problems and responses the French for the English phrases (a–h).**

a I have a headache
b I have earache
c I'm not eating much
d I'm ill
e they will examine her straightaway
f the doctor is going to call you
g I'm going to give you an appointment
h you are going to stay in bed

5 🎯 **Rewrite the sentences, changing the verb to the near future tense.**

a Je mange des légumes.
b Il joue au foot.
c Tu restes au lit?
d Elle voit ses copains.
e Je fais de l'exercice.
f Nous allons au parc.

Les verbes

The near future tense

Use the near future tense to say what you are going to do or will do. You need to use a form of *aller* in the present tense, followed by the main verb in the infinitive:

aller (to go)	
je vais	nous allons
tu vas	vous allez
il / elle / on va	ils / elles vont

\+ infinitive

Je **vais jouer** au tennis. I am going to play tennis.
Vous **allez rester** au lit. You are going to stay in bed.

Healthy living and lifestyle 2.1F

6 Read the texts and answer the questions (a–h).

Martin
Posté le 3 octobre

Ma mère a commencé à fumer des cigarettes à l'âge de vingt ans. Elle est souvent malade et le médecin dit que fumer, c'est dangereux. Ça va être difficile d'arrêter car elle a beaucoup de soucis et elle dit que fumer l'aide à rester calme.

Élise
Posté le 27 octobre

Mon ami Thomas prend des drogues. Il dit que ça le relaxe mais je sais que les drogues, ça peut tuer! Je ne suis pas d'accord avec ses choix de vie. Moi, je ne vais jamais prendre de drogues, car je veux rester en bonne santé. Je voudrais vivre très longtemps, alors je vais être active et manger de façon saine: beaucoup de légumes et pas trop de gâteaux!

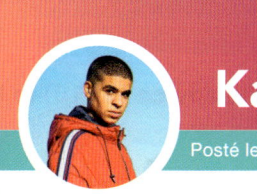

Karim
Posté le 23 novembre

Ma cousine boit de l'alcool et elle vapote. Elle va faire un effort pour boire moins car elle a peur de tomber malade. Elle va aussi arrêter de vapoter car on ne connaît pas bien les dangers de la e-cigarette.

a What does Martin's mother's doctor say about smoking?
b Why will Martin's mother find it difficult to stop smoking?
c How does smoking cigarettes help her?
d What can drugs do, according to Élise?
e Why will she never take drugs?
f How will Élise try to live a long life? Give **two** details.
g Why is Karim's cousin going to try to drink less alcohol?
h What else will she do and why?

7 Work out the plural form of the nouns.

a une drogue
b un corps
c un accident
d un neveu
e une maladie
f un château

8 Listen and write down the nouns you hear to complete the sentences.

« Je vais boire moins d'**1** ___ et je vais arrêter de fumer car c'est mauvais pour la **2** ___. Ça peut donner des **3** ___. »

« Aïe, j'ai mal au **4** ___ et aux **5** ___! Je vais aller voir un **6** ___. »

9 Translate the sentences into French.

a I have a headache.
b He is going to see the doctor.
c I am going to drink less coffee.
d My sister is going to eat fruit and vegetables.
e I am not going to take drugs.

Grammaire

Plural nouns

Most plural nouns end in -s:

un copain → des copain**s**

une oreille → des oreille**s**

If the singular noun ends in -eau, -au or -eu, the plural adds an -x instead of an -s:

un gât**eau** → des gât**eaux**

un chev**eu** → des chev**eux**

If the singular noun already ends in -s, -x or -z, there is no change in the plural:

un pay**s** → des pay**s**

un choi**x** → des choi**x**

vingt-neuf

2.2G Mon mode de vie

OBJECTIVES
- Lifestyle choices and habits
- Interrogative adjective: *quel*
- Imperatives in the *tu* form
- Phonics: *qu*

1 📖 Match the advice (1–10) to the pictures (a–j).

Pour arriver à ton mode de vie idéal…

1. Va faire les courses plus souvent!
2. Reçois tes amis à la maison!
3. Partage tes problèmes avec tes amis!
4. Crois en toi!
5. Fais plus de sport!
6. Bois souvent de l'eau pendant la journée!
7. Ris avec ta famille!
8. Suis tes rêves!
9. Va te coucher plus tôt!

2 🎧 Listen (1–4) and choose the correct picture from activity 1 for each speaker.

3 ✗ Translate the sentences (1–9) from activity 1 into English.

4 🎯 Copy and complete the sentences with the *tu* form of the imperative.

a ___ tes devoirs! (*faire*)
b ___ plus de légumes! (*manger*)
c ___ au lit plus tôt! (*aller*)
d ___ un médecin! (*voir*)
e ___ ton livre! (*lire*)
f ___ moins de café! (*boire*)

Les verbes

Imperatives in the *tu* form

The imperative is used to give instructions or advice. It is the same as the present tense but without the pronoun *tu*.

Bois *de l'eau!* Drink some water.
Fais *plus de sport!* Do more sport.

For -er verbs, drop the final 's' of the present tense (*tu manges*, *tu vas*, etc.):
Mange *des fruits!* Eat some fruit.
Va *chez le médecin!* Go to the doctor's.

30 trente

Healthy living and lifestyle — 2.2G

5 In pairs, take turns to read out the answers (A and B) two teenagers gave to each question (1–6) in a survey (*un sondage*) on lifestyle habits. Give each person advice from activity 1.

Example:
- Question 1. Quelles sont tes habitudes sportives?
  Personne A dit: Je fais du sport une fois par mois.
- Fais plus de sport!

Phonétique

qu

qu in French is always pronounced like the English sound 'k'.

quel   **qu**and   **qu**i   **qu**'est-ce **qu**e

Sondage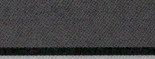
Il est comment, ton mode de vie?

1 Quelles sont tes **habitudes** sportives?
   A Je fais du sport une fois par mois.
   B Je ne fais jamais de sport.

2 Quelles **boissons** préfères-tu?
   A Je bois trop de café.
   B Je ne bois pas beaucoup d'eau.

3 Quelles sont tes **habitudes** le soir?
   A Je joue à des jeux vidéo.
   B Je me couche tard.

4 Quelle est ta **personnalité**?
   A Je n'ai pas confiance en moi.
   B Je suis timide.

5 Quelles **activités** fais-tu avec tes amis?
   A Je ne vois pas souvent mes amis.
   B On ne fait rien ensemble.

6 À l'avenir, quels **choix** vas-tu faire?
   A Je ne vais pas faire d'exercice.
   B Je ne vais pas manger de légumes.

6 Look at the questions in the quiz again. Decide if each noun in bold is masculine or feminine, and singular or plural.

7 Choose the correct option to complete each sentence.

   a **Quel** / **Quels** / **Quelles** sports préfères-tu?
   b Tu habites dans **quelle** / **quels** / **quel** maison?
   c Tu lis **quelle** / **quel** / **quels** livre en ce moment?
   d **Quelle** / **Quelles** / **Quels** couleurs aimes-tu?
   e Tu as mal à **quel** / **quelle** / **quels** bras?
   f Tu vas au lit à **quel** / **quelle** / **quels** heure?

8 Translate the sentences into French. You are addressing a friend, so use *tu* forms of the verbs.

   a Do more sport.
   b Share your problems with your friends.
   c Go to buy some milk.
   d Which vegetables do you eat?
   e Which sports do you do?
   f Which activities do you do on Saturdays?

Grammaire

Interrogative adjective: *quel*

Use *quel* before a noun to ask 'which…?' or 'what…?'
Quel works like an adjective, so make it agree with the noun.

	Singular	Plural
Masculine	quel	quels
Feminine	quelle	quelles

Quel fruit	aimes-tu?	Which fruit	do you like?
Quelle couleur		What colour	
Quels légumes		Which vegetables	
Quelles voitures		Which cars	

Attention

Masculine	Feminine
bras	couleur
livre	heure
sport	maison

2.2F Hier, j'ai...

OBJECTIVES
- Recent activities
- Indirect object pronouns
- The perfect tense of regular verbs with *avoir*

1 Read the blog and answer the questions (a–g).

Salut, je m'appelle Corentin et je suis vraiment très sportif. Aujourd'hui, je te parle de mon programme sportif de la semaine dernière.

Lundi, **j'ai joué** une partie de foot. C'est mon sport préféré et je joue pour l'équipe de ma ville, Mougins.

Mardi, **on a participé** à un match et **on a gagné** 3–0. On était super contents car **on a fini** premiers!

Ensuite, mercredi, **j'ai marché** avec mon chien. **J'ai perdu** mon chien dans la forêt et **j'ai attendu** pendant deux heures! Après, *je lui ai donné un bain* et de la nourriture.

Jeudi, **j'ai essayé** la natation pour la première fois et **j'ai vraiment aimé** ça.

Vendredi soir, j'ai fait une course de 15 kilomètres. Après, **j'ai beaucoup dormi** car j'étais fatigué.

Samedi, **j'ai mangé** au restaurant avec mes parents car c'était mon anniversaire: **ils ont choisi** du poisson avec des légumes mais moi, **j'ai choisi** de la viande et des frites. Et *ils m'ont acheté un nouveau portable* comme cadeau! Génial!

Dimanche, **j'ai fini** mes devoirs et **j'ai regardé** le Tour de France à la télé. Puis **j'ai retrouvé** mon meilleur ami au parc et *je lui ai vendu mon vieux portable*!

Quelle semaine!

a Which team does Corentin play football for?
b What did he do on Tuesday?
c How long did he wait for, when he lost his dog on Wednesday?
d What did he try for the first time on Thursday?
e What did he think of that activity?
f What did his parents choose at the restaurant on Saturday?
g Which **four** things did he do on Sunday?

2 Read the blog again and translate the phrases in bold into English.

3 Listen (1–9) and decide if each sentence is in the present (Pr) or perfect (P) tense.

Les verbes

The perfect tense with *avoir* (regular verbs)

Use the perfect tense to say what you did or have done. To form the perfect tense, use part of the verb *avoir* (to have) + a past participle.

Past participles:

for regular *-er* verbs, replace the *-er* with *-é*:
jou**er** → jou**é**

for regular *-ir* verbs, replace the *-ir* with *-i*:
chois**ir** → chois**i**

for regular *-re* verbs, replace the *-re* with *-u*:
vend**re** → vend**u**

Nous **avons joué** au foot. We **played** football.
J'**ai choisi** des frites. I **chose** chips.
Tu **as vendu** ta voiture? **Have** you **sold** your car?

Healthy living and lifestyle 2.2F

4 🎯 **Copy and complete the sentences, adding the past participle of the verb given in brackets.**

a J'ai ___ beaucoup de fruits. (*manger*)
b Elle a ___ son chien. (*perdre*)
c Nous avons ___ les devoirs. (*finir*)
d Ils ont ___ leur voiture. (*vendre*)
e J'ai ___ de la musique. (*écouter*)
f Elle a ___ pendant huit heures. (*dormir*)
g Il a ___ le film. (*aimer*)

5 💬 **In pairs, take turns to start and finish a sentence describing what Corentin (activity 1) did each day.**

- Alors, lundi, Corentin a…
- … joué au football. Et mardi, il a…
- … gagné un match de foot. Vendredi, il a…

6 🔀 **Translate into English the phrases in *italics* in the text in activity 1.**

7 ⭐ **Copy the sentences, replacing the bold words with an indirect object pronoun in the correct position.**

a Je demande (**à Marie**) de partir.
b Il dit (**à moi**) de manger des fruits.
c Je vends mon vélo (**à toi**).
d Votre frère ressemble (**à vous**).
e Amélie a parlé (**à son frère**).
f Tu as répondu (**à ton professeur**).

Grammaire

Indirect object pronouns

me / m' (before a vowel)	(to) me
te / t' (before a vowel)	(to) you (informal)
lui	(to) him / her / it
vous	(to) you (formal)

Indirect object pronouns replace a noun that would be introduced with the preposition *à* (to). They always go before the verb.

*Je **lui** donne de l'eau.* I give **him** some water. / I give some water **to him**.

*Ils **me** donnent un portable.* They are giving **me** a mobile phone.

When the verb is in the perfect tense, the pronoun goes before both parts of the verb:

*Je **lui** ai donné de l'eau.* I gave **him** some water.

*Ils **m'**ont donné un portable.* They gave **me** a mobile phone.

Be careful, because some French verbs need *à* while their English equivalent does not need the word 'to':

*Je **demande à** ma mère.* I ask (to) my mum.
→ *Je **lui** demande.* I ask **her**.

---

8 🎧 **Listen to Khalida (1–5) and decide which activity (a–e) she did on each day of the week.**

a ate out
b tried a new sport
c went shopping
d did schoolwork
e met up with a friend

9 ✏️ **Copy the storyboard. Think of something you did each day last week. Draw an emoji for each activity and write a caption in the perfect tense for each day.**

Example: Lundi. J'ai joué au foot pour l'équipe de mon école. On a gagné le match. C'était super.

lundi	mardi	mercredi	jeudi	vendredi	samedi	dimanche
⚽						

trente-trois 33

3.1G Les règles scolaires

OBJECTIVES
- School rules
- Ordinal numbers
- *pouvoir* and *devoir*

1 Match the French and the English phrases.

1 les ordinateurs	6 un stylo	a to wear	f a team
2 les règles scolaires	7 porter	b homework	g to forget
3 le collège / le lycée	8 une équipe	c secondary school	h a pen
4 une leçon / un cours	9 oublier	d a lesson	i computers
5 les devoirs		e school rules	

2 Read the texts and match them to the photos.

1 J'habite à Montréal au Québec. Je vais au lycée et on doit porter un uniforme. C'est nul! **Myriam**

2 Je vais dans un collège à Tunis. À l'école, je peux porter mes propres vêtements, c'est génial. **Latifa**

3 Je vais dans un lycée au Burkina Faso. Les règles scolaires sont assez strictes mais je peux travailler en équipe et j'adore ça. **Moussa**

4 Je vais au lycée en France et je suis en seconde. Je dois faire beaucoup de devoirs, c'est difficile. **Jonas**

5 Je vais dans un lycée français à Londres. Je suis en quatrième. Pour le cours de maths, on ne doit jamais oublier notre livre à la maison. Madame Sander est très stricte. **Arnaud**

6 Je suis en troisième dans un collège en Belgique. En cours d'informatique, on doit toujours avoir un stylo et du papier… Pourquoi?! Moi, je préfère utiliser un ordinateur. **Nathalie**

3 Read the texts again and answer the questions.

a What does Myriam think of her school uniform?
b What does Latifa wear to school?
c What does Moussa love doing?
d What does Jonas have to do?
e What is Arnaud's maths teacher like?
f How does Nathalie like to work?

Culture

School rules vary hugely across different francophone countries. For example, wearing school uniform is not common in Belgium, France or Switzerland, but it is compulsory in many schools in Burkina Faso, the Ivory Coast and French Guiana.

Classes in French schools are labelled like this:

	France	Equivalent in England and Wales
collège	sixième (6e)	Year 7
	cinquième (5e)	Year 8
	quatrième (4e)	Year 9
	troisième (3e)	Year 10
lycée	seconde (2nde)	Year 11
	première (1re)	Year 12
	terminale	Year 13

trente-quatre

Education and work 3.1G

4 Choose the correct option to complete each sentence.

a Au collège, je **peut** / **peux** / **pouvons** porter mes propres vêtements.
b On **doit** / **devons** / **dois** toujours arriver à l'heure.
c Ils **pouvez** / **peut** / **peuvent** travailler en équipe.
d À l'école, elle **doit** / **doivent** / **dois** porter un uniforme.
e À la récré, nous **peut** / **pouvons** / **pouvez** aller dehors.

5 Listen (1–5) and choose the correct school rule.

a No eating food in class.
b Help others.
c Do your homework.
d No mobile phones in class.
e Wear school uniform.

6 Listen again (1–5). Decide if each speaker has a positive (P) or negative (N) opinion of the rule.

7 Read the texts in activity 2 again. Which school years are Jonas, Arnaud and Nathalie in?

8 Turn these numbers into ordinal numbers.

a huit
b quinze
c dix
d sept
e vingt
f onze

9 In pairs, complete the role play. Take turns to ask and answer the questions.

> **You are talking to your French friend about your school.**
>
> 1 *Alors, ton école?*
>   Give your opinion of your school. (Give **one** detail.)
> 2 *Il y a des règles scolaires?*
>   Give **one** rule.
> 3 Ask your friend a question about their school.
>   *(Give an appropriate response.)*
> 4 *Et ta classe?*
>   Say which year group you are in.
> 5 *Que penses-tu de l'uniforme?*
>   Give your opinion on wearing a uniform. (Give **one** detail.)

Les verbes

pouvoir and devoir

The verbs *pouvoir* (to be able to / can) and *devoir* (to have to / must) are useful when writing about school rules.

pouvoir	devoir
je peux	je dois
tu peux	tu dois
il / elle / on peut	il / elle / on doit
nous pouvons	nous devons
vous pouvez	vous devez
ils / elles peuvent	ils / elles doivent

Je **peux** porter mon pantalon noir.
I **am able to** / **can** wear my black trousers.
Je **dois** faire mes devoirs.
I **have to** / **must** do my homework.

Grammaire

Ordinal numbers

Ordinal numbers indicate the **order** in which something is organised.
Add *-ième* to the end of the number. If the number ends in '-e', drop the '-e' first.

deux → deuxième   second
quatre → quatrième   fourth

Exceptions:
premier / première   first
second(e)   second (can be used instead of *deuxième*)

10 Write a short paragraph (50 words) on school. Mention:
- where you go to school
- which year group you're in
- whether you wear a uniform
- your school rules
- your opinion of the rules.

Example: Je vais au lycée…
  Je suis en…
  On porte…
  On doit / peut…
  C'est…

3.1F Lycée et université?

OBJECTIVES
- Studies post-16
- Nouns ending in *-ation*
- Negative constructions
- Phonics: *-tion*

1 🎧 Listen to and read Nathan's conversation with his school careers adviser and answer the questions.

Nathan Bonjour, Madame Colas. Je ne sais pas quoi étudier l'année prochaine. Pouvez-vous m'aider?

Mme Colas Oui, bien sûr. Quelle est votre personnalité, Nathan?

Nathan Je suis très patient et j'aime aider les gens. De plus, j'ai une bonne communication. Par contre, je ne suis pas toujours indépendant.

Mme Colas Et vous aimez quelles matières au collège?

Nathan J'adore les sciences. C'est ma passion et j'ai de très bonnes notes. Je n'aime pas l'histoire… je n'écoute jamais en cours d'histoire, c'est trop ennuyeux!

Mme Colas Vous voulez travailler dans un bureau ou dans un autre environnement?

Nathan Je ne veux pas travailler dans un bureau. Je veux aider les gens, je veux un métier dans une organisation publique.

Mme Colas Avez-vous déjà pensé à la médecine? Je pense que c'est une bonne idée pour vous.

Nathan Oui, ça m'intéresse. Qu'est-ce que je dois faire pour devenir médecin?

Mme Colas Alors, il faut continuer à bien travailler en sciences. Après le lycée, il faut aller à l'université pendant plusieurs années. Bonne chance!

Nathan Merci beaucoup. Je ne connais personne qui travaille dans la médecine. Je vais chercher des informations ce soir.

a What is Nathan not sure about for next year?
b What is Nathan's personality like? Give **three** details.
c Which school subject doesn't he like and why?
d Which type of working environment doesn't appeal to him?
e What will he have to do to work in medicine? Give **two** details.
f What is he going to do this evening?

2 ✏️ Rewrite the sentences in the correct order.

a n' Il apprend ses leçons jamais .
b Je rien écoute n' en classe .
c M. Marin personne aime n' .
d pas as Tu n' de cours de langues ?
e Elle veut pas ne à l'université aller .

3 🔀 Translate into French.

a I do not know what to study next year.
b I don't want to go to university.
c I don't know anyone.
d I am not very organised.
e I never have good grades in science.

Grammaire

Using negative constructions

To make a sentence negative, use *ne … pas* around the verb:

Je **ne** fais **pas** d'espagnol au collège.
I **do not** do Spanish at school.

ne is shortened to *n'* in front of a vowel or silent *h*:

Je **n'**ai **pas** de cours d'anglais aujourd'hui.
I **don't** have any English lessons today.

These other negative forms follow the same pattern:

Il **ne** fait **jamais** ses devoirs. He **never** does his homework.
Je **ne** comprends **rien**. I do **not** understand **anything**. / I understand **nothing**.
Je **ne** vois **personne**. I do **not** see **anyone**. / I see **no one**.

Education and work   **3.1F**

4 🎧 Listen (1–4) and write down the sentences you hear.

5 Turn these verbs into nouns.

   a   participer   c   situer
   b   informer   d   préparer

Phonétique

-tion
communica**tion**   organisa**tion**   informa**tion**

6 💬 In pairs, take turns to read the text aloud.

> J'ai une bonne communication et une bonne organisation. À l'avenir, je veux travailler avec des enfants mais je ne veux pas travailler dans une école. Je vais aller au lycée mais je ne veux pas aller à l'université.

7 💬 In pairs, take turns to ask and answer the questions.
- Qu'est-ce-que tu n'aimes pas dans ton collège? Pourquoi pas?
- Dans quel environnement ne veux-tu jamais travailler? Pourquoi?
- Tu veux aller au lycée l'année prochaine? Pourquoi (pas)?
- Tu veux aller à l'université à l'avenir? Pourquoi (pas)?

8 ✏️ Write a paragraph (90 words) on school and future studies. Describe:
- the subjects you like and dislike, and why
- what you want to do when you leave school
- whether you want to go to university and why (not).

Grammaire

Nouns ending in -ation

Some nouns ending in -ation are closely related to an -er verb, and their English equivalent also ends in -ation. Simply replace the final -er of the verb with '-ation'.
Knowing the connection can help you create nouns or understand new ones when you read.

inviter ⟶ invit**ation**

organiser ⟶ organis**ation**

Culture

In France, students aged 11 to 15 go to *le collège* and at the end, they take exams called *le brevet*, equivalent to GCSEs. For the next three school years, they go to *le lycée*, where the final exam is *le baccalauréat* or *le bac*. Many students then choose to go to university, often in or near their home town, and course fees are low.

J'aime	l'histoire.
Je n'aime pas	les maths.
Ma matière préferée, c'est…	les sciences.
Je veux	aller à l'université.
Je ne veux pas	faire un apprentissage de…
À l'avenir, je voudrais	travailler / voyager.
	gagner de l'argent.
	être chanteur / chanteuse.
	être médecin / professeur(e).
	être footballeur / footballeuse professionel(le).
	travailler dans un bureau.
	travailler avec les enfants.
	travailler avec les animaux.

3.2G   Quel métier pour toi?

OBJECTIVES
- Describing jobs
- Feminine person nouns
- *il faut* + infinitive

1 📖 Match the jobs (1–9) to the photos (a–i).

1 acteur / actrice
2 policier / policière
3 facteur / factrice
4 influenceur / influenceuse
5 écrivain / écrivaine
6 chef / cheffe de cuisine
7 chanteur / chanteuse
8 professeur / professeure
9 aidant / aidante

2 📖 Choose a job (1–9) from activity 1 for each statement.

a Il faut aimer travailler avec des jeunes.
b Il faut aimer la musique.
c Il faut rester calme et aimer travailler en équipe.
d Il faut aimer aider les personnes malades ou âgées.
e Il faut aimer écrire des livres et créer des histoires.
f Il faut passer beaucoup de temps sur les réseaux sociaux.
g Il faut savoir faire la cuisine.
h Il faut savoir jouer différents personnages.
i Il faut distribuer le courrier.

3 ⭐ Work out the feminine form of these professions.

a directeur
b écrivain
c facteur
d influenceur
e président
f artiste

Grammaire

Feminine person nouns

Many feminine words for a job or profession add an *-e* to the end of the noun, unless it already ends in *-e*:

un professeur   *une professeur**e***
un journaliste   *une journaliste*

Some word endings change in other ways:

-eur / -euse	un serv**eur**	une serv**euse**
-ier / -ière	un polic**ier**	une polic**ière**
-teur / -trice	un ac**teur**	une ac**trice**

Some words are the same for both masculine and feminine:
un(e) médecin, un(e) prof, un(e) secrétaire (and others ending in *-e*)

Attention

When talking about jobs in French, *un* and *une* are not used:

Je suis journaliste mais je veux être acteur.
I am **a** journalist but I want to be **an** actor.

Education and work 3.2G

4 🎧 Listen (1–4). Copy and complete the table in English.

	Job	To do this job, you must…
1		

> **Les verbes**
>
> **il faut + infinitive**
>
> *Il faut* means 'it is necessary to', 'you / we must' or 'you / we have to'. It is followed by an infinitive. Use *il faut* + infinitive to express ideas in a general sense.
>
> *Il faut être créatif pour être artiste.*
> You have to be creative to be an artist.

5 💬 In pairs, take turns to choose a job and describe it using *il faut* + infinitive, and to guess your partner's job.

Example:

• *Il faut travailler dans une école avec des enfants.*

• *Professeur?*

• *Oui! À toi!*

• *Il faut…*

6 ✏️ Write sentences to say whether you would like to do these jobs and why (not).

directeur / directrice d'entreprise

professeur(e) de maths

scientifique

chef / cheffe de cuisine

président(e)

| Je voudrais
Je veux
Je vais

Je ne voudrais pas
Je ne veux pas
Je ne vais pas | être | professeur(e) de maths
chef / cheffe de cuisine
président(e)
scientifique
directeur / directrice d'entreprise | parce qu'
car | il faut
il ne faut pas
il ne faut jamais | aimer…
avoir…
être…
travailler… |

trente-neuf

3.2F Mon métier créatif

OBJECTIVES
- Jobs in the creative industries
- Indefinite adjectives
- *il y a* and *il y aura*
- Phonics: *c* and *ç*, *s*, *qu* and *th*

1 Read the texts and answer the questions.

J'adore mon boulot!

Agnès

Thomas

Mehdi

J'adore chanter et j'ai commencé à l'âge de cinq ans. **Je chante dans quelques restaurants** et à des mariages. Je voudrais devenir célèbre mais il y a beaucoup d'autres chanteurs, alors c'est très dur de devenir connue! **Tous les chanteurs célèbres** ont de la chance et je rêve de donner un concert. Samedi prochain, il y aura un concours de musique et j'espère gagner.

Moi, je suis auteur de livres pour enfants. Ce métier, c'est le meilleur du monde car il y a un grand choix de thèmes: les animaux, les héros, les romans historiques… Et il n'y a pas d'entretien! **Chaque livre est différent** – c'est vraiment passionnant! Demain, dans ma bibliothèque locale, il y aura une soirée où je vais parler de mon dernier livre.

Je suis acteur et mon projet est de faire carrière dans le cinéma. Pour être acteur, je dois avoir confiance en moi car il y a beaucoup de compétition. **Il y a toujours d'autres personnes** qui ont plus d'expérience et **plusieurs fois**, on m'a dit que j'étais nul. En mai, je vais aller au festival du film de Cannes pour voir mes deux acteurs préférés.

a According to Agnès, why is it hard to become famous?
b What does she hope will happen next Saturday?
c According to Thomas, why is being a writer the best job in the world? (Give **two** details.)
d What is he going to do tomorrow evening?
e According to Mehdi, which quality is important for an actor?
f Why is he going to the Cannes film festival in May?

Les verbes

Il y a and il y aura

Il y a means 'there is' or 'there are'.
Il y a un concert ce soir. **There is** a concert this evening.
Il y a beaucoup de concerts. **There are** lots of concerts.

Il y aura means 'there will be'.
Il y aura un concert ce soir.
There will be a concert this evening.
Il y aura beaucoup de concerts.
There will be lots of concerts.

2 Find *six* phrases containing *il y a* or *il y aura* in activity 1 and translate them into English.

40 quarante

Education and work 3.2F

Grammaire

Indefinite adjectives

Indefinite adjectives are words like 'other' and 'all' that refer to people or things in a general way. They go before a noun. In French they have to agree with the noun, just like any other adjective.

*J'aime les **autres** acteurs.* I like the **other** actors.
*J'écris un livre **chaque** année.* I write a book **every** year.
*Elle va à **tous** les concerts ici.* She goes to **all** the concerts here.

Singular		Plural		English
Masculine	Feminine	Masculine	Feminine	
autre	autre	autres	autres	other
chaque	chaque	–	–	every, each
tout	toute	tous	toutes	all, every
–	–	plusieurs	plusieurs	several, many
–	–	quelques	quelques	some, a few

3 Translate the *five* bold phrases in activity 1 into English.

4 Listen (1–5) and answer the questions.
1. Where did Jonathan listen to Agnès for the first time?
2. Where does Agnès get her inspiration from?
3. Where has she already found success?
4. What happens every Saturday?
5. Why is that good, in his opinion?

5 Listen (1–4) and write down the sentences you hear.

6 In pairs, look at the photo and take turns to ask and answer the questions. Look at the ideas underneath to help you.
- Parle-moi de la photo.
- Que penses-tu du métier d'influenceur / d'influenceuse?
- Tu voudrais faire quel métier? Pourquoi?

7 Write *five* sentences to describe the photo.
Example: Je vois …
Il est …
Il a …
Sur la photo…

Phonétique

c and ç
soft *c*: ç, c + e, c + i
hard *c*: c + a, c + o, c + u

ça	**c**'est	
carrière	**c**onnue	**c**oncert

s, qu and th

mai**s**on	plu**s**ieurs	cui**s**ine
quelques	musi**qu**e	cha**qu**e
thème	bibilio**th**èque	

quarante et un 41

Theme 1 — Culture: Mon métier francophone

1 Read the texts and answer the questions (a–h).

Voici mon métier !

Je m'appelle Simone. J'ai le meilleur métier du monde: je suis physicienne au CERN à Genève en Suisse. Le CERN, c'est le conseil européen pour la recherche nucléaire. J'utilise des machines scientifiques très complexes pour découvrir plus d'informations sur l'univers. Je travaille avec une grande équipe et j'aime surtout trouver des solutions aux problèmes. C'est vraiment un métier passionnant.

Mon prénom, c'est Bruno. J'habite à Grasse en France et je fais le métier de « nez »! Un nez, c'est une personne qui crée des parfums. Grasse, c'est la capitale mondiale du parfum depuis le 17e siècle. La ville est classée au patrimoine mondial de l'UNESCO. Il est très difficile de devenir nez et ça prend plusieurs années: il faut se souvenir de milliers d'arômes. Je suis bien payé et j'adore mon métier car j'aime travailler seul dans un laboratoire.

Je m'appelle Akissi et j'habite à la campagne en Côte d'Ivoire. Mon métier? C'est ingénieur agronome. L'agronomie, c'est la « science de la terre cultivable ». Je travaille pour améliorer les techniques agricoles dans une plantation de cacao. Je suis bien organisée et j'ai une bonne communication avec mon équipe. C'est très important dans mon métier. Pour devenir agronome, il faut étudier cinq ans à l'université.

a For what purpose does Simone uses complex machinery?
b What does Simone like in particular?
c What does the job of a 'nose' involve?
d Why does it take years to become 'a nose'?
e What reason does Bruno give for loving his job?
f What does Akissi's role as an agronomist involve?
g Which **two** qualities does she have?
h How can you become an agronomist?

un(e) ingénieur(e) agronome	agronomist
l'agronomie	agronomy
cultivable	arable
la technique agricole	agricultural technique
la plantation de cacao	cocoa farm
un arôme	aroma, scent, flavour
le / la physicien(ne)	physicist

Theme 1

2 In pairs, discuss in English the jobs in activity 1.
- Do you find any of these jobs appealing?
- Why (not)?
- Can you think of any unusual jobs that are specific to your own country?

Culture

West African countries such as the Ivory Coast and Cameroon produce over 70% of the cocoa beans in the world. Millions of people work on cocoa farms and it is a major part of these countries' economies. Child labour and deforestation are two major problems linked to cocoa production. Fairtrade and organic chocolate producers work in more ethical and sustainable ways.

3 Listen to Martine, who works on a snail farm in France. Write down the order in which the statements (a–g) are mentioned.

a I work in the countryside.
b We give calcium to the snails.
c We eat snails in a certain way.
d I work with snails.
e We have to choose the right snails for reproduction purposes.
f We feed the snails.
g It is important to be well organised for this job.

un escargot	a snail
un(e) héliciculteur/-trice	a snail farmer
la farine	flour
ramasser	to collect
le beurre persillé à l'ail	parsley and garlic butter

4 Research an unusual job in a francophone country and create a fact file.

Culture

Snails have been eaten for thousands of years and they were much loved by the Romans. It is estimated that between 16,000 and 30,000 tons of *escargots* (snails) are consumed in France each year: on average, 6.5 snails per person per year! They are particularly popular at Christmas, when about two-thirds of French snails are consumed.

Métier	chocolatier / chocolatière
Salaire	jusqu'à 6 500 € par mois (pour un maître chocolatier)
Heures de travail	longues
Études (*studies*)	apprentissage
Qualités	patience, créativité

5 Write a short paragraph to describe the job you chose in activity 4.

Example: Pour faire le métier de chocolatier, il faut travailler de longues heures et être patient et créatif. Comme études, c'est bien de faire un apprentissage.

quarante-trois

Theme 1 — Grammar practice

The present tense

1 Conjugate the verbs in the present tense.

a je (*manger*)
b tu (*entendre*)
c nous (*vendre*)
d je (*choisir*)
e ils (*jouer*)
f vous (*écouter*)
g ma sœur (*attendre*)
h Marc et moi (*parler*)
i je (*finir*)

2 Copy and complete the sentences with the present tense of the verb in brackets.

a Je ___ travailleur. (*être*)
b Elle ___ quinze ans. (*avoir*)
c Nous ___ en ville. (*aller*)
d Je n'___ pas de sœur. (*avoir*)
e Je ___ attention à ma santé. (*faire*)
f Elle ___ actrice. (*être*)
g Ce soir, ils ___ dans un centre sportif. (*aller*)
h Au collège, nous ___ de l'anglais. (*faire*)

Adjectives

3 Copy the sentences, adding in the adjective(s) in the correct position, with agreement where needed. Then translate the sentences into English.

a J'ai un chien. (*grand*, *noir*)
b Elle aime les films. (*vieux*, *historique*)
c Ma prof s'appelle madame Howard. (*préféré*)
d Il a un frère. (*petit*, *travailleur*)
e Mon père a trois voitures. (*bleu*)
f Je mange toujours des repas. (*équilibré*)

> **Grammaire**
>
> Most adjectives **follow** the noun they describe, but a few (such as those describing appearance, age, goodness and size) go **before** the noun.
>
> Remember to make the adjective agree with the noun.

Reflexive verbs

4 Choose the correct reflexive pronoun to complete each sentence. Then translate the sentences into English.

a Elle **m'** / **s'** / **t'** entend bien avec son frère.
b Je **me** / **te** / **se** lève tôt le matin.
c Tu **te** / **me** / **se** laves après le petit-déjeuner.
d Il **t'** / **s'** / **m'** appelle Martin.
e Je **se** / **me** / **te** dispute souvent avec mes parents.
f Tu **me** / **se** / **te** souviens de ton école primaire?

qui

5 Copy and combine the pairs of sentences using *qui*.

Example: Il y a un enfant. Il joue au foot.
→ *Il y a un enfant qui joue au foot.*

a Je mange des légumes verts. Ils sont bons pour la santé.
b Elle va au restaurant. Il est cher.
c En juillet, il se marie avec sa fiancée. Elle est canadienne.
d Les élèves font beaucoup d'exercices. Ils sont difficiles.
e Je préfère mon collège. Il est très grand.
f Tu vois souvent ta grand-mère? Elle habite en France.

Theme 1

Comparative adjectives

6 Rewrite the comparative sentences in the correct order. Then translate the sentences into English.

a aussi   que   Le sport   difficile   le travail   est   .

b est   Il   toi   amusant   que   plus   .

c est   meilleure   que   Ma copine   en français   moi   .

d L'anglais   est   utile   aussi   les maths   que   .

e M. Marin   moins   Mme Colas   que   strict   est   .

f pire   le foot   Le vélo   que   est   .

Negative sentences

7 Rewrite the sentences using the negative construction in brackets. Then translate the sentences into English.

a Nous sommes actifs. (*ne … jamais*)
b Ma meilleure copine est allemande. (*ne … pas*)
c Mon frère va à une nouvelle école. (*ne … pas*)
d Je regarde la télé. (*ne … jamais*)
e Je mange après 21 heures. (*ne … rien*)
f Je tchatte avec mes amis. (*ne … personne*)

Grammaire

Remember that the **negative** sandwiches the verb:

*Je **ne** bois **pas** beaucoup d'eau.*

Position of adverbs

8 Rewrite the sentences, putting the adverb in brackets in the correct place.

a Je mange de la viande pour le déjeuner. (*souvent*)
b Je joue au foot le dimanche. (*parfois*)
c Elle aime faire ses devoirs. (*beaucoup*)
d Je vais au cinéma avec ma famille. (*normalement*)
e J'aime les fruits. (*seulement*)
f Il travaille. (*trop*)

The near future tense

9 Copy and complete the sentences in the near future tense, to match the English translation.

a Je ___ voir mes cousins. (*I am going to see my cousins.*)
b Elle ___ étudier les maths. (*She is going to study maths.*)
c ___-tu faire plus d'exercice? (*Are you going to do more exercise?*)
d Nous ___ ___ ce soir. (*We are going to go out tonight.*)
e Je ___ ___ moins de viande. (*I am going to eat less meat.*)
f Ils ___ ___ en France. (*They are going to work in France.*)

Les verbes

Remember that the near future tense uses a part of *aller* + an infinitive.

Theme 1 — Grammar practice

Plural nouns

10 Write the plural form of the nouns.

a un lieu → des ___
b un bras → des ___
c une leçon → des ___
d un château → des ___
e un cheveu → des ___
f un choix → des ___

Imperatives

11 Copy and complete the sentences with the correct *tu*-form imperative of the verb in brackets.

a ___ avec tes amis. (*parler*)
b ___ plus de vélo! (*faire*)
c ___ te coucher plus tôt! (*aller*)
d ___ tes devoirs. (*finir*)
e ___ moins de gâteaux! (*manger*)
f ___ beaucoup d'eau. (*boire*)

Les verbes

The imperative is formed from the *tu*-form of the present tense. For *-er* verbs, drop the 's'.

Interrogative adjective: *quel*

12 Copy and complete the sentences with the correct form: *quel*, *quelle*, *quels* or *quelles*.

a ___ est ta couleur préférée?
b ___ est ton projet pour l'avenir?
c ___ chanteuses préfères-tu?
d ___ métiers (*mpl*) aimes-tu?
e ___ film (*m*) veux-tu regarder?
f Tu vas à ___ école (*f*)?

Grammaire

Interrogative adjectives (meaning 'which') need to agree with the noun, just like any other adjective.

The perfect tense

13 Translate into French.

a I ate
b she played
c we sold
d they finished
e you changed
f I succeeded
g he lost
h we chose
i she waited

14 Correct the verb error in each sentence and write why it is wrong.

a Je joué au foot hier. (*I played football yesterday.*)
b Elle n'ai pas fini ses devoirs. (*She hasn't finished her homework.*)
c Tu as mange beaucoup de poisson. (*You ate a lot of fish.*)
d J'ai vendé ma voiture. (*I sold my car.*)
e Ils a attendu le train. (*They waited for the train.*)
f Il a travailler dans un restaurant. (*He worked in a restaurant.*)

Theme 1

Indirect object pronouns (singular)

15 Rewrite the sentences, replacing the words in brackets with the correct indirect object pronoun in the correct position: *me*, *te*, *lui*, *vous*.

Example: Mon cousin ressemble (**à moi**). → Mon cousine **me** ressemble.

a Je téléphone (**à ma sœur**).
b Il donne le cadeau (**à moi**).
c Je parle (**à toi**).
d J'ai dit (**à mon copain**) qu'il était sympa.
e Nous vendons notre voiture (**à vous**).
f J'ai répondu (**à ma mère**).

Grammaire

Indirect object pronouns replace a noun that would be introduced with the preposition *à* (to). They always go before the verb.

pouvoir and *devoir*

16 Rewrite the sentences in the correct order. Then translate them into English.

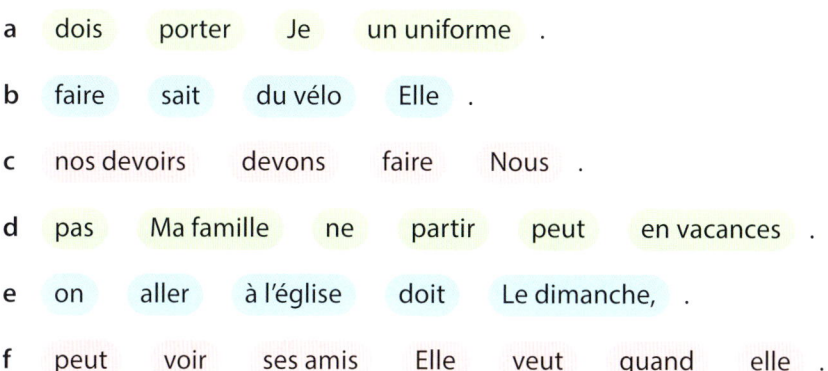

a dois · porter · Je · un uniforme .
b faire · sait · du vélo · Elle .
c nos devoirs · devons · faire · Nous .
d pas · Ma famille · ne · partir · peut · en vacances .
e on · aller · à l'église · doit · Le dimanche, .
f peut · voir · ses amis · Elle · veut · quand · elle .

Les verbes

Remember that modal verbs like *devoir* (to have to, must) and *pouvoir* (to be able to, can) are usually followed by an infinitive.

il faut + infinitive

17 Write school rules for a–f, using either *il faut* or *il ne faut pas*.

Example: utiliser un ordinateur → Il faut utiliser un ordinateur.

a porter un uniforme
b écouter les professeurs
c avoir un portable en classe
d arriver à l'heure
e manger en classe
f faire des devoirs

Feminine person nouns

18 Write the feminine form of these names for jobs.

a un policier → une ___
b un aidant → une ___
c un acteur → une ___
d un chanteur → une ___
e un écrivain → une ___
f un professeur → une ___

Theme 1 — Vocabulary

Words that are highlighted in grey in this list are words that may be useful, but you won't need to know them for the exam.

Introductory vocabulary

l' *acteur/actrice* actor, actress
actif/active active
adorer to love
l' *allemand (n.) (m.)* German (language)
aller to go
l' *ami(e) (m./f.)* friend
amusant(e) amusing, fun, funny, enjoyable
l' *anglais (n.) (m.)* English (language)
anglais(e) (adj.) English
s' *appeler* to be called
apporter to bring
après after
l' *après-midi (m.)* afternoon
assez quite, enough
au chômage unemployed
autre chose anything else
avoir to have
beaucoup (de) a lot (of)
le *beau-père* stepfather, father-in-law
la *belle-mère* stepmother, mother-in-law
la *bibliothèque* library
bien good, well
blanc (adj.) white
boire to drink
bon(ne) good
bonjour good morning, afternoon
brun(e) brown
ça it, that
le *café* coffee, coffee shop
car because
célèbre famous
cependant however
la *chanson* song
le/la *chanteur/chanteuse* singer
les *cheveux (m. pl.)* hair

le *chômage* unemployment
cinq five
le *collège* (secondary) school
comme such as, like, since
le *concert* concert
la *construction* construction
content(e) glad, pleased, happy
le *cours* lesson
court(e) short
le/la *cousin(e)* cousin
dernier/dernière last
détester to hate
deux two
devenir to become
difficile difficult
dix ten
du/de la/des/de l' some
l' *eau (f.)* water
l' *école (f.)* school
écrire to write
l' *éducation (f.)* education
en général in general
en plus in addition
en premier first of all, firstly
l' *enfant (m./f.)* child
enfin finally
ennuyeux/ennuyeuse boring
ensemble together
ensuite then
équilibré(e) balanced
l' *équipe (f.)* team
l' *espagnol (n.) (m.)* Spanish (language)
espagnol(e) (adj.) Spanish
être to be
facile easy
le/la *facteur/factrice* postman/postwoman
faire to do, to make
la *famille* family
la *femme* woman, wife
la *fille* girl, daughter
le *film* film
le *fils* son
le *football* football

le *français (n.)* French (language)
français(e) (adj.) French
la *France* France
les *frites (f. pl.)* chips
le *fromage* cheese
le *fruit* fruit
gagner to win, earn
le *gâteau* cake
gauche left
généralement generally
génial(e) great
la *géographie* geography
la *glace* ice, ice cream
le *gouvernement* government
la *grand-mère* grandmother
le *grand-père* grandfather
la *grève* strike
habiter to live
l' *heure (f.)* hour, time, o'clock
l' *histoire (f.)* history, story
important(e) important
l' *indépendance (f.)* independence
l' *informatique (f.)* IT, computer science
intéressant(e) interesting
jamais never
je voudrais (vouloir) I would like
jeune young
jouer to play
juillet July
le *lait* milk
le/la/l'/les the
le *légume* vegetable
la *lettre* letter
leur(s) (to) them, their
long(ue) long
la *maison* house
manger to eat
(le) *mardi* Tuesday
le *mari* husband
les *maths (f. pl.)* maths
le *matin* morning
méchant(e) naughty, nasty
la *mère* mother

le *métier* job
la *mode* fashion
moi me
la *musique* music
la *natation* swimming
non-binaire non-binary
nul(le) rubbish
l' *oncle (m.)* uncle
l' *ordinateur (m.)* computer
où where
le *pain* bread
par contre on the other hand
parce que because
parfois sometimes
passer to spend, to pass
le *père* father
la *personne* person
le *petit-déjeuner* breakfast
la *photo* photo
la *piscine* swimming pool
plusieurs several
le *poisson* fish
le/la *policier/policière* policeman/policewoman
la *politique* politics
porter to wear, to carry
pouvoir to be able to
préféré(e) favourite
le *professeur/professeure, prof* teacher
puis then
la *récréation* breaktime
rentrer to go back, to go home
le *restaurant* restaurant
le *rêve* dream
le *riz* rice
la *rue* street
sain(e) healthy
le *salaire* salary
(le) *samedi* Saturday
les *sciences (f. pl.)* sciences
la *sécurité* safety, security
la *semaine* week
le/la *serveur/serveuse* waiter/waitress
la *sœur* sister
sourire to smile

Theme 1

souvent often
le sport sport
sportif/sportive sporty
strict(e) strict
le studio studio
le succès success
la Suisse Switzerland
super great, super
sûr(e) safe, secure
sympa nice
la technologie DT
le temps time, weather
le thé tea
le théâtre drama
toujours always
tous les jours every day
transgenre transgender
travailler to work
trop de too much, many (of)
trouver to find
le t-shirt t-shirt
un peu a little
un(e) a
le vélo bike
vers towards
la viande meat
le Vietnam Vietnam
le village village
la ville town, city
le vin wine
voici here is
vouloir to want
voyager to travel
vraiment really

1.1G Qui suis-je?

aimer to like
l' an (m.) year
avec with
beau/belle beautiful, handsome
la Belgique Belgium
bleu(e) blue
le chien dog
comment how
la couleur colour
la cuisine kitchen, cooking
dans in
douze twelve
elle she
facilement easily
le fast-food fast food
le frère brother
gentil(le) kind
grand(e) big, large, tall
les grand-parents (m. pl.) grandparents
il he
je/j' I
joli(e) pretty
mais but
le Maroc Morocco
mauvais(e) bad
le million million
mon, ma, mes my
la montagne mountain
nous we
noir(e) black
nouveau/nouvelle new
on we, one
le pantalon trousers
parler to speak, to talk
petit(e) small, little, short
préférer to prefer
le Québec Quebec
qui who, which
regarder to look, to watch
rouge red
le Sénégal Senegal
sénégalais(e) (adj.) Senegalese
surtout especially
la table table
la télé TV
très very
tu you (singular)
vert(e) green
les vêtements (m. pl.) clothes
vieux/vieil/vieille old
les yeux (m. pl.) eyes

1.1F Ma personnalité

acheter to buy
alors so, well, then
arriver to arrive
attendre to wait
au revoir goodbye
aussi also
bavard(e) chatty
bonne chance good luck
calme (adj.) calm, quiet
la catastrophe catastrophe
la clé key
connaître to know (person, place)
le copain friend, boyfriend
la copine friend, girlfriend
de plus besides, moreover
descendre to go down, descend, get off
devoir to have to, must
drôle funny
embêtant(e) annoying
en fait in fact, in reality
en retard late
entendre to hear
fier/fière proud
fort(e) strong
gentil(le) kind
inquiétant(e) worrying
intelligent(e) intelligent
Internet (m.) internet
le judo judo
maintenant now
même same
la mission mission
neuf/neuve new
non no
la note grade, mark
oui yes
paresseux/paresseuse lazy
partir to leave
passionnant(e) exciting
penser to think
perdre to lose
la personnalité personality
personne nobody
la qualité quality
quand when
que that
quel(le) what, which
répondre to answer
salut hi, hello
sérieux/sérieuse serious
son/sa/ses his/her
le téléphone phone
timide timid, shy
toi you (singular)
ton/ta/tes your (singular)
le train train
travailleur/travailleuse hard-working
triste sad
trop too
vendre to sell
vite quick
la voiture car
vrai(e) true

1.2G Voici ma famille

l' année (f.) year
ce/cet/cette/ces this, these
se disputer to argue
s' entendre avec to get on with
s' excuser to apologise
handicapé(e) (adj.) disabled
se marier to get married
ou or
le petit copain boyfriend
la petite copine girlfriend
se séparer to split up, separate
la tante aunt
terrible terrible
tout le temps all the time

1.2F Les familles de nos jours

à at, to
adopté(e) adopted
aussi … que as … as
canadien(ne) Canadian
chez moi at my place, at mine
choisir to choose
la chose thing
le cinéma cinema
comprendre to understand
la Côte d'Ivoire Ivory Coast
les courses (f. pl.) (grocery) shopping
le déjeuner lunch

quarante-neuf 49

Theme 1 Vocabulary

le **demi-frère** half-brother
la **demi-sœur** half-sister
les **devoirs** (m. pl.) homework
(le) **dimanche** Sunday
écouter to listen (to)
l' **émission** (f.) TV programme
encore again, still, yet
finir to finish
le **frigo** fridge
grandir to grow (up)
le **jeu** game
le **jeu vidéo** video game
là-bas over there
la **lecture** reading
meilleur(e) que better than
moins … que less than
le **mois** month
né(e) born
Noël Christmas
normalement normally
nous we
les **parents** (m. pl.) parents
Paris Paris
pire que worse than
la **plage** beach
plus more
plus … que more than
pour for, in order to
le **problème** problem
remplir to fill up
réunir to gather
réussir to succeed
rire to laugh
le **sac** bag
séparé separated
septembre September
la **télé** television
tolérant(e) tolerant
tous all, every
le **travail** work
les **vacances** (f. pl.) holidays
(le) **vendredi** Friday
vivre to live

2.1G On mange!

la **boisson** drink
d'habitude usually
le **dîner** dinner
donner to give
du tout at all
l' **énergie** (f.) energy
la **faim** hunger
la **ferme** farm
le **hamburger** hamburger
le **marché** market
la **mer** sea
le **poisson-frites** fish and chips
préparer to prepare
le **produit** product
la **recette** recipe
le **repas** meal
rien nothing
seul(e) alone
seulement only
la **soif** thirst
végan(e) vegan
végétarien(ne) vegetarian

2.1F Aïe aïe aïe!

à l'âge de at the age of
l' **accident** (m.) accident
aider to help
l' **alcool** (m.) alcohol
arrêter to stop
aujourd'hui today
avoir mal to hurt
avoir peur to be scared
la **bouche** mouth
le **bras** arm
le **château** castle
le **choix** choice
la **cigarette** cigarette
commencer to start
le **corps** body
d'accord ok, agreed
la **dame** lady
le **danger** danger
dangereux/dangereuse dangerous
demain tomorrow
dire say, tell
le **dos** back
la **drogue** drug
l' **effort** (m.) effort
envoyer to send
examiner to examine
l' **exercice** (m.) exercise
la **façon** way, manner
fatigué(e) tired
fumer to smoke
la **gorge** throat
il faut (falloir) it is necessary, must
immédiatement immediately
inquiet/inquiète worried
la **jambe** leg
lever to raise
le **lieu** place
le **lit** bed
le **mal** ache
malade ill
le **médecin** doctor
le **médicament** medication
l' **oreille** (f.) ear
peut-être maybe
le **pied** foot
prendre to take
se **relaxer** to relax
le **rendez-vous** rendez-vous, appointment
sain(e) healthy
la **santé** health
savoir to know
le **souci** worry
la **tête** head
tomber to fall
tuer to kill
l' **urgence** (f.) emergency
vapoter to vape
la **vie** life
voir to see

2.2G Mon mode de vie

à l'avenir in the future
se **coucher** to go to bed
croire to believe
l' **habitude** (f.) habit
la **journée** day
le **livre** book
le/la **meilleur(e) ami(e)** best friend
le **mode de vie** lifestyle
le **mois** month
partager to share
pendant during
poser to ask
la **question** question
recevoir to receive
le **soir** evening
suivre to follow
tard late
tôt early

2.2F Hier j'ai…

l' **anniversaire** (m.) birthday
le **bain** bath
le **cadeau** present
demander to ask
essayer to try
… fois … time, times
hier yesterday
(le) **jeudi** Thursday
lui (to) him, (to) her
(le) **lundi** Monday
le **match** match
(le) **mercredi** Wednesday
la **nourriture** food
la **nuit** night
participer to participate, contribute, take part
le **portable** mobile phone
premier / première first
le **programme** schedule
rencontrer to meet
ressembler to look like
le **surf** surf
te / t' (to) you
le **Tour de France** Tour de France
la **partie (de foot)** (football) match, game
vous (to) you (polite, plural)

3.1G Les règles scolaires

la **cinquième** fifth, Year 8
la **classe** class, classroom, year group
le **lycée** school, 6th form
Londres London
madame Mrs, Ms
normal normal
oublier to forget
le **papier** paper

Theme 1

pourquoi why
la première first, Year 12
propre clean, own
la quatrième fourth, Year 9
la règle rule, ruler
la seconde second, Year 11
la sixième sixth, Year 7
le stylo pen
la terminale last, Year 13
la troisième third, Year 10
l' uniforme (m.) uniform
utiliser to use

3.1F Lycée et université?

apprendre to learn
bien sûr of course
le bureau desk, office
chercher to research, to look for
la classe class, classroom
la communication communication
continuer to continue
l' environnement (m.) environment
étudier to study
les gens (m. pl.) people
indépendant(e) independent
l' information (f.) information
intéresser to interest
la langue language
la matière subject
la médecine medicine (field, profession)
merci thank you
l' organisation (f.) organisation
l' organisation caritative charity
organisé(e) organised
la participation contribution
la passion passion
prochain(e) next
progresser to progress
quoi what
la situation situation

situer to locate
l' université (f.) university

3.2G Quel métier pour toi?

l' adresse (f.) address
âgé(e) old, older
l' aidant/aidante carer
l' artiste (m./f.) artist
le/la chef/cheffe chef, boss
le courrier post
créer to create
différent(e) different
le/la directeur/directrice (company) director, headteacher
distribuer to distribute
l' écrivain(e) (m./f.) author, writer
l' élève (m./f.) pupil, student
l' influenceur/influenceuse (m./f.) influencer
patient(e) (adj.) patient
le personnage character
le/la policier/policière policeman/policewoman
le/la président/présidente president
les réseaux sociaux (m. pl.) social media
le/la scientifique scientist

3.2F Mon métier créatif

l' animal (m.) animal
l' auteur/autrice author
la carrière career
chanter to sing
chaque each, every
la compétition competition
connu(e) famous, known
dur(e) hard
espérer to hope
l' Europe (f.) Europe
l' expérience (f.) experience
le festival festival
l' héroïne (female) hero
le héros (male) hero
historique historical
local(e)(s)/locaux local

mai May
le mariage marriage
le monde world
montrer to show
le/la musicien(ne) musician
le quartier neighbourhood
quelque(s) some, several
le roman novel
la soirée evening
le thème theme

Culture

l' agronomie (f.) agronomy
améliorer to improve
l' apprentissage (m.) work experience
le beurre persillé à l'ail parsley and garlic butter
le calcium calcium
le chocolatier chocolatier
cinq five
classé(e) classified
la communication communication
complexe complex
le conseil a piece of advice
la Côte d'Ivoire Ivory Coast
la créativité creativity
cultivable arable
d'abord first of all
l' escargot (m.) snail
l' étude (f.) study
étudier to study
européen(ne) European
la farine flour
l' héliciculteur/hélicicultrice snail farmer
l' Ingénieur(e) agronome agronomist
jusque until
le laboratoire laboratory
la machine machine, equipment
les milliers (m. pl.) thousands
mondial(e) universal, international
le nez nose
(le) nucléaire nuclear
organisé(e) organised
le parfum perfume, scent

la patience patience
le patrimoine mondial worldwide heritage
le prénom first name
payé(e) paid
le/la physicien(ne) physicist
la plantation de cacao cocoa farm
le problème problem
la qualité quality
ramasser to collect
la recherche research
la reproduction reproduction
se souvenir (de) remember
le siècle century
la solution solution
les techniques agricoles (f. pl.) agricultural techniques
la terre earth, soil
l' univers (m.) universe

French is a language with grammatical genders, so some of the words in this list have a masculine and feminine form, which are used for referring to different people. You will not be marked down in the exam for your preferred ways of referring to yourself and others through the use of pronouns, gendered language and grammatical agreements.

Theme 1 — Test and revise: Foundation Listening

1 You hear some Belgian teenagers (1–4) talking about health and lifestyle.

What do they mention? Write the correct letter for each person.

A	Swimming
B	Relaxing
C	Riding a bike
D	Eating fruit
E	Sleeping well
F	Drinking water

4 marks

Conseil

For this task, you are likely to hear the exact French for the words given in the answer options. Before you listen, you could jot down the French words if you know them, so you have something to refer to when listening.

You will hear four extracts and there are six options to choose from, so there are two options in the box that you won't be using. These are called distractors.

2 You hear this conversation on the radio about friendship.

Which aspects are necessary for a solid friendship?

Write the **two** correct letters for each extract (1–2).

A	Good communication
B	Kindness
C	Spending time together
D	Listening to the friend's problems
E	Having similar interests
F	Laughter

4 marks

Conseil

There are two extracts to listen to and each extract has two correct letters. So there are two options (distractors) in the list that won't be used.

Before listening, try to predict which French words might come up for each option. For example, for option F (laughter), the word used might be a verb (*rire* – to laugh) or an adjective (*amusant* – fun, funny).

3 You hear this radio programme about marriage. Complete the sentences in **English**.

1 a These days, young people choose…   1 mark

    b First, they prefer to…   1 mark

2 a At the moment, more and more couples…   1 mark

    b This is sometimes because they…   1 mark

Conseil

For this task, you are given the beginnings of four sentences to complete in English. There are two sentences for each audio extract. The answer may be a short phrase or just a single word. You can write in English exactly what you hear in the recording or paraphrase it (write in your own words).

4 You hear some French people talking about their jobs. What is their opinion on the following aspects?

Write   **P** for a **positive** opinion
        N for a **negative** opinion
        P+N for a **positive** and **negative** opinion.

1 Colleagues
2 Salary
3 Working hours
4 The boss

4 marks

Conseil

Listen to the whole statement each time before making your decision. Listen out for words such as *mais, cependant* and *par contre*, which can introduce a negative opinion even if the sentence started positively.

Theme 1

5 You hear some French students talking about their health. Complete the sentences in **English**.

1 I like running with…   **1 mark**
2 I swim in a pool near…   **1 mark**
3 I have made… at the book club.   **1 mark**
4 I play football because…   **1 mark**

Conseil

This task requires you to listen for specific details and complete sentences in English. Read the sentences carefully and think about language you might hear. For example, in sentence 4, you will need to listen out for a reason, possibly preceded by *car* or *parce que*.

6 You hear this podcast about a school in Burkina Faso. Choose the correct answer and write the letter.

1 Issa thinks…

A	his class is very quiet.
B	there are too many students in his class.
C	he can work well in his class.

1 mark

2 Issa says that the school day…

A	includes a long break for lunch.
B	is too short.
C	is longer on Saturdays.

1 mark

3 Last year…

A	Issa didn't do his homework.
B	there was no homework set.
C	there was homework set.

1 mark

4 In the future, Issa wants to work…

A	as an actor.
B	on a farm.
C	with his cousin.

1 mark

Dictation A

You will now hear **four** short sentences.

- Listen carefully and, using your knowledge of French sounds, write down in French exactly what you hear for each sentence.
- You will hear each sentence **three** times: the first time as a full sentence, the second time in short sections and the third time again as a full sentence.
- Use your knowledge of French sounds and grammar to make sure that what you have written makes sense. Check carefully that your spelling is accurate.

8 marks

Dictation B

You will now hear **four** more sentences.

Write down in French exactly what you hear for each sentence.

8 marks

Conseil

This task requires you to understand all the details in the audio extract. For the first question, for example, Issa mentions all three options: noise levels, number of students and concentration. You need to listen to the whole audio extract before choosing an answer.

cinquante-trois **53**

Theme 1 — Test and revise: Foundation Speaking

Role play

You are talking to your Belgian friend.
Your teacher will play the part of your friend and will speak first.
You should address your friend as *tu*.
When you see this – ? – you will have to ask a question.

In order to score full marks, you must include a verb in your response to each task.

1 Say who you get on with in your family. (Give **one** detail.)
2 Say **one** activity you do with your family.
3 Give **one** opinion on marriage.
? 4 Ask your friend a question about their family.
5 Describe your best friend. (Give **one** detail.)

10 marks

> **Conseil**
> Remember that you are allowed to take notes for all tasks in the speaking exam. You can refer to these at any point during the test. Use this to help you!

> **Conseil**
> For the role play, the most important thing is to convey the message clearly. Make sure you double-check how many pieces of information you are required to give for each point. Keep your sentences short and accurate.

Reading aloud

When your teacher asks you, read aloud the following text **in French**.

J'adore mon collège.
Ma matière préférée, c'est les sciences.
À la récréation, je joue au foot avec mes copains.
Mon copain, il n'aime pas les devoirs.
À l'avenir, il veut être chanteur ou acteur.

You will then be asked four questions **in French** that relate to the topic of **Education and work**. Make sure you **answer all four questions as fully as you can**.

15 marks

> **Conseil**
> For the reading aloud task, you can obtain a maximum of 5 marks for reading the text aloud. When reading aloud, focus carefully on your pronunciation. Try to remember all the French sounds and sound combinations you have learnt.
>
> For the second part of the task, you can obtain a maximum of 10 marks for your responses to the follow-up questions. These need to be communicated clearly and in as much detail as possible. Try to answer all questions and extend your sentences by giving opinions and using other tenses and conjunctions.

Theme 1

Photo card

- During your preparation time, look at the two photos. You may make as many notes as you wish on an Additional Answer Sheet and use these notes during the task.
- Your teacher will ask you to talk about the content of these photos. The recommended time is approximately **one minute**. You must **say at least one thing about each photo**.
- After you have spoken about the content of the photos, your teacher will then ask you questions related to **any** of the topics within the theme of **People and lifestyle**.

25 marks

Conseil

For the photo card task, you can obtain a maximum of 5 marks for describing the two pictures. You must say at least one thing about each photo. Try to give as much information as possible, even if your message is not always communicated clearly.

For the follow-up conversation, you can obtain a maximum of 20 marks. Try to develop your answers by giving and justifying opinions using *parce que* or *car*, for example.

Photo 1

Photo 2

cinquante-cinq 55

Theme 1 — Test and revise: Foundation Reading

1 These French students are talking about school rules. Which rule does each student mention? Write the correct letter.

1. Dans mon école, il faut arriver à l'heure. **Armelle**

2. Dans mon collège, on doit faire beaucoup de devoirs. **Élodie**

3. Au lycée, il ne faut pas utiliser son portable en classe. **Vincent**

4. Dans mon école, on doit toujours écouter les professeurs. **Mathis**

A	Wearing a uniform
B	Doing homework
C	Respecting others
D	Not using mobile phones
E	Arriving on time
F	Listening to the teachers

4 marks

Conseil
If you don't understand exactly what a word means, move on to the next sentence and then use a process of elimination to choose your answer. Use cognates and near-cognates to help you too.

2 You see an online forum about families. What do these people think about their family members?

Write **P** for a **positive** opinion
      N for a **negative** opinion
      P+N for a **positive** and **negative** opinion.

5 marks

 1 Jérôme
Ma tante est toujours embêtante. Elle n'arrête pas de me demander quand je vais me marier avec ma petite copine.

 2 Catherine
Mon frère est très sympathique. Il aide toujours les autres quand ils ont besoin de quelque chose.

3 Margaux
Ma belle-mère a de bons côtés: elle m'achète souvent des vêtements et on s'entend bien. Le seul problème, c'est qu'elle travaille beaucoup alors on ne passe pas beaucoup de temps ensemble.

 4 Medhi
Mon vieil oncle m'a toujours raconté des histoires sur son passé et je trouve ça intéressant. En plus, il fait très bien la cuisine.

 5 Ludovic
Mes parents me donnent de l'argent pour sortir avec mes copains, c'est gentil. Cependant, ils sont très stricts avec mon travail scolaire: je trouve ça vraiment embêtant.

Conseil
In this task, you only need to work out the gist (overall meaning) of each text, focusing on clues that tell you whether each person's opinion is positive or negative. Look out for words like *mais* or *cependant,* which can change the meaning of a sentence from positive to negative or the other way round.

Theme 1

3 You read an article about a singer. What does the article say about these events?

Write **P** for something that happened **in the past**
N for something that is happening **now**
F for something that will happen **in the future**.

> Dans quelques semaines, Benji va donner son premier concert devant des milliers de personnes. À dix-huit ans, il a fait partie d'une émission de télévision française; il n'a pas gagné le concours mais il a adoré participer. Il est maintenant célèbre, surtout parmi les jeunes qui adorent sa musique. Il chante des chansons qui parlent d'amour mais bientôt, il va commencer à chanter sur des thèmes différents. Il adore chanter car c'est le métier de ses rêves.

a	His first concert	1 mark
b	Taking part in a TV programme	1 mark
c	Young people loving his music	1 mark
d	Singing about love	1 mark
e	Singing about different themes	1 mark

Conseil

In this task, you need to use your knowledge of grammar, especially verbs and tenses, to choose the correct answer. Use your knowledge of adverbs of time to help you too. For example, *bientôt* means 'soon' and is therefore referring to the future.

4 Translate these sentences into **English**.

a Tu es trop fatigué. Couche-toi plus tôt!
b Je m'entends bien avec ma petite sœur.
c Je ne mange jamais entre les repas.
d L'année prochaine, elle va étudier l'informatique à l'université.
e L'année dernière, nous avons essayé le volley pour la première fois.

10 marks

5 Translate these sentences into **English**.

a À l'avenir, je vais choisir de me marier.
b Mon meilleur ami est plus gentil que mon frère.
c Quels sports n'as-tu pas encore essayés?
d Hier, ils ont oublié de faire leurs devoirs de français.
e Parfois, elle aime porter son uniforme scolaire.

10 marks

Conseil

When translating into English, you need to give the meaning of the whole sentence without necessarily translating word for word. Identify the verb and tense the sentence is in before you start. When you have finished, make sure you haven't forgotten to translate any words, and proofread your English translation to check for accuracy. If there is a word that you don't know at all, it is better to include a similar word (e.g. noun, adjective, adverb) than to leave a gap in your translation

cinquante-sept 57

Theme 1 — Test and revise: Foundation Writing

1 **You are sharing photos about school with a French friend on Snapchat**

What is in this photo? Write **five** sentences in **French**.

> **Conseil**
>
> For this task, you must only describe what you see in the photo (not give your opinion of it). You can write in short sentences. You need to include a conjugated verb to obtain two marks. For example, you could use *Il y a* (there is / there are) or *Je vois* (I see) at the beginning of the sentence.

10 marks

2 **You are writing to your French friend about your life at home. Write a short description of your family and health for your friend.**

Write approximately **50** words in **French**. You must write something about each bullet point.

Mention:
- your personality
- your family
- your best friend
- your meals on a typical day
- what you do to stay healthy.

10 marks

> **Conseil**
>
> For this task, you must write something about all the bullet points but there is no need to cover them equally. You must try to be as accurate as possible so that your message is clearly communicated. You don't have to write in more than one tense if you don't want to. You should show a variety of vocabulary: for example, different adjectives, verbs and pronouns.

Theme 1

3 Using your knowledge of grammar, complete the following sentences in **French**.

Choose the correct French word from the three options in the grid.

Write the correct word, as shown in the example.

Example: *Le garçon* **a** *trois sœurs.*

ont	a	ai

a Nous ___ faire du sport.

aimons	aime	aimez

1 mark

b Ma prof est très ___.

gentils	gentil	gentille

1 mark

c Le samedi, ___ finissent leurs devoirs.

je	elle	ils

1 mark

d Mon frère ___ très ennuyeux.

es	est	suis

1 mark

e Hier, j'ai ___ dans un hôpital.

travailler	travaille	travaillé

1 mark

Conseil

For this task, read the sentences very carefully as each word is a clue to the answer.
- If you need to fill in the blank with a verb, look carefully at the subject of the verb.
- If you are given a verb in three tenses as your options, look at time indicators to decide which tense to choose.
- If you need to fill in an adjective, decide whether the noun it relates to is feminine or masculine.

4 Translate the following sentences into **French**.

   a I have a sister.

   b My best friend is beautiful and kind.

   c At school, there is too much homework.

   d My mother works in an office.

   e Yesterday, I ate some fruit.

10 marks

Conseil

For this task, you need to convey your message clearly. Check the tense required and conjugate your verbs correctly. If you don't know the exact word, you can use a synonym (a word with a similar meaning). Check you have translated all the words.

Either question **5.1** or question **5.2**

5.1 **You are emailing your Belgian friend about yourself, your family and friends.**

Write approximately **90** words in **French**.

You must write something about each bullet point.

Describe:
- the type of person you are
- what you did with your friends recently
- your future relationships.

15 marks

5.2 **You are emailing your Swiss friend about school and jobs.**

Write approximately **90** words in **French**.

You must write something about each bullet point.

Describe:
- the advantages and disadvantages of your school
- what you did recently at school
- what you plan to do once you leave school.

15 marks

Conseil

For this task, you must write something about all the bullet points but there is no need to cover them equally. Make sure you make accurate references to all three time frames. Try to include opinions and justify them using *parce que* or *car*.

Theme 2
Popular culture

Free-time activities

1 **Match the sentence halves.**

1	Tu écoutes	a	son roman préféré.
2	Nous jouons	b	au théâtre.
3	Vous allez	c	aux cartes.
4	Je fais	d	la radio.
5	Elle lit	e	du camping.

le camping	camping
les cartes	cards
la radio	radio
le roman	novel
le théâtre	theatre

2 **Read the blog post and answer the questions.**

Zoé

Le soir, j'aime beaucoup jouer à des jeux vidéo. C'est passionnant. Le week-end, je vais parfois au cinéma avec mes copines, mais je préfère aller au théâtre car c'est plus intéressant. Mon frère aime lire après le dîner, mais son activité préférée, c'est la danse. Il fait ça le mercredi.

posté le 26 septembre à 12:43

a When does Zoé play video games?
b What does she think of playing video games?
c What does Zoé sometimes do at the weekend, and who with?
d What does Zoé prefer doing, and why?
e When does Zoé's brother read?
f What is his favourite activity?
g When does he do that activity?

le soir	(in the) evening
le week-end	weekend
le dîner	dinner
le jeu vidéo	video game
le cinéma	cinema
la danse	dance
passionnant	exciting

3 **Listen (1–6) and choose the correct picture (a–f).**

détester	to hate
préférer	to prefer
le livre	book
autre chose	something else
ennuyeux	boring
tous les jours	every day

4 **Listen again (1–6) and decide whether each person's opinion is positive (P) or negative (N).**

Popular culture — Theme 2

Sport and leisure

1 📖 **Choose the correct word from the box to match the places (a–j).**

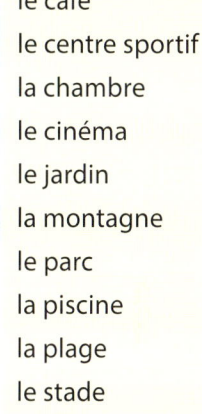

le café
le centre sportif
la chambre
le cinéma
le jardin
la montagne
le parc
la piscine
la plage
le stade

2 📖 **Read the email. Copy and complete the sentences (a–f).**

Mon frère et moi, nous aimons être actifs. Nous allons au centre sportif trois fois par semaine. Pendant les vacances, nous allons à la campagne. Nous faisons du vélo sur les petites routes. Ce n'est pas dangereux. Parfois mon frère va à la montagne et il court. Ça, c'est très dur! Moi, j'aime mieux courir dans le parc car je trouve ça plus facile.

Mustapha

la campagne	countryside
la fois	time
la route	road
les vacances	holidays
aimer mieux	to prefer
courir	to run
faire du vélo	to go cycling
actif	active
dur	hard
facile	easy

a Mustapha and his brother enjoy being…
b They go to the… three times a week.
c In the holidays they go to…
d They cycle on… because it's…
e Sometimes Mustapha's brother runs in…
f Mustapha prefers… because it's…

3 🎧 **Listen and write down the order in which the activities (a–f) are mentioned.**

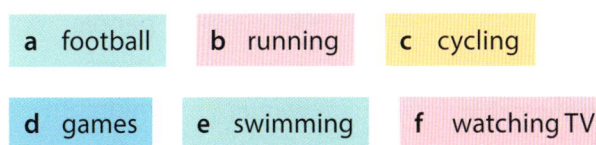

le chien	dog
une équipe	team
la famille	family
la sœur	sister
sportif/sportive	sporty

4 🎧 **Listen again and write down who they do each activity with.**

soixante et un 61

# Theme 2 — Popular culture

Customs, festivals and celebrations

1 Match the sentences (1–6) to the celebrations (a–f).

1. Demain, c'est l'anniversaire de ma mère. On va au restaurant.
2. Le jour de l'An, nous invitons des amis chez nous.
3. C'est la fin du Ramadan. Après une visite à la mosquée, on célèbre ça à la maison.
4. À Noël, on fait la fête avec la famille et on donne des cadeaux à tout le monde.
5. Quand on aime quelqu'un, le 14 février, c'est un jour important.
6. Aujourd'hui, c'est la fête des Mères, alors j'achète des fleurs.

a Valentine's Day   b Mother's Day   c a birthday

d New Year's Day   e Christmas   f Eid

le cadeau	present
la fin	end
les fleurs	flowers
la mosquée	mosque
à la maison	at home
célébrer	to celebrate
faire la fête	to party
inviter	to invite

2 Match the sentence halves.

1	Cet été, je vais à	a	des billets en ligne.
2	D'abord, je réserve	b	notre groupe préféré.
3	Les billets coûtent	c	un festival.
4	Le festival commence	d	beau.
5	Nous allons voir	e	le 4 août.
6	Il va faire	f	cher.

le billet	ticket
le groupe	band
coûter	to cost
réserver	to book
il fait beau	the weather is fine
cher	expensive
en ligne	online

3 Read the comments. Copy and complete the sentences (a–f).

- C'est bien d'envoyer des cartes pour le jour de l'An.
- En France, le 26 décembre n'est pas un jour férié.
- À Hanouka, chaque famille a ses propres traditions.
- Certaines personnes se marient à l'église.
- Souvent, on mange un gâteau à une fête d'anniversaire.
- Le dimanche de Pâques, on peut se lever tard.

a At New Year, it's good to…
b 26 December is not…
c At Hanukkah, each family…
d Some people get married…
e At a birthday party, people often…
f On Easter Sunday, you can…

la fête	party
Pâques	Easter
envoyer	to send
certains	some
chaque	each
propre	own
tard	late

4 Listen to find out about the *fête nationale*. Write down the order in which the different aspects (a–f) are mentioned.

a dancing   c music   e lots of people
b procession   d cafés   f fireworks

le défilé	procession
le feu d'artifice	firework display
les gens	people
la rue	street
minuit	midnight
écouter	to listen
voir	to see
partout	everywhere

Popular culture — Theme 2

Celebrity culture

1 Listen (1–6) and choose the correct profession (a–f) for each person.

 a
 b
 c
 d
 e
 f

2 Listen again (1–6) and write down *one* further detail for each person.

3 Read the advice and choose the correct tip (a–e) that each celebrity gives.

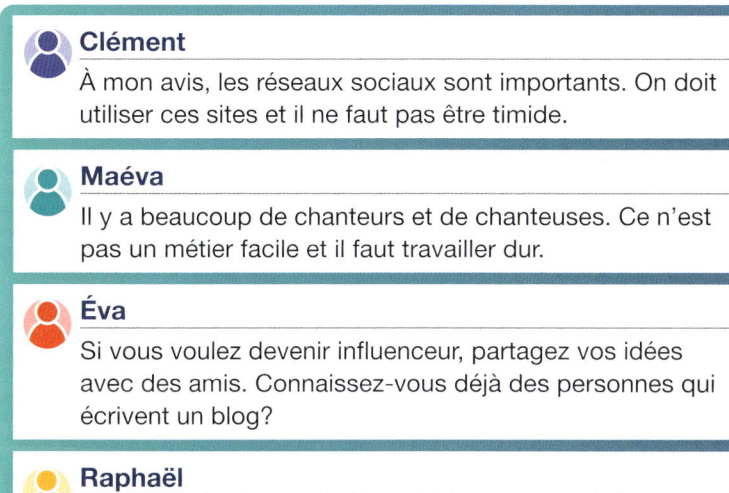

Clément
À mon avis, les réseaux sociaux sont importants. On doit utiliser ces sites et il ne faut pas être timide.

Maéva
Il y a beaucoup de chanteurs et de chanteuses. Ce n'est pas un métier facile et il faut travailler dur.

Éva
Si vous voulez devenir influenceur, partagez vos idées avec des amis. Connaissez-vous déjà des personnes qui écrivent un blog?

Raphaël
Essayez de vivre une vie normale. On peut être célèbre et avoir un partenaire et une famille en même temps.

Adam
Si vous voulez voyager, acceptez cette proposition. Partez, visitez le monde et rencontrez plus de personnes intéressantes!

a Share your ideas!   b Work hard!   c Travel!
d Use social media!   e Live a normal life!

4 Read the advice again (activity 3). Copy and complete the sentences.

a Clément says you mustn't…
b Maéva thinks that singing isn't…
c Éva asks if you know anyone who…
d Raphaël says that you can be famous and…
e Adam believes that you will meet…

un acteur	actor
une chanteuse	female singer
un chef de cuisine	head chef
un écrivain	writer
une femme politique	female politician
une championne de natation	swimming champion

la recette	recipe
devenir	to become
espérer	to hope
s'intéresser à	to be interested in
à l'étranger	abroad
francophone	French-language / from the French-speaking world

le concours	competition
un métier	career, job
la vie	life
connaître	to know
partager	to share
rencontrer	to meet
vivre	to live
il faut	it is necessary to
il ne faut pas	you must not
timide	shy
quelqu'un	someone
en même temps	at the same time
déjà	already

soixante-trois

4.1G Qu'est-ce que tu aimais faire?

OBJECTIVES
- Hobbies and sports
- Adverbs ending in *-ment*
- The imperfect tense of regular verbs

1 Match the activities (1–6) to the pictures (a–f).

Quand j'étais petit(e)…
1. j'écoutais de la musique.
2. j'adorais faire du vélo.
3. j'aimais faire de la cuisine.
4. je regardais tous les jours la télé.
5. je jouais au foot.
6. je dansais avec mes amis.

2 Read the texts and decide which activity / activities each person liked.

Karim
Quand j'étais petit, **j'aimais regarder la télévision**. Normalement, j'adorais les émissions comme *Qui veut gagner des millions?*

Clémentine
Comme passe-temps, j'aimais la natation. Généralement, j'allais à la piscine trois fois par semaine. J'aimais aussi faire du vélo et courir… très rapidement!

Sophie
Quand j'avais huit ans, **je dansais et chantais souvent avec mes copines**. J'aimais danser lentement. Mais plus récemment, quand j'avais onze ans, **je préférais jouer au foot**. Je trouvais ça génial.

Paul
Moi, quand j'étais petit, j'adorais la lecture. Je lisais couramment à l'âge de quatre ans et j'aimais lire toutes sortes de livres, mais surtout des romans. **Je trouvais Jules Verne vraiment génial.**

a reading
b swimming
c a team sport
d cycling and running
e watching TV
f dancing

3 Read the texts again. Note down *six* different verbs in the imperfect tense.

4 Translate the bold phrases in activity 2 into English.

Les verbes

The imperfect tense of regular verbs

The imperfect tense is used to say what you used to do or were doing in the past.

Use the present tense *nous* form of the verb, remove the *-ons* ending and add the imperfect tense endings:

| j'aim**ais** |
| tu aim**ais** |
| il / elle / on aim**ait** |

À l'âge de huit ans, je jouais au foot.
At the age of eight, I **used to play** football.

Mon frère **aimait** faire du vélo.
My brother **used to like** cycling.

Free-time activities   **4.1G**

5 Choose the correct form of the imperfect tense to complete each sentence.

a J'**aimais** / **aimait** la mode.
b Cédric **adorais** / **adorait** le théâtre.
c Tu **regardais** / **regardait** la télé?
d Je **préférais** / **préférait** sortir le soir.
e Mon frère **jouais** / **jouait** au foot.
f On **mangeais** / **mangeait** des fruits.

6 In pairs, take turns to play the part of Karim, Clémentine, Sophie or Paul from activity 2. Your partner guesses who you are.

Example:

• *J'aimais danser.*

• *Tu es Sophie?*

• *Oui!*

7 Listen (1–4). Copy and complete the table in English.

	What they liked doing	One more detail
1	camping	it was sunny

8 Listen (1–4). Copy and complete the sentences with adverbs from the box.

> généralement   lentement
> normalement   rapidement

1 ___, il y avait du soleil.
2 J'allais très ___ !
3 J'aimais courir assez ___.
4 ___, je jouais sur mon ordinateur.

9 Copy and complete the sentences with an adverb formed from the adjective in brackets.

a Je courais ___ parce que j'étais fatiguée. (*lent*)
b ___, on regardait la télé dans la cuisine. (*normal*)
c Tu gagnais ___ les concours! (*facile*)
d On marchait ___ parce qu'on était en retard. (*rapide*)
e ___, j'allais à la plage pendant les vacances. (*général*)
f ___, je suis allée à la plage. (*récent*)

Grammaire

Adverbs ending in -*ment*

French adverbs often add -*ment* to the feminine form of the adjective:

lent (slow) → *lentement* (slowly)

général (general) → *généralement* (generally)

If the adjective ends in -*i*, the adverb just adds -*ment*:

vrai (true, real) → *vraiment* (really)

Adjectives that end in -*ent* or -*ant* (except *lent*) replace those letters with -*emment* or -*amment*:

récent (recent) → *récemment* (recently)

courant (fluent) → *couramment* (fluently)

10 Write *five* sentences to describe what you used to do in your free time when you were younger. Try to include some adverbs ending in -*ment*. Use activities 1 and 2 for to help you.

Example: Normalement, quand j'étais petit(e), je dansais et je chantais avec mes copains.

soixante-cinq   **65**

4.1F Le week-end dernier

OBJECTIVES
- Leisure activities in the past
- Emphatic pronouns (*moi, toi*)
- The perfect tense: irregular past participles
- Phonics: *u* and *ou*; *oi* and *oy*

1 Read the texts and decide which activity (a–f) each person did.

Qu'est-ce que tu as fait le week-end dernier?

 **Nina**

J'ai passé le week-end à Genève chez une copine. Elle a visité toute la ville avec moi. On a fait beaucoup de promenades et on a pris le bus pour faire la visite de la ville. Nous avons vu des sites comme l'église Saint-Pierre et le jardin des Alpes. C'était génial! J'ai reçu un petit cadeau de ma copine – elle est très gentille.

 **Henri**

Samedi, j'ai fait les courses, comme toujours! J'ai vu mon meilleur copain et nous avons écrit un blog ensemble. Le soir, j'ai téléchargé un film amusant et mon beau-père a regardé ce film avec moi – nous avons beaucoup ri. Dimanche, j'ai vu mes grands-parents. J'ai mis mon pantalon noir préféré. On a joué à un jeu de société et on a bu du thé. J'ai beaucoup aimé!

 **Yasmine**

Samedi matin, j'étais fatiguée. J'ai lu mon livre préféré, *Le Petit Prince*. L'après-midi, mon frère et moi, nous avons fait des gâteaux. Mon frère n'a pas eu de chance – il a trop mangé de gâteau et il a été malade! Dimanche, j'ai eu plus d'énergie et j'ai couru sur la plage près de chez moi. J'ai adoré.

un jeu de société — a board game

a met up with family
b did some sport
c went sightseeing
d went online
e made cakes with a family member
f took public transport

2 Read the texts again and answer the questions.

a Who was Nina in Geneva with?
b What did that person give Nina?
c What did Henri do with his friend?
d What did Henri do with his stepdad?
e What did Yasmine do on Saturday morning?
f Where was the beach that Yasmine went to?

3 Find *eight* irregular past participles in the text (activity 1) and work out their infinitive.

Les verbes

The perfect tense: irregular past participles

Many common verbs have an irregular past participle in the perfect tense. These include:

Infinitive	Perfect tense	English
avoir	j'ai eu	I had
être	j'ai été	I was
faire	j'ai fait	I did / have done
mettre	j'ai mis	I put / have put
prendre	j'ai pris	I took / have taken
courir	j'ai couru	I ran / have run
lire	j'ai lu	I read / have read
rire	j'ai ri	I laughed / have laughed
voir	j'ai vu	I saw / have seen
recevoir	j'ai reçu	I received / have received
boire	j'ai bu	I drank / have drunk
écrire	j'ai écrit	I wrote / have written

Free-time activities 4.1F

4 Copy and complete the email with the correct past participles.

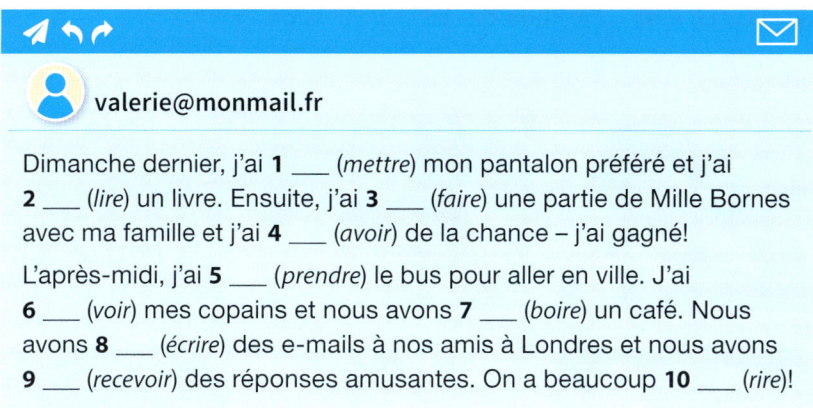

valerie@monmail.fr

Dimanche dernier, j'ai **1** ___ (*mettre*) mon pantalon préféré et j'ai **2** ___ (*lire*) un livre. Ensuite, j'ai **3** ___ (*faire*) une partie de Mille Bornes avec ma famille et j'ai **4** ___ (*avoir*) de la chance – j'ai gagné!

L'après-midi, j'ai **5** ___ (*prendre*) le bus pour aller en ville. J'ai **6** ___ (*voir*) mes copains et nous avons **7** ___ (*boire*) un café. Nous avons **8** ___ (*écrire*) des e-mails à nos amis à Londres et nous avons **9** ___ (*recevoir*) des réponses amusantes. On a beaucoup **10** ___ (*rire*)!

Phonétique

u and *ou*, *oi* and *oy*

j'ai b**u**	j'ai v**u**	tu as l**u**
n**ou**s	v**ou**s	
c**ou**rses	p**ou**r	c**ou**ru
s**oi**r	m**oi**	hist**oi**re
v**oy**ager	env**oy**er	empl**oy**é

Mille Bornes '1000 milestones', a classic French card game

5 🎧 Listen to Hugo and Alice and decide which activities (a–h) each person mentions.

a watching a film
b drinking coffee
c reading
d writing a letter
e shopping
f going running
g going into town
h doing homework

6 🎧 Listen (1–4) and write down the sentences you hear.

7 💬 In pairs, take turns to read aloud one of the texts from activity 1: Nina, Henri or Yasmine.

8 💬 In pairs, ask and answer the questions.
- Tu es allé(e) où le week-end dernier?
- Qui était avec toi?
- Qu'est-ce que tu as fait?
- Qu'est-ce que tu as vu?

9 ✏️ Write a paragraph (50 words) to describe what you did last weekend. Mention:
- where you went
- who was with you
- what you saw
- what you did
- your opinion.

Grammaire

Emphatic pronouns (*moi*, *toi*)

We use the pronouns *moi* and *toi* after a preposition or for emphasis:

*Amélie a fait les courses **avec moi**.* Amélie went shopping **with me**.
*J'ai un cadeau **pour toi**.* I have a present **for you**.
*Ils ont bu un café **sans moi**.* They drank a coffee **without me**.
*J'ai lu la recette **chez toi**.* I read the recipe **at your house**.

Culture

Le Petit Prince was written and illustrated by Antoine de Saint-Exupéry. Since publication in 1943, it has sold over 140 million copies worldwide. It has been translated into more than 500 different languages and dialects, and has even appeared on stamps!

soixante-sept

4.2G Sport ou musique?

OBJECTIVES
- Plans for leisure activities
- Partitive articles (*du, de la, de l', des*)
- Revising the near future tense
- Phonics: *-tion, -sion, -ssion*

1 📖 Match the sentences (1–6) to the pictures (a–f).

1 On va chanter.
2 Je vais faire des promenades.
3 Ils vont faire de la danse.
4 Elle va écouter de la musique.
5 Tu vas jouer du piano?
6 Il va se relaxer.

2 📖 Read the texts. Decide whether each person is going to do something sporty, musical or both.

Ce week-end, je vais faire des promenades. Ma sœur va venir avec moi. Je vais aussi faire de la natation. J'adore faire de l'exercice! **Zoé**

Mes copains et moi, nous allons jouer de la guitare. Nous allons chanter et danser aussi. Ça va être relaxant. **Victor**

Ma famille et moi, nous allons faire de l'équitation à la campagne. Le soir, on va écouter de la musique en ville car ma sœur va jouer de la flûte dans un concert. Ça va être génial. **Livia**

Cet après-midi, je vais faire de l'escalade en salle. Ensuite, je vais faire du vélo avec ma copine. C'est notre activité préférée. **Alex**

l'escalade en salle   climbing (on a climbing wall)

3 📖 Read the texts again. Find the French for the English phrases (a–h).

a to go for walks
b to go swimming
c to play the guitar
d to go horse riding
e to listen to music
f to play the flute
g to go climbing
h to go cycling

Les verbes

Revising the near future tense

Use the near future tense to say what you are going to do.
You need to use a form of ***aller*** in the present tense, followed by the main verb in the infinitive:
*Je **vais** danser*. I **am going to** dance.
*Livia **va** se relaxer*. Livia **is going to** relax.

soixante-huit

Free-time activities 4.2G

4 Copy and complete the sentences with the correct form of the verb *aller*.

a Jamel, tu __ faire du vélo?
b Chiara et sa copine __ faire des promenades.
c Salomé __ écouter de la musique.
d Moi, je __ faire de l'exercice.

5 Find *four* examples of *faire + de* and *two* examples of *jouer + de* in the texts in activity 2.

6 Copy and complete the sentences with the correct form of the partitive article: *du*, *de la*, *de l'* or *des*.

a Je vais faire __ vélo.
b Nous allons faire __ natation.
c Ils vont faire __ danse.
d Vous allez faire __ promenades?
e Elle va faire __ exercice.
f Tu vas faire __ sport?

7 Listen (1–4). Copy and complete the table.

	What they are going to do	When	One more detail
1			

8 In pairs, take turns to choose which activity you are going to do. Your partner guesses.

Example:

• *Tu vas jouer du piano?*
• *Non!*
• *Tu vas écouter de la musique?*
• *Oui, je vais écouter de la musique!*

faire du sport	faire de la natation
faire du vélo	faire des promenades
faire du camping	jouer de la guitare
faire de la danse	jouer du piano

9 Write *seven* sentences about what a friend or family member is going to do each day next week.

Example:
Lundi, ma copine va faire du sport.
Mardi, elle va écouter de la musique à un concert.

Grammaire

Partitive articles: *du*, *de la*, *de l'*, *des*

A partitive article is used in front of a noun when the quantity is not specific. In English, it is often translated as 'some' or 'any', or is missed out altogether. The partitive article in French needs to agree with the noun that follows:

du sport, ***de la*** musique, ***de l'*** exercice, ***des*** promenades

The same articles are used after *faire* to talk about sports and other activities:

*On va faire **de la** natation.*
We're going to go swimming.

They are also used after *jouer* when referring to musical instruments:

*Elle va jouer **de la** guitare.*
She is going to play the guitar.

But for sports, *jouer* is followed by ***à*** not ***de***:

*Tu joues **au** foot?* Do you play football?

Phonétique

Phonics: *-tion*, *-sion*, *-ssion*

na**tion**   équita**tion**   ac**tion**   Atten**tion**!
télévi**sion**   déci**sion**   occa**sion**
émi**ssion**

soixante-neuf 69

4.2F   En voyage!

OBJECTIVES
- Leisure activities around the world
- *en* and *à* with places
- The perfect tense with *être*
- Phonics: *e* and *eu*; *-é*, *-er* and *-ez*

1 📖 Read the texts. Copy and complete the sentences (a–h).

Accueil   À propos   **Blog**   Derniers articles   Intérêts

L'année dernière, je suis partie au Maroc avec ma famille. Nous sommes arrivés à Tanger après un long voyage en bateau. À Tanger, j'ai fait du surf – c'était super! Pendant les vacances, nous avons aussi pris le bus. **Nous sommes descendus du bus à Fez**, une ville historique. À Fez, nous sommes allés à un concert de musique traditionnelle. **Anna**

Moi, **je suis née à La Réunion**. L'automne dernier, je suis retournée là-bas. **Je suis allée voir ma cousine** et nous sommes parties à la montagne ensemble. Nous avons vu le « Grand Raid de La Réunion » – c'est un ultra-marathon de 162 kilomètres, un vrai défi! **Le soir, nous sommes retournées à Saint-Louis** où habite ma cousine. **Lucie**

Pendant les vacances, je suis parti au Canada. **Ma sœur est venue avec moi**. Nous sommes restés trois semaines à Montréal. Ma sœur a joué au hockey sur glace, un sport très populaire au Canada. **Elle est tombée** mais ce n'était pas grave. Après, ma sœur et moi, nous sommes allés voir un match de foot. **Thomas**

L'année dernière, j'ai passé mes vacances en France. **Je suis resté une semaine** à Avignon pendant le célèbre Festival d'Avignon, et mon frère a joué dans une pièce de théâtre. La ville était pleine de vie! Après le festival, **nous sommes rentrés chez nous ensemble**. **Max**

a Anna and her family went to Morocco by ___.
b They went to Fez by ___.
c Lucie went to La Réunion last ___.
d Her cousin lives in ___.
e Thomas went to Montréal with ___.
f He saw a ___ with his sister.
g Max visited Avignon during the ___.
h His brother took part in a ___.

2 🔀 Translate the phrases in bold in activity 1 into English.

3 🎯 In the texts in activity 1, find and list all the verbs in the perfect tense with *être*.

Phonétique 🎤

e and *eu*

je   le   de   deux   un peu   le jeu

70 soixante-dix

Free-time activities 4.2F

Les verbes

The perfect tense with *être*

14 common verbs use *être* instead of *avoir* in the perfect tense. You can learn them in pairs of opposites:

aller (to go)	venir (to come)
arriver (to arrive)	partir (to leave)
entrer (to go in)	sortir (to go out)
monter (to go up)	descendre (to go down)
tomber (to fall)	retourner (to go back)
rester (to stay)	rentrer (to come back / to return home)
naître (to be born)	mourir (to die)

With these verbs, the past participle agrees with the subject: add *-e* for the feminine form and *-s* for plural.

arriver (to arrive)	
je suis arrivé(e)	nous sommes arrivé(e)s
tu es arrivé(e)	vous êtes arrivé(e)(s)
il est arrivé	ils sont arrivés
elle est arrivée	elles sont arrivées
on est arrivé(e)(s)	

4 Copy and complete the sentences with the perfect tense of the verb in brackets.

a Mon frère ___ aux États-Unis. (*aller*)
b Ta sœur ___ à quelle heure? (*arriver*)
c Nous ___ deux semaines au bord de la mer. (*rester*)
d Ils ___ à la maison. (*rentrer*)
e Ma mère ___ au concert avec nous. (*venir*)
f Charlotte et Mélanie ___ à midi. (*partir*)

5 In pairs, read aloud one of the texts in activity 1.

6 In pairs, ask and answer the questions.
- L'année dernière, tu es allé(e) où pendant les vacances?
- Qu'est-ce que tu as fait là-bas?
- Les vacances, c'était comment?

7 Listen (1–4) and answer the questions.
a Which new activity did Victor try in Marseille?
b What did he think of it? Give **two** details.
c How long did Aurélie stay in Dakar?
d Which sport is popular there?
e What did Nader think of the journey to La Réunion?
f What did he think of the holiday in general?
g Where did Jasmine spend her holiday?
h What did she do with her friend?

8 Listen (1–4) and write down the sentences you hear.

9 Write a paragraph (50 words) about what you did on a recent holiday. Use the details on the profile card. Mention:
- where you went
- who you went with
- where and how long you stayed
- what you did
- your opinion of the holiday.

Grammaire

en, *au*, *aux*, *à* with countries and towns

To say 'in' or 'to' a feminine name of a country, use *en*:
*Elle habite **en** Suisse. Il va **en** Suisse.*

To say 'in' or 'to' a masculine name of a country, use *au*:
*Je travaille **au** Maroc. Nous partons **au** Maroc.*

To say 'in' or 'to' a plural name of a country, use *aux*:
*Vous habitez **aux** États-Unis?*

To say 'in' or 'to' a town or island, use *à*:
*Ils travaillent **à** Paris. Je vais **à** La Réunion.*

Phonétique

-é, *-er*, *-ez*
je suis all**é**   all**er**   vous all**ez**

- France
- with family
- in Paris, for five days
- visited historic sites, went to a football match
- great!

soixante et onze 71

5.1G Les journées spéciales

OBJECTIVES • Customs and celebrations • *c'est* and *il y a*
• Question words and subject–verb inversion

1 📖 Match the words and phrases (1–6) to the pictures (a–f).

1. une carte d'anniversaire
2. un livre
3. un stylo
4. un jeu vidéo
5. un gâteau
6. un tee-shirt

2 🎧 Listen and read (1–6). Write down the missing words that you hear.

> 1 Moi, je vais acheter des ___. C'est pour l'anniversaire de mon ___.

> 2 Comme ___ de vacances, je vais acheter un ___. C'est pour ___!

> 3 Moi, je vais acheter des ___. C'est un cadeau pour ___. Il y a de jolies ___ ici.

> 4 Ce week-end, je vais acheter une ___ d'anniversaire pour ma ___. Il y a beaucoup de choix.

> 5 Je vais acheter ce ___ pour ma ___ car elle aime lire. C'est un nouveau ___.

> 6 Ici, il y a un ___ rouge. C'est le cadeau parfait pour mon ___. Alors je vais l'acheter.

3 🎧 Listen again (1–6). Copy and complete the table in English.

	Present	Who for?
1	chocolates	brother

4 💬 In pairs, take turns to read aloud the completed sentences in activity 2.

5 ✂ Translate the sentences into French.

a. It is a pretty birthday card.
b. Here, there are some flowers.
c. It is my mum's birthday.
d. There is a cake.
e. It is a perfect present.

6 💬 In pairs, take turns to choose a present from activity 1. Your partner guesses what it is and who it is for.

Example:
• *C'est quelque chose pour ma mère.*
• *C'est un stylo?*
• *Non.*
• *C'est un livre?*
• *Oui! C'est un livre pour ma mère.*

7 ✏ Write *six* sentences to say which presents you have for which people.
Example: Pour mon copain, il y a un tee-shirt rouge.

Grammaire ⭐

c'est and **il y a**

C'est un cadeau très cher. **It is** a very expensive present.
Il y a un cadeau pour toi. **There is** a present for you.

Customs, festivals and celebrations — 5.1G

8 📖 Read the text about festivals in Quebec. Write down the order in which the statements (a–f) appear in the text.

Au Québec, on aime faire la fête. On organise des festivals de chanson, de musique, de cinéma, de danse, de sport, d'humour…

Quand peut-on aller à un festival?
Toute l'année! L'été, par exemple, il y a le Festival International de Jazz de Montréal. C'est un festival de jazz très important.

Pourquoi est-il populaire, ce festival?
On organise environ 650 concerts avec des artistes de plus de 30 pays différents.

Combien de temps dure le festival?
Le festival dure dix jours.

Combien doit-on payer?
Il y a des concerts dehors et ils sont gratuits. Il y a aussi des concerts en salle, bien sûr!

Et l'hiver, que recommandez-vous?
La Fête des Neiges, pendant quatre week-ends en janvier et février, est le grand festival d'hiver à Montréal.

Comment peut-on participer à la Fête des Neiges?
Les familles peuvent essayer différentes activités comme des concours de sculpture sur glace et des jeux de neige. C'est idéal pour tous les âges.

a The jazz festival lasts ten days.
b There are different activities, ideal for people of all ages.
c There are many different festivals in Quebec.
d The snow festival takes place over four weekends.
e Quebec hosts an important jazz festival.
f Outdoor performances are free of charge.

Grammaire

Question words and subject–verb inversion

Que…? What…?   Comment…? How…?
Quand…? When…? Combien de…? How many…?
Où…? Where…?

In more formal situations, after the question word, change the word order so that the verb comes first before the person (the subject pronoun):
Que **faites-vous**? What are you doing?
Où **vas-tu**? Where are you going?

9 ✂ Translate the *six* questions (in bold) in the article into English.

10 ⭐ Match the questions (1–4) to the answers (a–d).

1 Quand allons-nous au festival?
2 Comment célébrez-vous Noël?
3 Où mangeons-nous?
4 Que fais-tu?

a Nous faisons la fête chez nous.
b Dans le jardin, car il fait beau.
c Je cherche un cadeau pour ma copine.
d Demain, après le petit-déjeuner.

11 🎧 Listen and check your answers to activity 10.

soixante-treize 73

5.1F Bon anniversaire!

OBJECTIVES
- Birthdays and other personal special days
- Direct object pronouns: *me, te, vous, le, la*
- The present tense of common irregular verbs
- Phonics: *-eur / -œur* and *r*

1 📖 Match the dates (1–8) to the special days (a–h).

1	🎄 le 25 décembre	a	C'est la fête du Travail en France.
2	🇫🇷 le 14 juillet	b	C'est Noël.
3	💗 le 14 février	c	C'est la Saint-Valentin, la fête des amoureux.
4	🎉 le 1er janvier	d	C'est l'Aïd-el-Fitr.
5	✊ le 1er mai	e	C'est Pâques.
6	🌙 un jour entre le 22 mars et le 25 avril	f	C'est la fête nationale en France.
7	🐰 un jour en mars ou avril	g	C'est le Rosh Hashanah.
8	🍇 pendant trois jours, en septembre ou octobre	h	C'est le jour de l'An.

2 📖 Read the text and choose the *five* correct statements.

L'anniversaire de mon frère

Aujourd'hui, c'est l'anniversaire de Xavier, mon petit frère. Cette année, il a onze ans. C'est un bon âge, je crois. Xavier reçoit toujours beaucoup de cadeaux et il court dans le salon où il ouvre les paquets. Il rit quand il voit ma carte d'anniversaire car je le connais bien et j'écris toujours un message amusant.

Le cadeau préféré de Xavier, c'est un billet pour un match de foot. Il adore le Paris Saint-Germain et normalement il suit les matchs en ligne. Moi aussi, je suis fan de foot et je vais aller au match avec lui.

Le soir de son anniversaire, il invite plusieurs amis à la maison. On mange un gâteau délicieux – c'est notre père qui le prépare – et on boit du cola. On joue à des jeux et on écoute de la musique. On ne se couche pas tôt!

Mathilde

a Mathilde is older than Xavier.
b Xavier opens his presents in the kitchen.
c Mathilde always writes a funny message on Xavier's birthday card.
d Xavier's favourite present is a football shirt.
e Mathilde likes football too.
f Xavier's friends come over in the evening.
g Mathilde baked her brother's birthday cake.
h They go to bed late.

3 🎯 Find in the text (activity 2) examples of the *ten* irregular verbs given in *Les verbes*. List them and translate them into English.

Example: je crois – I believe

4 🎯 Choose the correct option to complete each sentence.

a Ma sœur **reçoit / reçois / recevoir** beaucoup de cadeaux.
b Tu **courir / cours / court** très vite!
c J'ai soif, alors je **boit / boire / bois** de l'eau.
d Tu **connais / connaître / connaît** la Saint-Valentin?
e J'**écris / écrit / écrire** une carte d'anniversaire pour ma copine.
f On **rire / ris / rit** souvent pendant le spectacle.

Customs, festivals and celebrations — 5.1F

Les verbes

Irregular verbs in the present tense

These verbs are irregular and you will need to learn them:

	voir (to see)	boire (to drink)	croire (to believe)	écrire (to write)	rire (to laugh)
je/j'	vois	bois	crois	écris	ris
tu	vois	bois	crois	écris	ris
il/elle/on	voit	boit	croit	écrit	rit

	courir (to run)	connaître (to know)	recevoir (to receive)	suivre (to follow)	ouvrir (to open)
je/j'	cours	connais	reçois	suis	ouvre
tu	cours	connais	reçois	suis	ouvres
il/elle/on	court	connaît	reçoit	suit	ouvre

5 Listen (1–4) and decide if each person has a positive (P), negative (N) or positive and negative (P+N) opinion of Christmas.

6 Listen again and answer the questions.
1. What does Morgane's little sister enjoy?
2. Why is Christmas a double celebration for Tanguy?
3. Name **two** types of presents that Chloé says children ask for.
4. What does Vincent do instead of celebrating Christmas? Give **two** details.

7 Listen (1–4) and write down the sentences you hear.

8 Copy and complete the sentences with the correct pronoun.
a. Je ___ connais. (*her*)
b. Il ___ aide. (*me*)
c. Tu ___ vois. (*him*)
d. Je ___ suis. (*you, formal*)
e. Elle ___ invite. (*you, informal*)

9 In pairs, complete the role play. Take turns to ask and answer the questions. Answer in full sentences.

> **You are talking to your French friend about special days.**
> 1. *Que penses-tu de Noël?*
>   Give **one** opinion of Christmas.
> 2. *Tu aimes quelle fête?*
>   Say what your favourite festival is. (Give **one** detail.)
> 3. *Le jour de ton anniversaire, tu aimes faire quoi?*
>   Say what you like to do on your birthday. (Give **one** detail.)
> 4. *Tu aimes passer les occasions spéciales avec qui?*
>   Say who you like spending special days with. (Give **one** detail.)
> 5. Ask your friend a question about their birthday.

Phonétique

-eur / -œur and r

These words have an open -*eu* sound:

l**eur**   plusi**eur**s   c**œur**   s**œur**

Roll the 'r' a little in these words:

j'ado**r**e   annive**r**sai**r**e   pa**r**ents   décemb**r**e
raison   aut**r**es   ch**r**étien   **r**ecevoi**r**

Grammaire

Direct object pronouns: *me, te, vous, le, la*

Direct object pronouns (*me, te, vous, le, la*) replace nouns and help avoid repetition. In French, they always go before the verb, unlike in English where they go after.

*Tu **me** crois.* You believe **me**.
*Je **te** suis.* I follow **you** (informal).
*Elle **vous** invite.* She invites **you** (polite).
*Ils **le** mangent.* They eat **it** (masculine).
*Nous **la** prenons.* We take **it** (feminine).

The pronouns *me, te, le* and *la* are shortened before a vowel:
*Il **t'**aide.* He helps you.

10 Write *five* sentences in French to describe how someone you know (it could be a friend or family member) spends a special day.

soixante-quinze **75**

5.2G On a fait la fête!

OBJECTIVES
- Recent festivals
- Irregular plural nouns
- Revising the perfect tense with *avoir* and *être*
- Phonics: liaison

1 📖 Match the sentences (1–6) to the images (a–f).

1 Nous sommes allés à un festival de musique.
2 Nous avons acheté des billets pour le festival.
3 Nous avons pris la voiture pour aller au festival.
4 Nous avons dansé avec beaucoup d'autres jeunes.
5 Nous avons dormi au camping.
6 Nous sommes rentrés à la maison, fatigués mais heureux.

2 📖 Read Sophie's blog about a music festival and find the French for the English phrases (a–f).

Accueil   À propos   Blog   Nouveau   Intérêts

Sophie

Au printemps dernier, je suis allée à un festival de musique avec deux copines. D'abord, j'ai réservé les billets en ligne. Les billets ont coûté 80€ par personne.

Nous sommes parties le jeudi matin et nous sommes arrivées au festival en fin d'après-midi. Mon chien, Rio, est resté à la maison.

À l'entrée du festival, nous avons montré nos billets et nous avons trouvé un bel endroit au camping. Il a fait mauvais, alors nous n'avons pas perdu de temps.

Le festival était très bien organisé. Nous avons écouté notre groupe préféré et plusieurs autres artistes connus. Au festival, nous avons vu la fille de mon voisin – quelle surprise!

Le jeudi, nous avons préparé notre repas au camping. Le vendredi, nous avons acheté du fast-food car c'était plus facile. Nous avons parlé avec d'autres jeunes jusqu'à une heure du matin.

Le samedi, j'étais fatiguée et triste de quitter le festival. Nous avons pris le train et nous sommes rentrées à la maison le soir.

a I booked the tickets online.
b We left on the Thursday morning.
c We showed our tickets.
d We listened to our favourite band.
e We prepared our meal on the campsite.
f We went back home.

3 📖 Answer the questions in English.

a When in the year did the festival take place?
b How much did the tickets cost?
c Who is Rio and what did he do?
d What was the weather like?
e Who was Sophie surprised to see?
f How late did Sophie stay up chatting?
g How did Sophie and her friends feel as they left the festival?

Culture 🌐

One of Belgium's biggest music festivals is *Les Ardentes*, which takes place every year in the city of Liège. In 2022 it attracted around 200,000 fans, and performers included the Belgian hip-hop star Stromae and the French rapper Orelsan.

soixante-seize

Customs, festivals and celebrations 5.2G

4 💬 In pairs, take turns to read aloud Sophie's blog about the festival.

5 🎯 Find in the blog *five* examples of verbs in the perfect tense with *être*.

6 🎯 Choose the correct option to complete each perfect tense sentence.

a Nous avons **réservé** / **réservée** / **réservés** des billets.
b Mon oncle **a** / **est** / **sont** arrivé le matin.
c Vous **avez** / **avons** / **êtes** parti à quelle heure?
d Nous sommes **arrivé** / **arrivée** / **arrivées** à midi.
e Tu **a** / **as** / **es** bien dormi?
f Mes copains **est** / **ont** / **sont** restés toute la journée.

7 🎧 Listen (1–4) and decide which type of festival each person attended (a–d).

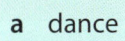 a dance
 b film
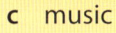 c music
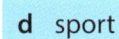 d sport

8 🎧 Listen (1–4) and write down the sentences you hear.

9 ⭐ Write the plural of these nouns.

a un bateau
b un repas
c un journal
d un gâteau
e un concours
f un hôpital

10 💬 In pairs, take turns to say something about a festival you went to with family or friends. Use activities 1 and 2 to help you.

Example:
Person A: Nous sommes allés à un festival de cinéma.
Person B: J'ai acheté les billets en ligne.
Person A: Nous avons vu...

11 ✏️ Write *five* sentences using the perfect tense about a festival your friend or family member went to.

Example:
Ma sœur est allée à un festival du sport.
Elle est arrivée…

Les verbes

Revising the perfect tense with *avoir* and *être*

To form the perfect tense, use a part of *avoir* or *être* + the past participle of the verb.

-er verbs: *j'ai mangé, je suis arrivé(e)*
-ir verbs: *tu as choisi, tu es sorti(e)*
-re verbs: *elle a perdu, elle est descendue*

Remember:
- Some past participles don't follow those three patterns. For example:

  être: vous avez **été**   voir: ils ont **vu**
  prendre: nous avons **pris**   venir: ils sont **venus**

- For verbs that take *être*, the past participle must agree in gender and number with the subject.

Phonétique

Liaison

Sometimes the normally silent last consonant of a word is pronounced: it happens when the next word begins with a vowel or a silent 'h'. This is called a liaison.

The pronouns *nous* and *vous* always form a liaison before a verb beginning with a vowel.

*Nou**s a**vons acheté des livres.*
*Vou**s a**vez rencontré des amis.*
*Mon frère es**t a**rrivé ce matin.*
*J'ai vu mo**n o**ncle.*
*On a découvert de nouvea**ux e**ndroits.*

Grammaire

Irregular plural nouns

Most French nouns add *-s* in the plural, just as they do in English: *un billet* → *des billets*

However, there are some exceptions, including most nouns that end in *-al*, *-eau* and *-eu*:

un animal → des anim**aux**
un cadeau → des cadeau**x**
un jeu → des jeu**x**

Nouns ending in *-s*, *-z* or *-x* don't change at all:

un bras → des bras   un choix → des choix

One common noun is completely irregular:

un œil → des **yeux**

5.2F Les fêtes dans le passé et à l'avenir

OBJECTIVES
- Past and future festivals
- Definite and indefinite articles
- Two tenses together: past and near future

1 📖 Read the texts and find the French for the English phrases (a–h).

Jaël: Ma famille est juive et chaque année, nous célébrons Hanouka, la fête des Lumières. C'est une fête qui dure huit jours. L'année dernière, elle a commencé le jeudi 7 décembre. Nous sommes restés à la maison et nous avons fait la fête avec nos voisins. Cette année, nous allons passer Hanouka chez mes cousins qui habitent à la campagne.

Inaya: Ici au Cameroun, nous avons beaucoup de festivals. L'année dernière, le pays a connu son premier festival Diaspora Kitchen, un festival de cuisine. Pendant deux jours, plus de vingt chefs camerounais et américains ont partagé des recettes traditionnelles et familiales. J'espère que ce festival va se passer tous les ans parce que **je vais étudier la cuisine** pour devenir chef.

Sacha: En France, le 14 juillet, c'est la fête nationale. On célèbre la fin de la monarchie française en 1789. **L'année dernière, je suis allé à Paris** et j'ai vu le grand défilé. **Il y avait des gens partout**. Cette année, je vais rester dans ma ville. Il y aura un feu d'artifice et **je vais faire la fête avec mes copains.**

Hugo: J'habite en France, à 20 km de la Suisse. En décembre dernier, j'ai passé une journée en Suisse pour voir la fête de l'Escalade. **On a écouté des chansons traditionnelles.** Les habitants ont servi de la soupe aux légumes et du vin chaud – et c'était gratuit! En décembre prochain, nous allons retourner à cette fête. Nous allons manger dans un café au marché.

le vin chaud — mulled wine

a a festival that lasts eight days
b we celebrated with our neighbours
c traditional and family recipes
d I'm going to stay in my town
e there will be a firework display
f the local people served vegetable soup
g it was free
h we are going to return to this festival

2 📖 Copy and complete the sentences.

a Last year Hanukkah ___ on 7 December.
b Jael's cousins live ___.
c More than 20 ___ took part in the *Diaspora Kitchen* festival.
d Inaya hopes that the festival will take place ___.
e Sacha saw the big ___ for the *fête nationale* in Paris.
f Next year Sacha will celebrate with ___.
g At the last *Escalade* festival Hugo listened to ___.
h Next December Hugo and his family will eat at ___.

Customs, festivals and celebrations 5.2F

3 Listen (1–4). For each person, write down:
- whether they are talking about the past or the future
- one further detail.

4 Choose the correct options to complete each sentence.

a Hier, nous **sommes restés** / **allons rester** à la maison, mais demain, nous **avons passé** / **allons passer** la journée en ville.

b L'année dernière, **j'ai vu** / **je vais voir** le grand défilé militaire à Paris et **je suis retourné** / **je vais retourner** à Paris l'été prochain.

c L'année prochaine, ma famille **a fait** / **va faire** la fête mais l'année dernière, nous **avons été** / **allons être** malades.

d Demain, on **a chanté** / **va chanter** dans la rue. Hier, on **a écouté** / **va écouter** les autres groupes.

Attention

When choosing a tense, look for adverbs of time to give you clues.
Hier and *l'année dernière* refer to the past.
Demain and *l'année prochaine* refer to the future.
Aujourd'hui and *cette année* could refer to past, present or future.

5 Translate the bold phrases in the texts (activity 1) into English.

6 In pairs, prepare a presentation about a recent visit to the *Festival Terre et Nature* and your plans to go there together again next year.

Photo
Cinéma
Musique
Jeux

Rencontres
Promenades
Spectacles
Sandwicherie

Festival TERRE ET NATURE

Venez passer une journée agréable en famille ou entre amis! Il y a des activités pour les petits et pour les grands!

Entrée gratuite pour les moins de 18 ans
Le dimanche 3 septembre 10h00–18h00

7 Write a description (90 words) of a festival or special day. Describe:
- your favourite festival or special day
- what you did on that day last year
- how you are planning to celebrate that day next year.

Les verbes

Two tenses together: past and near future

In your writing and speaking, you will often need to use different tenses in the same sentence or paragraph. This also sounds natural and adds more interest.

Hier, **nous avons pris** *le train, mais demain* **nous allons prendre** *la voiture.*
(perfect + near future)

Quand **j'étais** *petite,* **je partais** *en vacances avec ma famille. L'année prochaine,* **je vais partir** *avec des copines.*
(imperfect + near future)

Grammaire

Definite and indefinite articles

The definite article (*le, la, l', les*) and the indefinite article (*un, une, des*) are sometimes used in French when they are not needed in English:

J'aime **les** *films.* I like films. (literally: I like **the** films.)

L'*année dernière, elle est restée à* **la** *maison.* Last year, she stayed at home. (literally: **The** last year…)

Mon jour / festival préféré, c'est…
Normalement, je vais… / je reste…
Je passe la journée avec…
Je mange… / Nous mangeons…
Je bois… / Nous buvons…
J'aime ce jour parce que…
L'année dernière, j'ai passé / nous sommes allé(e)s…
L'année prochaine, je vais aller / on va passer…

soixante-dix-neuf 79

6.1G J'ai eu du succès!

OBJECTIVES
- Routes to fame
- *de* to show possession
- The perfect tense of *avoir*, *être*, *faire* and *prendre*

1 Match the paragraphs (1–5) to the photos (a–e).

1 Quand j'avais dix ans, **j'ai pris des cours de danse**. Deux ans plus tard, j'ai gagné mon premier prix. Maintenant, la danse, c'est mon métier.
Benoît

2 D'abord, **j'ai fait des vidéos** YouTube. Ensuite, je suis entrée dans le monde du cinéma car j'adorais les films de Luc Besson. C'est une carrière extraordinaire.
Chloé

3 J'adore la mode, surtout le style d'Olivier Rousteing, et j'aime influencer les autres. Avec mon blog, **j'ai eu du succès** presque immédiatement. Cela m'a beaucoup encouragé.
Karim

4 J'ai appris à jouer de la guitare et **ça a été facile**. J'ai aussi écrit des chansons. Après quelques années, j'ai fait des concerts partout en Europe.
Émilie

5 Moi, **j'ai eu l'occasion** de jouer pour l'équipe nationale. Quelle chance! Récemment, **j'ai donné ma première interview** à la télévision et ça s'est bien passé.
Noémie

| l'occasion | chance, opportunity |
| la chance | (good) luck |

2 Find the French for the English words (a–j) in activity 1.

a	prize	d	career	g	everywhere
b	job	e	fashion	h	team
c	world	f	others	i	interview

3 Translate the bold phrases in activity 1 into English.

4 In pairs, take turns to read aloud the texts in activity 1.

Les verbes

The perfect tense of *avoir*, *être*, *faire* and *prendre*

When using these four verbs in the perfect tense, remember their irregular past participles:

avoir: eu Elle **a eu** une carrière extraordinaire.
She's had an extraordinary career.

être: été Le concert **a été** super.
The concert was great.

faire: fait Il **a fait** un concert au festival.
He did a concert at the festival.

prendre: pris **J'ai pris** des photos du groupe.
I took photos of the group.

Celebrity culture 6.1G

5 **Listen to people talking about how they became famous (1–4). Copy and complete the sentences.**

   a Ambre's ___ encouraged her to sing.
   b Ambre entered her first competition at the age of ___.
   c Luc's ___ gave him the idea of taking part in a TV show.
   d To begin with, Luc felt ___ about it.
   e Emma took photos of ___ in Morocco.
   f Her videos of ___ are popular.
   g After a few months in Belgium, Aaron took part in ___.
   h Aaron thinks cycling as a sport is ___ but ___.

Grammaire

de to indicate possession

French doesn't use an apostrophe + 's' after a name to indicate possession. Instead, use the preposition *de* (meaning 'of') + the name or noun. Remember that *de* becomes *d'* before a vowel.

*les films **de** Céline Sciamma*
Céline Sciamma's films

*le style **d'**Olivier Rousteing*
Olivier Rousteing's style

6 **Rewrite the sentences in the correct order.**

   a de | C'est | ma sœur | le sport préféré .
   b Charlotte Dipanda | J'aime | de | les chansons .
   c paroles | Grand Corps Malade | J'adore | les | de .
   d le | ma | de | C'est | mère | nouveau métier .
   e style | Je | le | cet auteur | déteste | de .

7 **Translate the sentences (activity 6) into English, using an apostrophe + 's'.**

8 **Listen (1–4) and write down the sentences you hear.**

9 **Translate into French, using the perfect tense.**

   a She took some lessons.
   b You made some videos.
   c We had some success.
   d The concert was extraordinary.
   e He learnt to play the guitar.

Culture

Céline Sciamma has quickly become one of the most successful French film directors in recent years. She puts women at the heart of her films, and offers her own vision of feminism. Her best-known film, *Portrait of a Lady on Fire*, won several prestigious prizes including the Best Screenplay and the Queer Palm at the Cannes Film Festival

6.1F Vous voulez être célèbre?

OBJECTIVES
- Tips on becoming famous
- Infinitives used as nouns
- The imperative (*tu* and *vous* forms)
- Phonics: *i*, *y* and *-ien*

1 📖 Read the advice given by three successful people. Decide who says each statement below (a–h).

Maël
Suivez mon exemple! Si vous êtes sportif comme moi, **jouez bien et participez à des concours** aussi souvent que possible. Il ne faut pas être timide! Perdre un match, ce n'est pas la fin du monde. Il y aura toujours une autre occasion. **Écoutez vos amis** et votre famille quand ils veulent vous aider.

Céleste
Si vous avez une compétence, développez-la! **Montrez aux autres que vous pouvez faire quelque chose de spécial.** Pour moi, c'était la musique. Chanter, c'est ma vie! Je suis handicapée. Mon quotidien est parfois difficile, mais je veux vraiment suivre ma passion. Être handicapé n'est pas une raison pour éviter de faire quelque chose.

Amir
J'ai eu de la chance et je suis devenu célèbre à l'âge de vingt ans. J'ai eu l'occasion de voyager partout dans le monde et j'ai gagné beaucoup d'argent. Mais **faites attention**! Les célébrités ne sont pas toujours heureuses. On peut être célèbre mais seul. Parfois, je voudrais vivre une vie calme avec ma famille, sans paparazzi.

a Losing a match is not the end of the world.
b Being disabled is no reason for avoiding doing something.
c Singing is my life.
d I had the opportunity to travel throughout the world.
e Famous people are not always happy.
f My daily life is sometimes difficult, but I really want to follow my passion.

2 🔀 Translate the bold sentences in the texts into English.

3 🎯 Copy and complete the instructions with the *vous*-form imperative of the verb in brackets.

a ___ l'écran. (*regarder*)
b ___ la musique. (*écouter*)
c ___ du vélo. (*faire*)
d ___ les paroles. (*lire*)
e ___ ici. (*attendre*)
f ___ un blog. (*écrire*)

4 💬 In pairs, take turns to choose a text from activity 1 and read it aloud.

Les verbes 🎯

The imperative

The imperative is used to give someone advice or instructions.

For most verbs, the *vous*-form imperative is the same as the normal *vous* form of the present tense, but without the pronoun.

Venez ici! Come here!
Dormez bien. Sleep well.
Faites du sport. Do some sport.

The *tu*-form imperative is usually the same as the *tu*-form of the present tense but without the pronoun. For *-er* verbs and *aller*, drop the final *-s*.

Viens ici! Come here!
Regarde! Look!
Va dans la cuisine. Go into the kitchen.

Celebrity culture 6.1F

5 🎧 Listen to the advice (1–6). Copy and complete the table.

	Instruction	Reason
1		

6 🎯 Find *three* examples of an infinitive used as a noun in activity 1.

Example: Perdre un match, ce n'est pas la fin du monde.

7 ⤫ Translate the sentences into English.
   a Arrêter de fumer est une bonne décision.
   b Lire me relaxe.
   c Faire du yoga est une activité saine.
   d Chanter me fait oublier mes problèmes.
   e Vouloir, c'est la clé du succès!
   f Organiser un voyage, c'est difficile.

8 🎧 Listen (1–4) and write down the sentences you hear.

9 💬 In pairs, complete the role play. Take turns to ask and answer the questions. Answer in full sentences.

> **You are talking to your Belgian friend about celebrities.**
>
> 1 *Qui est ta célébrité préférée et pourquoi?*
>   Name a celebrity you like and give **one** reason for liking them.
> 2 Ask your friend whether she / he has a favourite celebrity.
>   *Name your favourite celebrity.*
> 3 *Quelle sorte de musique aimes-tu?*
>   Say what kind of music you like. (Give **one** detail.)
> 4 *Comment écoutes-tu de la musique?*
>   Say how you listen to music. (Give **one** detail.)
> 5 *Que penses-tu des réseaux sociaux?*
>   Say what you think of social media. (Give **one** detail.)

10 ✏️ You are helping to write an article about becoming famous. Write *five* sentences giving advice, using the *vous*-form of the imperative.

Example: Écoutez votre famille!
Partagez vos idées avec…

Les verbes

Infinitives used as nouns

French infinitives can be used as nouns, often at the beginning of a sentence. In English, they correspond to present participles ending in '-ing'.

Faire des photos est simple.
Taking photos is simple.

Apprendre à lire est important.
Learning to read is important.

Phonétique

i, y and -ien

fac**i**le l**i**sez **i**l **y** aura
s**y**stème ph**y**sique les P**y**rénées
b**ien** v**ien**s ch**ien** entret**ien**

Attention

In the role play, keep your responses short and simple. Use language that you know and are sure of.

Make sure you use a verb in each response.

Culture

Assia El Hannouni is a French Paralympian who is almost blind. Her main event is the 800m sprint, which she runs against athletes both with and without disabilities. She has won several gold medals at the Paralympics and in 2007, she established a new world record in her disability category for the women's 800m sprint.

quatre-vingt-trois 83

6.2G Je sais réussir!

OBJECTIVES
- Abilities and achievements
- Demonstrative adjectives: *ce, cet, cette, ces*
- *savoir* + infinitive
- Phonics: *è / ê / ai* and *c'est / ces / sais*

1 Match the French verbs to the English translations.

| courir | communiquer | chanter | raconter |
| influencer | écrire | exprimer | parler |

| to write | to influence | to sing | to speak |
| to run | to communicate | to tell | to express |

2 Listen to and read the texts about five famous people from francophone countries. Copy and complete the table.

	Profession	Abilities
1	athlete	running, influencing others

Marie-Josée Ta Lou

Cette athlète de la Côte d'Ivoire sait courir et influencer les autres. Elle gagne beaucoup de médailles et elle est fière de son pays. Marie-José Ta Lou est un symbole de détermination pour les jeunes filles qui rêvent de devenir championnes.

French Montana
(de son vrai nom Karim Kharbouch)

Ce chanteur et rappeur vient du Maroc mais il a quitté ce pays quand il avait treize ans. Non seulement il sait chanter, mais c'est aussi un sportif: il joue au foot et au basket.

Marc Labrèche

Cet acteur est né à Montréal. Il a eu des rôles dans plus de trente films et au théâtre. C'est aussi un humoriste qui sait raconter des histoires et amuser son public. On le voit souvent à la télévision au Canada.

Roxana Maracineanu

Née en Roumanie, cette sportive est arrivée en France à l'âge de neuf ans. Elle est devenue la première championne du monde française de natation. Aujourd'hui, elle travaille dans la politique, un monde où elle sait bien communiquer.

Mohamed Mbougar Sarr

Cet écrivain est né au Sénégal en 1990. Il a étudié en France avant de retourner en Afrique. Dans ses romans, il sait parler de problèmes comme le racisme ou la discrimination. Il a gagné plusieurs prix internationaux.

3 Find the French for the English phrases.

a she wins lots of medals
b he left this country
c he's also a sportsperson
d he has had roles
e she became the first world champion
f she works in politics
g he studied
h he has won several prizes

quatre-vingt-quatre

Celebrity culture 6.2G

4 Rewrite the sentences using *savoir* + infinitive.

Example: Nous chantons. → *Nous savons chanter.*

a Je fais la cuisine.
b Nous dansons.
c Vous jouez au foot.
d Les enfants écrivent.
e Mon petit frère lit.
f Elle réussit.

5 Find the *six* examples of demonstrative adjectives in activity 2 and translate them into English.

6 Choose the correct option to complete each sentence.

a Tu veux aller à **cette** / **ce** / **cet** concert (*m*)?
b **Cette** / **Cet** / **Ce** équipe (*f*) joue très bien.
c **Cet** / **Ce** / **Cette** livre (*m*) est intéressant.
d J'aime bien **ce** / **cet** / **cette** photo (*f*).
e **Cette** / **Ces** / **Ce** gâteaux (*pl*) sont très bons.
f Qui est **ce** / **cette** / **cet** acteur (*m*)?

7 Listen (1–4). Write down in English *three* things about each person's opinion of what makes the ideal celebrity.

8 Listen (1–4) and write down the sentences you hear.

Phonétique

è / *ê* / *ai* and *c'est* / *ces* / *sais*

| très | célèbre | rêve | fête | j'ai | français |
| c'est | ces | je sais | | | |

9 In pairs, take turns to choose a text from activity 2 and read it aloud.

10 In pairs, take turns to choose a celebrity from activity 2 and guess who it is.

Example:
• *Cette célébrité sait faire de la natation et elle est devenue championne du monde.*
• *C'est Roxanna Maracineanu?*
• *Oui!*

11 Choose any celebrity and write *five* sentences in French about their abilities and achievements.

Les verbes

savoir + infinitive

Use **savoir** (to know) followed by an infinitive to mean 'to know how to…'

Tu **sais** faire la cuisine.
You **know how** to cook.

je sais	nous savons
tu sais	vous savez
il / elle / on sait	ils / elles savent

Grammaire

Demonstrative adjectives

French has one set of words for both 'this / these' and 'that / those':

Masculine	Feminine	Plural
ce	cette	ces
cet (+ vowel)		

Ce film est super.
Cet influenceur a beaucoup de succès.
Cette célébrité travaille en Belgique.
Ces photos sont extraordinaires.

Cette célébrité s'appelle…	
C'est un / une	acteur / actrice. influenceur / influenceuse. écrivain(e) / musicien(ne) / athlète. sportif / sportive.
Il / Elle sait	écrire / parler / chanter / courir / jouer. communiquer / exprimer des idées.
Il / Elle gagne Il / Elle a gagné	beaucoup de médailles / un prix.
Il / Elle est devenu(e) champion(ne) de…	
Il / Elle travaille Il / Elle a travaillé	dans la politique / le cinéma / le sport / la musique. comme bénévole.
Il / Elle participe à	des concours (internationaux).
Il / Elle a étudié en / au…	

quatre-vingt-cinq 85

6.2F La vie de célébrité

OBJECTIVES
- Pros and cons of being famous
- Possessive adjectives
- The present tense of *avoir*, *être*, *faire* and *aller*
- Phonics: *j*, *g*, *ch*, and *gn*

1 📖 Match the interview questions (1–6) to the responses (a–f).

Interview avec une célébrité

1 Que faites-vous comme travail?
2 Voyagez-vous beaucoup?
3 Quelle personnalité avez-vous?
4 Est-ce que l'argent est important pour vous?
5 Êtes-vous prête à partager votre vie personnelle avec le public?
6 Que faites-vous pour rester en bonne santé?

a Quand je ne travaille pas, je vais souvent à la salle de sport. Je fais aussi de la natation. J'ai de la chance car j'ai ma propre piscine.

b Je suis positive et souvent heureuse. Je ne suis jamais paresseuse.

c Oui, il faut accepter cela si on est célèbre. J'ai choisi cette carrière. Mais j'essaye de protéger mon mari et mes enfants.

d Oui, je vais souvent à l'étranger. Cet été, mon groupe et moi allons au Canada pour participer à un spectacle.

e Je suis danseuse et chanteuse. Je fais surtout du hip-hop, mais j'aime d'autres styles comme le jazz.

f Oui et non. La vie est plus facile quand on est riche, mais certaines célébrités riches sont tristes malgré leur succès.

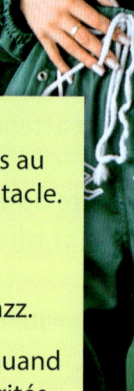

2 💬 In pairs, read the interview aloud.

3 🎧 Listen (1–4) and write down the sentences you hear.

Phonétique

j, ch and gn

je proté**g**e les **g**irafes

j'ai de la **ch**ance   **j**'ai **ch**oisi

ga**gn**er   espa**gn**ol   monta**gn**e

4 Copy and complete the sentences using the present tense of the verb in brackets.

a Elle ___ en Suisse. (aller)
b Vous ___ beaucoup de chance. (avoir)
c Nous ne ___ pas paresseux. (être)
d Qu'est-ce que tu ___ pour rester en bonne santé? (faire)
e Ma famille ___ beaucoup d'influence sur moi. (avoir)
f Il ___ de belles chansons. (faire)

5 🔀 Translate the sentences (activity 4) into English.

Les verbes

The present tense of *avoir*, *être*, *faire* and *aller*

These very common verbs are irregular in the present tense:

	avoir (to have)	*être* (to be)	*faire* (to do)	*aller* (to go)
je/j'	ai	suis	fais	vais
tu	as	es	fais	vas
il/elle/on	a	est	fait	va
nous	avons	sommes	faisons	allons
vous	avez	êtes	faites	allez
ils/elles	ont	sont	font	vont

86 quatre-vingt-six

Celebrity culture   **6.2F**

6 Read about one actor's lifestyle and answer the questions (a–f) in English.

La vie d'un acteur sénégalais

Ousmane est acteur. Il est fier de son métier et de son succès. Mais comment est sa vie quotidienne? Comment voit-il ses fans? Ousmane répond à nos questions.

« Ma vie quotidienne n'est pas complètement différente de votre vie quotidienne! Le matin, je me lève, je prends le petit-déjeuner, je travaille pendant la journée, je rentre à la maison, je mange, je me relaxe et je me couche. Mais mon travail est extraordinaire! J'ai la chance de découvrir des endroits fantastiques et de rencontrer des gens passionnants. Mes collègues sont super et ils m'encouragent beaucoup quand je suis fatigué. C'est bien d'avoir un grand nombre de fans et je reçois souvent des messages. »

Ousmane a aussi une vie de famille. Sa partenaire est également bien connue: elle est journaliste et a son propre site. Le couple vit à Dakar, la capitale du Sénégal, avec ses deux enfants. Pour Ousmane, sa famille est aussi importante que sa carrière. Par exemple, il aime passer du temps avec ses parents et son oncle qui habitent près de la plage.

a How does Ousmane compare his daily life with that of others?
b What does he say he is lucky to do? (Give **two** details.)
c How do Ousmane's colleagues support him?
d What does Ousmane say about his fans? (Give **two** details.)
e What do we learn about his partner? (Give **three** details.)
f How does Ousmane view his family compared with his career?

7 Translate the sentences into French.
a I am proud of my job.
b Her life is interesting.
c Your (*familiar*) colleagues are great.
d We have our own website.
e She lives with her two children.

8 Listen to an extract from a podcast about the YouTube star, Michou. Copy and complete the sentences.

a Michou was born in ___.
b Michou has more than ___ followers.
c Michou doesn't always find his YouTube work ___.
d Having a large number of fans is sometimes ___.
e Michou likes sharing ___ with other young people.
f Michou hopes to have a long ___.

9 In pairs, take turns to ask and answer the questions.
- Quels sont les avantages d'être célèbre?
- Quels sont les inconvénients d'être célèbre?

Example:

On peut voyager / faire / rencontrer…

On doit travailler / avoir…

C'est dur / difficile / embêtant…

10 Write a paragraph describing the pros and cons of being a celebrity.

Grammaire

Possessive adjectives

In French, the words for 'my', 'your', 'his', etc. agree with the noun that follows.

	masculine singular*	feminine singular	plural
my	mon	ma	mes
your (familiar, singular)	ton	ta	tes
his / her	son	sa	ses
our	notre	notre	nos
your (formal, plural)	votre	votre	vos
their	leur	leur	leurs

* and feminine singular before a vowel or silent 'h' (*mon amie*)

*Elle adore **son** métier.* She loves **her** job. (*métier* is masculine singular)

***Notre** vie est facile.* **Our** life is easy. (*vie* is feminine singular)

*Je rencontre **mes** fans.* I meet **my** fans. (*fans* is plural)

Theme 2 — Culture: Les Jeux de la Francophonie

1 Read the fact file about *Les Jeux de la Francophonie*. Copy and complete the sentences.

Quoi:	Concours sportifs et culturels
Qui:	Entre 1 700 et 4 000 participants de plus de 50 pays
Quand:	Tous les quatre ans
Où:	Différents pays francophones
Durée:	10 jours
Premier événement:	1989

a *Les Jeux de la Francophonie* consist of ___ and ___ competitions.
b Between ___ and ___ people take part. They come from ___ countries.
c The games take place ___ years.
d The games take place in different ___ countries.
e The games last ___ .
f The games first took place ___ .

Culture

Les Jeux de la Francophonie might be compared to the Commonwealth Games. What are the similarities and differences? What other events bring together people who speak the same language but live in different countries?

2 Read the article below and answer the questions.
   a Where exactly did the first *Jeux de la Francophonie* take place?
   b How often does the host country change?
   c Which country hosted the games in 2023?
   d Name **one** aim of the games.
   e Name **two** different categories of sport that are included in the games.
   f Which **three** non-sporting competitions are mentioned?
   g Who are the non-sporting competitions for?
   h What do the competitions help these people to do?

Les premiers *Jeux de la Francophonie* ont eu lieu en 1989 dans deux villes du Maroc: Casablanca et Rabat. Tous les quatre ans, un pays francophone différent reçoit les Jeux. En 2023, c'était le tour de la République démocratique du Congo.

Les Jeux ont plusieurs buts, y compris:
- encourager les rencontres entre jeunes francophones
- célébrer la diversité des cultures francophones
- promouvoir la langue française.

Aux Jeux, on trouve des sports traditionnels comme l'athlétisme, le cyclisme et le football, mais aussi des sports moins traditionnels comme par exemple le beach volley, la lutte sénégalaise et le tennis de table.

De plus, on propose des concours culturels de danse, de chanson et de photographie. Ces concours sont ouverts aux personnes de 18 à 35 ans. Pour les jeunes talents, c'est l'occasion idéale de commencer une carrière professionnelle.

y compris	including	promouvoir	to promote
la rencontre	meeting	la lutte	wrestling
la diversité	diversity		

Theme 2

3 Read the article again and find the French for the English phrases (a–i).

a took place
b receives, hosts
c the turn of
d several goals
e in addition
f they offer
g competitions
h the ideal opportunity
i a professional career

4 In pairs, each choose a different year of the *Jeux de la Francophonie*. Research the following details. Then take turns to present the information in French.

- city/country where the games took place: *En 2017, les Jeux ont eu lieu à … en …*
- dates: *Les Jeux ont eu lieu du … au …*
- number of nations taking part: *… pays ont participé aux Jeux.*
- sports involved: *Il y a eu des compétitions dans … sports différents, comme par exemple …*
- non-sporting competitions: *Il y a eu aussi des concours de …*

5 Listen to an interview with Anaïs, who took part in the games (1–4). Write down the phrases you hear to complete the sentences.

1 ___ a été une expérience extraordinaire. Je suis ___ .
2 J'ai rencontré ___ et d'artistes d'autres pays.
3 Pour moi, c'est ___ pour les jeunes francophones de tous les continents de gagner et de ___ .
4 Beaucoup de ___ m'ont aidée à ___ aux Jeux. Merci à ___ !

6 Choose a French-speaking country named in the Culture box below. Research and create a fact file.

Nom du pays:	
Continent:	
Population:	
Population francophone:	
Autre(s) langue(s) parlée(s)	

Culture

La Francophonie is an international organisation of 88 countries and regions where French is either spoken or culturally significant. Some of those countries are former French colonies in Africa, where French is still used alongside other languages.

About two-thirds of the world's 98 million native French speakers live in France. There are also significant numbers of French speakers in Canada, Haiti, Belgium, the Democratic Republic of the Congo, Switzerland and Mali.

Curious fact: The French-speaking country with the largest population is the Democratic Republic of the Congo (DRC), not France. However, less than 5% of the DRC's population speaks French as their first language.

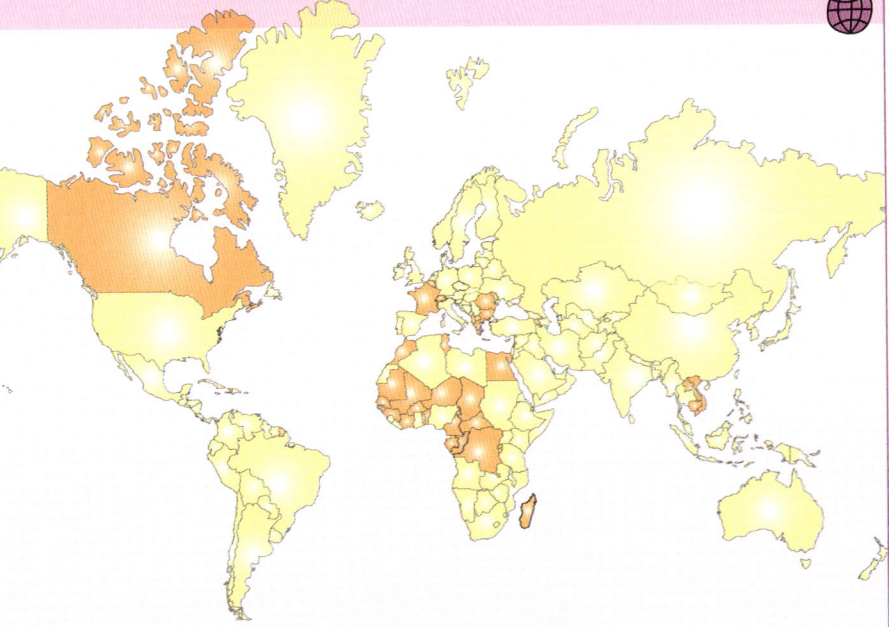

États membres de l'Organisation internationale de la Francophonie

quatre-vingt-neuf 89

Theme 2 — Grammar practice

The imperfect tense

1 Conjugate the verbs in the imperfect tense.

a je ___ (*regarder*)
b mon frère ___ (*aimer*)
c je ___ (*jouer*)
d tu ___ (*adorer*)
e je ___ (*préférer*)
f ma sœur ___ (*écouter*)

Adverbs ending in *-ment*

2 Copy and complete the sentences with the adverb formed from the adjective in brackets.

a Tu lis ___ . (*rapide*)
b ___ , il fait beau ici. (*normal*)
c ___ , nous allons à la plage. (*général*)
d Je cours ___ . (*lent*)
e Elle gagne ___ . (*facile*)
f J'ai vu mon cousin ___ . (*récent*)

Grammaire

Most adverbs are formed by adding -ment to the feminine form of the adjective. Adjectives ending in -ant and -ent change to -amment and -emment respectively.

The perfect tense: irregular past participles

3 Copy and complete the sentences with the correct past participle of the verb. Then translate the sentences into English.

a Tu as ___ le bus. (*prendre*)
b Nous avons beaucoup ___ . (*rire*)
c Elle a ___ un cadeau. (*recevoir*)
d J'ai ___ mes copains. (*voir*)
e Le chien a ___ très vite. (*courir*)
f Tu as ___ le livre. (*lire*)

Emphatic pronouns

4 Copy and complete the sentences with the correct preposition (*pour, sans, avec, chez, avant* or *sur*) and emphatic pronoun (*moi* or *toi*).

a J'ai choisi quelque chose ___ . (*for you*)
b C'est difficile ___ . (*without you*)
c Tu veux jouer aux cartes ___ ? (*with me*)
d Vous venez ___ ? (*to my home*)
e Je vais arriver ___ . (*before you*)
f Tu as ton portable ___ ? (*on you*)

Popular culture — Theme 2

The near future tense

5 Rewrite the sentences in the near future tense. Change the verb in bold to the correct form of *aller* + infinitive.

a Tu **écoutes** la chanson.
b Je **regarde** la télévision.
c Mon frère **arrive** ce soir.
d Elles **jouent** au football.
e Nous **chantons** ce soir.
f Vous **dansez** à la fête.

Partitive articles

6 Choose the correct form of the partitive article to complete each sentence.

a Nous faisons **du** / **des** / **de la** promenades.
b Vous écoutez **des** / **de la** / **du** musique (*f*)?
c Tu fais **de l'** / **de la** / **du** natation (*f*)?
d Je bois **du** / **de l'** / **de la** café (*m*).
e Elle fait **de l'** / **des** / **du** exercice (*m*).
f On réserve **des** / **du** / **de la** billets.

Grammaire

The partitive article conveys the idea of 'some'. Use *du* before a masculine singular noun, *de la* before a feminine singular noun, *de l'* before a singular noun beginning with a vowel or silent *h* and *des* before a plural noun.

The perfect tense with *être*

7 Copy and complete the sentences with the past participle of the verb in brackets. Then translate the sentences into English.

a Ma sœur est ___ en ville. (*aller*)
b Mon copain et moi, nous sommes ___ à la maison. (*rester*)
c Pierre, tu es ___ à quelle heure? (*rentrer*)
d Ma mère est ___ tôt. (*partir*)
e Mes copines sont ___ avec nous. (*venir*)
f Mon frère est ___ de vélo. (*tomber*)

Les verbes

Remember that for verbs that take *être* in the perfect tense, the past participle must agree in number and gender with the subject of the sentence.

Prepositions

8 Choose the correct preposition to complete each sentence.

a Vous allez **au** / **en** / **à** Maroc (*m*)?
b Je pars **à** / **au** / **en** Suisse (*f*).
c On va **à** / **en** / **au** Paris.
d Tu pars **au** / **aux** / **en** États-Unis?
e Elles vont **en** / **au** / **à** Canada (*m*).
f Nous passons les vacances **au** / **en** / **aux** Antilles.

Grammaire

To say 'to' or 'in' a place, use *à* with a town or city, *au* with a masculine country name, *aux* with a plural country name and *en* with a feminine country name.

quatre-vingt-onze

Theme 2 — Grammar practice

c'est and *il y a*

9 Copy and complete the sentences with *c'est* or *il y a*.

a Je vais acheter des fleurs. ___ un cadeau pour ma mère.
b Nous habitons à Montréal. ___ une grande ville.
c On va à la plage car ___ du soleil aujourd'hui.
d J'aime voir des films. ___ un nouveau cinéma ici.
e Quel est cet animal sur la photo? ___ un chien?
f J'ai soif. ___ un café dans cette rue?

The present tense of common irregular verbs

10 Choose the correct form of the verb in each sentence.

a Tu **bois** / **boit** / **boire** de l'eau?
b Je **courir** / **court** / **cours** dans le parc.
c Mon frère **ris** / **rit** / **rire** tout le temps.
d Je **connais** / **connaître** / **connaît** très bien mon voisin.
e Tu **recevoir** / **reçois** / **reçoit** souvent des cadeaux?
f Mon chien **voir** / **vois** / **voit** quelque chose.

Direct object pronouns

11 Rewrite the sentences in the correct order. Then translate them into English.

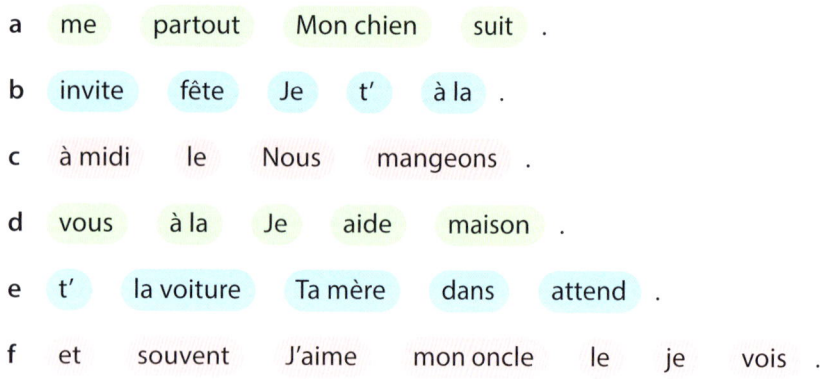

Grammaire

Direct object pronouns (*me*, *te*, *vous*, *le*, *la*) go before the verb.

The perfect tense with *avoir* and *être*

12 Copy and complete the sentences with the correct form of the auxiliary verb *avoir* or *être*. Then translate the sentences into English.

a Tu ___ pris le train ce matin?
b Elle ___ arrivée à cinq heures.
c Je ___ descendu du bus au cinéma.
d Nous ___ réservé des billets pour le concert.
e Mes parents ___ sortis ce matin.
f Vous ___ bien dormi au festival?

Les verbes

Most verbs use *avoir* as their auxiliary verb in the perfect tense. Some use *être*, particularly those describing movement, such as *aller*, *partir* and *retourner*.

Popular culture   Theme 2

de to show possession

13 Rewrite the sentences in the correct order.

a   les paroles   cette chanson   Je déteste   de .

b   de   J'emprunte   ma sœur   le vélo .

c   cet auteur   les romans   Nous aimons   de .

d   de   le nom   J'ai oublié   son équipe .

e   Nous écoutons   notre groupe préféré   de   la musique .

f   mon frère   la chambre   dort   dans   de   Le chien .

The perfect tense of *avoir*, *être*, *faire* and *prendre*

14 Copy and complete the sentences with the correct form of the perfect tense. Then translate the sentences into English.

a Le spectacle ___ extraordinaire. (*être*)
b Vous ___ le bus? (*prendre*)
c Elle ___ l'occasion de jouer pour son pays. (*avoir*)
d Tu ___ des vidéos pendant les vacances? (*faire*)
e Nous ___ des cours de natation. (*prendre*)
f Ils ___ du succès immédiatement. (*avoir*)

The imperative

15 Copy and complete the sentences with the correct form of the imperative.

a ___ le défilé, Théo! (*regarder*)
b Tu as faim? ___ ton repas! (*finir*)
c S'il vous plaît, ___ devant la porte, madame. (*attendre*)
d ___ les paroles de la chanson, Amir! (*écouter*)
e ___ son exemple si vous voulez réussir. (*suivre*)
f ___ votre nom ici, s'il vous plaît. (*écrire*)

Possessive adjectives

16 Choose the correct form of the possessive adjective to complete each sentence. Then translate the sentences into English.

a Je passe beaucoup de temps avec **mon** / **ma** / **mes** famille (f).
b Elle a célébré **son** / **sa** / **ses** succès (m).
c Tu t'entends bien avec **ton** / **ta** / **tes** collègues?
d Il a choisi **son** / **sa** / **ses** carrière (f) quand il était petit.
e Nous n'avons pas **notre** / **nos** propre piscine (f).
f Ils partagent **leur** / **leurs** vie (f) avec le public.

Demonstrative adjectives

17 Choose the correct demonstrative adjective to complete each sentence.

a **Ce** / **Cet** / **Cette** travail (m) est intéressant.
b Je n'aime pas **ce** / **cette** / **ces** vidéos.
c **Ce** / **Cet** / **Cette** chanteuse est travailleuse.
d Je m'intéresse à **ce** / **cette** / **ces** festival (m).
e **Ce** / **Cet** / **Cette** été (m), je vais au Maroc.
f J'ai écouté **ce** / **cette** / **ces** chanson (f) hier.

quatre-vingt-treize

Theme 2 — Vocabulary

Words that are highlighted in grey in this list are words that may be useful, but you won't need to know them for the exam.

Introductory vocabulary

- accepter to accept
- acheter to buy
- l' acteur/actrice actor, actress
- l' activité (f.) activity
- adorer to love
- aimer to like
- aimer mieux to prefer
- aller to go
- l' ami(e) (m./f.) friend
- l' an (m.) year
- l' anniversaire (m.) birthday
- août August
- après after
- attendre to wait
- aujourd'hui today
- autre other
- l' avis (m.) opinion
- avoir to have
- beaucoup a lot
- le billet ticket
- le blog blog
- boire to drink
- bon(ne) good
- ça it, that
- le cadeau present
- le café coffee, coffee shop
- la campagne countryside
- le camping camping, campsite
- car because
- la carte card/map
- célèbre famous
- célébrer to celebrate
- le centre centre
- certain(e)(s) some, certain
- la chambre bedroom
- chanter to sing
- le/la chanteur/chanteuse singer
- chaque each, every
- le/la chef (de cuisine) chef
- cher/chère expensive
- chez nous at/to our place
- le chien dog
- la chose thing
- le cinéma cinema
- commencer to start
- le concours competition
- connaître to know (person, place)
- le copain friend, boyfriend
- la copine friend, girlfriend
- courir to run
- coûter to cost
- créatif/créative creative
- d'abord first of all
- dangereux/dangereuse dangerous
- la danse dancing
- le/la danseur/danseuse dancer
- décembre December
- le défilé parade
- déjà already
- demain tomorrow
- détester to hate
- devenir to become
- devoir to have to, must
- (le) dimanche Sunday
- le dîner dinner
- donner to give
- dur(e) hard
- écouter to listen (to)
- écrire to write
- l' écrivain(e) (m./f.) author, writer
- l' église (f.) church
- en ligne online
- ennuyeux/ennuyeuse boring
- entendre to hear
- envoyer to send
- l' équipe (f.) team
- espérer to hope
- essayer to try
- l' été (m.) summer
- à l'étranger abroad
- être to be
- facile easy
- faire to do, make
- faire beau to be nice (weather)
- la famille family
- il faut it is necessary, must
- la femme politique politician (female)
- le festival festival
- la fête party, celebration
- le feu d'artifice firework display
- le film film
- la fin end
- la fleur flower
- la fois time, occasion
- le football football
- français(e) (adj.) French
- francophone French-language
- le frère brother
- le gâteau cake
- les gens (m. pl.) people
- grand(e) big
- le groupe group, band
- l' hiver (m.) winter
- l' homme politique politician (male)
- l' idée (f.) idea
- important(e) important
- intéressant(e) interesting
- s' intéresser à to be interested in
- inviter to invite
- le jardin garden
- le jeu game
- jeune (adj.) young
- jouer to play
- le jour day
- le jour de l'An New Year's Day
- le jour férié public holiday
- la lecture reading
- se lever to get up
- lire to read
- le livre book
- mais but
- la maison house
- manger to eat
- marcher to walk
- se marier to get married
- le match match
- même same
- (le) mercredi Wednesday
- la mère mother
- le métier job
- minuit midnight
- la mode fashion
- moi me
- la montagne mountain(s)
- la mosquée mosque
- la musique music
- la natation swimming
- national(e)(s)/nationaux national
- Noël Christmas
- l' occasion (f.) occasion, chance, opportunity
- l' offre (f.) offer
- ouvert(e) open
- Pâques Easter
- le parc park
- parfois sometimes
- partager to share
- le/la partenaire partner
- partout everywhere
- passionnant(e) exciting
- pendant during
- la personne person
- petit(e) small
- la piscine swimming pool
- la place place, square, spot
- la plage beach
- plus more
- possible possible
- poster to post
- pourquoi why
- pouvoir to be able to
- préféré(e) favourite
- préférer to prefer
- la proposition proposition
- quand when
- quelqu'un someone
- la radio radio
- la recette recipe
- regarder to watch
- rencontrer to meet
- le réseau network
- les réseaux sociaux (m. pl.) social media

Theme 2

réserver to book
le restaurant restaurant
le roman novel
la route road
la rue street
la semaine week
si if
social social
le site web website
la sœur sister
le soir evening
souvent often
sportif/sportive sporty, athletic
le stade stadium
la star star, celebrity
tard late
la télé(vision) television
télécharger to download
le temps time, weather
le théâtre theatre
timide shy
tous les jours every day
tout le monde everyone
la tradition tradition
travailler to work
trouver to find
utiliser to use
les vacances (f. pl.) holidays
le vélo bike
la vidéo video
la vie life
la visite visit
vivre to live
voir to see
vouloir to want
voyager to travel
le week-end weekend

4.1G Qu'est-ce que tu aimais faire?

l' âge (m.) age
assez (de) quite, enough
comme such as, like, since
couramment fluently
la cuisine cooking, kitchen
l' émission (f.) TV programme
en retard late

fatigué(e) tired
le fruit fruit
gagner to win, earn
généralement generally
génial(e) great
lentement slowly
libre free
normalement normally
onze eleven
l' ordinateur (m.) computer
le passe-temps pastime
rapidement quickly
récemment recently
le soleil sun
sorte sort, kind
sortir to go out
super super
surtout especially
tout all

4.1F Le week-end dernier

les Alpes (f. pl.) Alps
amusant(e) amusing, fun, funny, enjoyable
l' après-midi (m.) afternoon
le beau-père stepfather, father-in-law
britannique British
le bus bus
la chance luck, opportunity
les courses (f. pl.) (grocery) shopping
dernier/dernière last
les devoirs (m. pl.) homework
l' e-mail (m.) e-mail
l' énergie (f.) energy
ensuite then
gentil(le) kind
la grand-mère grandma
les grands-parents (m. pl.) grandparents
le jeu de société board game
malade ill, sick
le matin morning
meilleur(e) best, better
mettre to put (on)
le pantalon trousers
la partie part, round of (game)

le portable mobile phone
prendre to take
la promenade walk, stroll
puis then
quelque some
recevoir to receive
la réponse answer
rire to laugh
(le) samedi Saturday
sans without
le site (tourist) site
le SMS text message
le thé tea
toujours always
trop too
venir to come
la ville town, city
visiter to visit (place)

4.2G Sport ou musique?

l' action (f.) action
Attention! Watch out!
la décision decision
l' équitation (f.) horse riding
l' escalade en salle (f.) climbing (on a climbing wall)
l' exercice (m.) exercise
la flûte flute
la guitare guitar
la santé health

4.2F En voyage!

l' année (f.) year
arriver to arrive
l' automne (m.) autumn
le bateau boat
le bord edge
le Canada Canada
la capitale capital city
cependant however
comment how
le défi challenge
descendre to go down, descend, get off
difficile difficult
ensemble together
entrer (dans) to go into
les États-Unis (m. pl.) United States

grave serious
habiter to live
haut high
l' heure (f.) hour, time, o'clock
historique historical
le hockey sur glace ice hockey
l' île (f.) island
le kilomètre kilometre
là-bas over there
le Maroc Morocco
la mer sea
le midi midday
le mois month
monter to go up
mourir to die
naître to be born
partir to leave
passer to spend (time)
le pays country
la pièce (de théâtre) play (theatre)
plein(e) full
populaire popular
les Pyrénées (f. pl.) Pyrenees
rentrer to go back, to go home
rester to stay
retourner to return
la Réunion Reunion (island)
la salle room
le Sénégal Senegal
le sport sport
la Suisse Switzerland
le surf surfing
tomber to fall
traditionnel(le) traditional
l' ultra-marathon (m.) ultramarathon
le voyage journey
vrai(e) real, true

5.1G Les journées spéciales

l' artiste (m./f.) artist
la belle-mère stepmother, mother-in-law
le chocolat chocolate
le choix choice

quatre-vingt-quinze

Theme 2   Vocabulary

combien how many
dehors outside
le demi-frère half-brother
la demi-sœur half-sister
durer to last
la glace ice, ice cream
gratuit(e) free
l' humour (m.) humour
ici here
le jazz jazz
joli(e) pretty
la journée day
la neige snow
noir(e) (adj.) black
organiser to organise
parfait(e) perfect
par exemple for example
participer (à) to participate, take part (in)
payer to pay
que that
quelque chose something
rouge (adj.) red
recommander to recommend
la sculpture sculpture
le souvenir souvenir
spécial(e) special
le stylo pen
le tee-shirt T-shirt
très very
vert(e) green

5.1F Bon anniversaire!

Aïd-el-Fitr Eid al-Fitr
l' amoureux / amoureuse lover
les autres (m./f. pl.) others
avril April
la célébration celebration
chrétien(ne) (adj.) Christian
le cola coke
la collecte collection
commercial(e) (adj.) commercial
content(e) pleased, happy, glad
croire to believe

délicieux / délicieuse delicious
dîner (v.) to have dinner
divorcé(e) divorced
donc so
double double
entre between
le fan fan
février February
janvier January
juillet July
mai May
mars March
le message message
moins less
musulman(e) (adj.) Muslim
octobre October
ouvrir to open
le paquet parcel
plusieurs several
préparer to prepare
la raison reason
rarement rarely
le salon lounge, living room
septembre September
suivre to follow
le travail work
triste sad
les vêtements (m. pl.) clothes

5.2G On a fait la fête!

alors so, well, then
connu(e) famous, known
l' endroit (m.) place
l' entrée (f.) entrance
faire mauvais to be bad (weather)
le fast-food fast food
la fille girl, daughter
heureux / heureuse happy
l' hôpital (m.) hospital
(le) jeudi Thursday
le/la jeune (n.) young person
le/les journal / journaux (m. pl.) newspaper(s)
jusque until
le mois month
montrer to show
l' organisation (f.) organisation

parler to speak, to talk
perdre to lose
le printemps spring
quitter to leave
le repas meal
la surprise surprise
le/la voisin(e) neighbour
(le) vendredi Friday

5.2F Les fêtes dans le passé et à l'avenir

américain(e) (adj.) American
l' avenir (m.) future
le Cameroun Cameroon
la chanson song
la date date
étudier to study
extraordinaire extraordinary
familial(e) (adj.) family
le goût taste
Hanouka Hanukkah
l' histoire (f.) history, story
juif / juive (adj.) Jewish
les légumes (m. pl.) vegetables
la lumière light
le marché market
militaire (adj.) military
la monarchie monarchy
la nature nature
le passé past
la rencontre meeting
la sandwicherie sandwich bar
la soupe soup
le spectacle show
la Terre Earth
le vin chaud mulled wine

6.1G J'ai eu du succès!

apprendre to learn, to teach
avoir peur to be scared
bientôt soon
la carrière career
cela that, it
le cours lesson
drôle funny

encourager to encourage
énormément hugely
ensuite then
l' entretien (m.) interview
le fils son
immédiatement immediately
influencer to influence
maintenant now
le membre member
musical(e) musical
la nature nature
se passer to happen, go (well / badly)
la photographie photography
presque almost
le progrès progress
quelques some, a few
le style style
la télé-réalité reality TV
la vue view

6.1F Vous voulez être célèbre?

accessible accessible
l' argent (m.) money
le basket basketball
calme (adj.) calm, quiet
la célébrité celebrity
classique (adj.) classical
la compétence skill
découvrir to discover
développer to develop
l' exemple (m.) example
faire attention to be careful
le/la footballeur / footballeuse footballer
handicapé(e) (adj.) disabled
l' influenceur / influenceuse (m./f.) influencer
le/la joueur / joueuse player
l' opinion (f.) opinion
organiser to organise
oublier to forget
les paroles words, lyrics
réussir to succeed
sourire to smile
le yoga yoga

6.2G Je sais réussir!

- actuel(le) current
- amuser to entertain
- l' athlète (m./f.) athlete
- le/la bénévole volunteer
- le/la champion(ne) champion
- communiquer to communicate
- la Côte d'Ivoire Ivory Coast
- danser to dance
- la détermination determination
- l' enfant (m./f.) child
- exprimer to express
- fier/fière proud
- l' humoriste (m./f.) humorist, comedian
- idéal(e) ideal
- la médaille medal
- le/la musicien(ne) musician
- non seulement not only
- la politique politics
- le public audience
- raconter to tell
- le/la rappeur/rappeuse rapper
- rêver to dream
- le rôle role, part
- la Roumanie Romania
- savoir to know
- seulement only
- le/la sportif, sportive (n.) sportsman/sportswoman
- le symbole symbol
- travailleur/travailleuse hard-working

6.2F La vie de célébrité

- l' Amérique (f.) America
- l' avantage (m.) advantage
- complètement completely
- le couple couple
- devant in front of
- espagnol(e) (adj.) Spanish
- fantastique fantastic
- le hip-hop hip-hop
- l' influence (f.) influence
- malgré despite
- le mari husband
- la nuit night
- l' oncle (m.) uncle
- par by
- paresseux/paresseuse lazy
- personnel personal
- positif/positive positive
- prêt(e) ready
- le problème problem
- propre clean, own
- protéger to protect
- quotidien(ne) daily
- répondre to answer
- riche rich
- le site web website

Culture

- l' athlétisme (m.) athletics
- avoir lieu to take place
- le but goal
- la compétition competition
- le continent continent
- la culture culture
- culturel(le) cultural
- le cyclisme cycling
- démocratique democratic
- la diversité diversity
- en plus in addition
- entre between
- excellent(e) excellent
- la langue language
- la lutte wrestling
- merci thank you
- le/la participant(e) participant
- present(e) present
- promouvoir to promote
- la rencontre meeting
- République démocratique du Congo Democratic Republic of the Congo
- représenter to represent
- le tennis de table table tennis
- y compris including

Theme 2 — Test and revise: Foundation Listening

1 Your Belgian friend has sent you some voice messages.

What is each message (1–4) about?

Write the correct letter.

A	Running
B	Swimming
C	Cycling
D	Walking
E	Playing football
F	Dancing

4 marks

Conseil

In this type of task, look at the list of English options first and work out the French equivalents so that you know what to listen out for.

2 You hear this report about a Canadian festival. For each section (1–2), which **two** aspects of the festival are mentioned?

Write the **two** correct letters.

A	The length of the festival
B	The food
C	The languages people sang in
D	The number of people taking part
E	The cost of the festival
F	The weather

4 marks

Conseil

In this type of task, make sure you are prepared to listen out for **two** aspects within each question.

3 You hear some Senegalese students talking about their free time.

Complete the sentences in **English**.

1 My club meets on Wednesdays to…   1 mark
2 Football is a good pastime even when…   1 mark
3 I like to be… as often as possible.   1 mark
4 I have bought a novel and am going to read it…   1 mark

Conseil

Before listening, try to anticipate the French words you will hear that match the English words in the question. Sometimes it will be an exact translation, such as *mercredi* for Wednesday, but sometimes it may be less obvious.

4 You hear some well-known French people talking about fame. What is their opinion on the following aspects?

Write   **P** for a **positive** opinion
       N for a **negative** opinion
       P+N for a **positive** and **negative** opinion.

1 The press   1 mark
2 Travel   1 mark
3 Social media   1 mark
4 Money   1 mark

Conseil

In this type of task, listen out for adjectives and verbs that convey positive and negative opinions. Be aware of different linking words that may indicate a contrast of opinion, but don't always expect something as obvious as *mais*.

Theme 2

5 You hear two Swiss teenagers talking about Christmas.

Choose the correct answer and write the letter.
Answer all parts of the question.

1a Lucas celebrates with…

A	friends.
B	family.
C	neighbours.

1 mark

1b He says he can…

A	help others.
B	relax.
C	receive presents.

1 mark

2a Aurélie likes going to…

A	church.
B	town.
C	her father's house.

1 mark

2b In the evening, Aurélie is often…

A	sad.
B	tired.
C	ill.

1 mark

Conseil

In this type of task, remember that you are answering **two** questions for each section that you hear.

6 You hear this news item on the radio about a new theatre.

Choose the **two** correct statements for each section (1–3) and write the letters.

1

A	The theatre will open in seven days' time.
B	The theatre is in the market square.
C	The theatre is located near the church.
D	The church closed two years ago.

2 marks

2

A	The theatre can seat more than 100 people.
B	10 seats are reserved for disabled people.
C	There is a café in a separate building nearby.
D	The café will serve hot and cold food.

2 marks

3

A	It is hoped that the theatre will attract tourists.
B	The nearest theatre used to be 30km away.
C	The ticket prices have been decided on.
D	Young people will pay less.

2 marks

Conseil

In this type of task, beware of choosing an option based on a single word or phrase. Read the four sentences for each section carefully and take note of details such as verb tenses, and positive or negative expressions.

Dictation A

You will now hear **four** short sentences.

Listen carefully and, using your knowledge of French sounds, write down in French exactly what you hear for each sentence.

You will hear each sentence **three** times: the first time as a full sentence, the second time in short sections and the third time again as a full sentence.

Use your knowledge of French sounds and grammar to make sure that what you have written makes sense. Check carefully that your spelling is accurate.

10 marks

Dictation B

You will now hear **four** more sentences.

Write down in French exactly what you hear for each sentence.

10 marks

quatre-vingt-dix-neuf 99

Theme 2 — Test and revise: Foundation Speaking

Role play

You are talking to your French friend.
Your teacher will play the part of your friend and will speak first.
You should address your friend as *tu*.
When you see this – ? – you will have to ask a question.

> In order to score full marks, you must include at least one verb in your response to each task.
>
> 1 Say what your favourite day of the year is. (Give **one** detail.)
>
> 2 Say what you like to do on your birthday. (Give **one** detail.)
>
> ? 3 Ask your friend a question about their favourite festival.
>
> 4 Say when you see your friends. (Give **one** detail.)
>
> 5 Say what you like to eat at the weekend. (Give **one** detail.)

10 marks

Conseil

For the role play, try to include at least one verb in your response to each task (1–5) on the card. Keep your sentences short and accurate and be ready to ask the examiner a question where you see the question mark symbol.

Reading aloud

When your teacher asks you, read aloud the following text **in French**.

> J'aime la musique et je vais à des concerts.
>
> Ma chanteuse préférée est française.
>
> J'écoute ses chansons dans ma chambre.
>
> Les paroles sont toujours belles.
>
> Elle chante dans des films et à la radio.

You will then be asked four questions **in French** that relate to the topic of **Celebrity culture**. Make sure you **answer all four questions as fully as you can**.

15 marks

Conseil

Focus carefully on your pronunciation when undertaking the reading aloud task. Try to remember all the French sounds and sound combinations you have learnt.

Answer the follow-up questions as fully as possible. Extend your sentences by giving justified opinions and using a range of tenses, intensifiers and adverbs.

Theme 2

Photo card

- During your preparation time, look at the two photos. You may make as many notes as you wish on an Additional Answer Sheet and use these notes during the task.
- Your teacher will ask you to talk about the content of these photos. The recommended time is approximately **one minute**. You must **say at least one thing about each photo**.
- After you have spoken about the content of the photos, your teacher will then ask you questions related to **any** of the topics within the theme of **Popular culture**.

25 marks

Conseil

Make sure you say at least one thing about each photo and give as much information as you can, using accurate language.

Try to extend your answers to the follow-up questions as much as possible. Give opinions with reasons, and use a variety of tenses, adjectives, adverbs, pronouns and intensifiers.

Photo 1

Photo 2

cent un **101**

Theme 2 — Test and revise: Foundation Reading

1 Four French teenagers are talking about free-time activities. Which activity (A–F) does each person (1–4) mention? Write the correct letter.

A	Cycling
B	Running
C	Reading
D	Walking
E	Singing
F	Shopping

4 marks

1 Mathis
Moi, j'adore les romans!

2 Rose
Je fais souvent une promenade.

3 Amir
Tous les samedis, je fais les courses.

4 Jade
Faire du vélo, c'est super!

Conseil

In this type of task, the English won't necessarily be a literal translation of the French. For example, if one of the options were 'cooking', you might see a reference to food rather than the actual word *cuisine*.

2 You read this blog by Arnaud about celebrities.

Complete the sentences in **English**.

> J'aime regarder les célébrités à la télévision. Ma célébrité préférée est Baptiste Lecaplain. Il est très amusant. L'été prochain, il va donner un spectacle dans ma ville. J'espère le voir.
>
> Je n'aime pas trop les influenceurs. Je ne comprends pas pourquoi certains influenceurs sont célèbres. Tout le monde peut poster des vidéos sur les réseaux sociaux – ce n'est pas extraordinaire!

a   Arnaud thinks that Baptiste Lecaplain is…   **1 mark**
b   Next summer, Baptiste Lecaplain is…   **1 mark**
c   Arnaud doesn't understand why some influencers…   **1 mark**
d   Everyone can…   **1 mark**

Conseil

In this type of task, look for a word or phrase that links each question with the correct part of the text. Don't write more than you need to – sometimes a single word is enough.

Theme 2

3 You receive this email from a friend in Senegal who is a keen swimmer. What does your friend say about these activities (a–e)?

Write **P** for something she did **in the past**
       N for something she does **now**
       F for something she wants to do **in the future**

Louise
Pour ma famille, Noël est un jour comme les autres. Ma mère est policière et elle doit souvent travailler le 25 décembre. Cependant, mes copines aiment bien faire la fête. Elles aiment aussi donner et recevoir des cadeaux.

Arthur
Je ne peux pas imaginer le 25 décembre sans un repas de fête et sans cadeaux. Mais je sais que Noël est triste pour certaines personnes qui n'ont pas de famille. Cette année, nous allons inviter notre voisine car elle vit seule.

Yasmine
Je suis musulmane, mais j'aime bien le 25 décembre – comme beaucoup de gens dans le monde. Ma tante vient chez nous. Mes parents ne travaillent pas et tout le monde se relaxe. Les cadeaux n'ont pas beaucoup d'importance pour nous.

a	Being in a club	1 mark
b	Competing for the first time	1 mark
c	Using the pool at school	1 mark
d	Swimming in the sea	1 mark
e	Watching swimming on TV	1 mark

Conseil

For some questions you will need to infer the answer, i.e. work it out based on information from the text. In this task, the English statements are not direct translations of the French but the text gives enough information for you to work out the answers.

3 You see an online forum. Three Belgian teenagers are talking about Christmas. Who says each of these statements (a–e)?

Write **L** for **Louise**
       A for **Arthur**
       Y for **Yasmine**.

a	A neighbour is visiting us.	1 mark
b	Christmas is not a special day.	1 mark
c	I celebrate with family.	1 mark
d	My friends like presents.	1 mark
e	Christmas is a sad time for some.	1 mark

4 Translate these sentences into **English**.

a   Le festival d'été commence aujourd'hui.
b   Demain, je vais voir le défilé dans la rue.
c   Le soir, il y aura beaucoup de bruit.
d   Les chanteurs viennent de Belgique et ils sont célèbres.

Conseil

If there is a word or expression that you do not understand, write something that makes sense in the context. You need to take account of every detail in the French, including small words, such as *assez*, that are easy to miss.

Theme 2 — Test and revise: Foundation Writing

1 A friend has sent you some photos.

What is in this photo? Write **five** sentences in **French**.

> **Conseil**
>
> Keep your French simple and make sure the message is clear. Remember to include a verb in each sentence.

10 marks

2 Your Canadian friend is coming to stay with you in the summer holidays. Write a short description of what you normally do at home in the holidays.

Write approximately **50** words in **French**.

You must write something about each bullet point.

Mention:
- when you get up and go to bed
- sport
- music
- people you see
- meals.

10 marks

> **Conseil**
>
> Keep your French simple and relevant to the bullet points, and make sure you cover all five. All the verbs can be in the present tense.

104 cent quatre

Theme 2

3 Using your knowledge of grammar, complete the following sentences in **French**.

Choose the correct French word from the three options in the grid.

Write the correct word, as shown in the example.

Example: *Le concert commence à trois heures.*

commences	commence	commencent

a Nous ___ au football.

jouons	jouez	jouent

1 mark

b Ce livre est ___.

excellent	excellente	excellents

1 mark

c ___ va à la bibliothèque.

Je	Tu	Elle

1 mark

d La musique est ___.

beau	belle	beaux

1 mark

e Hier, je suis ___ au parc.

vais	allé	aller

1 mark

Conseil

In this task, look for clues in the words already in the sentence. For example, if the gap is a verb, is the subject singular or plural? If the gap is an adjective, is the accompanying noun feminine or masculine?

4 Translate the following sentences into **French**.

a The tickets are expensive.
b There are a lot of good concerts.
c My brother doesn't like the music.
d Normally we prefer the songs in French.
e Yesterday I listened to my favourite band.

10 marks

Conseil

The priority in the translation task is to convey the correct meaning. It is crucial to get the verb tense right and to distinguish correctly between the subject pronouns ('I', 'you', etc.).

Either question 5.1 or question 5.2

5.1 You are emailing your French friend about your free-time activities.

Write approximately **90** words in **French**.

You must write something about each bullet point.

Describe:

- what you normally do in the evening
- how you spent last weekend
- your free-time activities in the future.

15 marks

5.2 You are emailing your Canadian friend about celebrities.

Write approximately **90** words in **French**.

You must write something about each bullet point.

Describe:

- the advantages and disadvantages of being famous
- a celebrity you saw on screen or in person recently
- why you would like (or not like) to be famous one day.

15 marks

Conseil

For this task, you must write something about all the bullet points, but there is no need to cover them equally. You should, make accurate references to all three time frames. Try to include opinions and develop your ideas, using different linking words such as *mais*, *quand* and *si*.

cent cinq 105

Theme 3
Communication and the world around us

Travel and tourism

1 📖 Read the statements about travel. Choose the correct opinion, means of transport and reason for each one.

1 Quand je vais en vacances, j'aime voyager en avion car c'est rapide.
2 Pour partir en vacances, je préfère prendre le train parce que ce n'est pas cher.
3 J'adore voyager en bateau quand je vais en vacances mais j'ai le mal de mer.
4 Je déteste voyager à vélo parce que ce n'est pas rapide.
5 Je n'aime pas voyager en voiture car c'est mauvais pour l'environnement.
6 J'aime beaucoup voyager en car parce que c'est pratique.

Opinion	Transport	Reason
a I really like	a 🚗	a It is bad for the environment.
b I hate	b 🚆	b It is quick.
c I do not like	c ✈️	c I get seasick.
d I like	d 🚌	d It is convenient / practical.
e I love	e 🚢	e It is not quick.
f I prefer	f 🚲	f It is not expensive.

rapide	quick / fast	mauvais bad
cher	expensive	le mal de mer seasickness
pratique	convenient / practical	

2 🎧 Listen (1–4) and match each speaker to their perfect holiday (a–d).

a
b
c
d

il fait chaud	it's hot
il fait froid	it's cold
il y a du soleil	it's sunny
il pleut	it's raining

3 📖 Read the forum. Write down in English the activities each person does on holiday. Add whether they love, like, dislike or hate each activity.

Marion
Quand il fait beau, j'aime bien marcher dans la campagne et faire du vélo. J'adore faire de la natation dans la mer et jouer sur la plage avec mon frère.

Thomas
Quand je suis en vacances avec ma famille, j'aime faire du shopping dans les magasins en ville mais je déteste visiter des sites historiques. C'est ennuyeux, surtout quand il fait chaud.

a shopping
b walking
c visiting sites
d cycling
e swimming
f playing on the beach

marcher	to walk
passer du temps	to spend time
la campagne	the countryside
la plage	beach
les magasins	shops

Communication and the world around us — **Theme 3**

Media and technology

1 Match the phrases (1–5) to the pictures (a–e).

1. un journal
2. les réseaux sociaux
3. la radio
4. une émission
5. les devoirs

a

b

c

d

e

2 Listen (1–4) and choose the *two* activities (a–f) mentioned by each person.

a read newspapers   b use social media   c watch TV
d download music   e listen to the radio   f do homework online

regarder	to watch
écouter	to listen to
poster	to post
télécharger	to download

3 Listen again (1–4) and decide whether their opinion of each activity is positive (P) or negative (N).

4 Read the posts and decide who says each statement (a–f).

Abdel
J'ai un ordinateur dans ma chambre. Je recherche des informations sur Internet et je fais mes devoirs mais je ne vais pas souvent sur les réseaux sociaux.

Suzanne
Normalement, je télécharge de la musique sur Internet mais j'aime aussi écouter la radio.

Karim
Je passe tous les soirs deux heures en ligne car j'aime parler avec mes amis sur les réseaux sociaux et partager mes photos sur Internet.

a I download music.
b I have a computer.
c I share photos online.
d I don't use social media often.
e I go online every evening.
f I listen to the radio.

un ordinateur	a computer
la chambre	bedroom
souvent	often
en ligne	online
tous les soirs	every evening
partager	to share

cent sept 107

Theme 3 — Communication and the world around us

The environment

1 📖 Read the sentences and decide if each one has a positive (P) or negative (N) impact on the environment.

a J'utilise tous les jours ma voiture.
b Je vais au collège à pied.
c Je prends le bus.
d Je ne prends jamais de bain, je préfère la douche.
e Je fais du recyclage.
f Je mange de la viande à chaque repas.

utiliser	to use
prendre	to take
un bain	a bath
une douche	a shower
un repas	a meal
le recyclage	recycling
à pied	on foot

2 📖 Read the messages and answer the questions (a–h).

Amis

Ahmed
Je ne prends pas l'avion car c'est mauvais pour l'environnement. Je préfère utiliser les transports publics.

Issa
Le plastique est dangereux pour les animaux. Je fais souvent du recyclage car je ne jette pas le plastique dans la poubelle.

Martin
La pollution est un problème. Il y a trop d'usines et de voitures et le réchauffement du climat est de plus en plus dangereux.

mauvais	bad
les transports publics	public transport
jeter	to throw away
la poubelle	dustbin
une usine	a factory
le réchauffement du climat	global warming

a Which means of transport does Ahmed **not** use?
b Why doesn't he use it?
c What does he use instead?
d What does Issa say plastic is dangerous for?
e What does she do with plastic?
f What does Martin think is a problem?
g What does he say there are too many of? Give **two** details.
h What is becoming more dangerous?

3 🎧 Listen to three people's aims for environmental actions (1–3) and choose the correct picture (a–c).

a  b 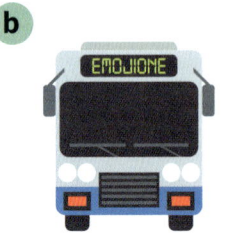 c

4 🎧 Listen again (1–3) and write down the order in which the actions (a–f) are mentioned.

a Do more recycling.
b Eat less meat.
c Don't have a bath.
d Eat more fruit and vegetables.
e Use public transport.
f Don't travel by plane.

108 cent huit

Communication and the world around us — Theme 3

Where people live

1 Match each property advert (1–3) to a potential tenant (a–c).

1 C'est une maison avec un étage, à la campagne. Il y a une cuisine, un salon, une salle de bains et un grand jardin.

2 La maison est au centre-ville et elle a deux étages. Il y a trois chambres et deux salles de bains. Il n'y a pas de jardin.

3 C'est un appartement au bord de la mer. Il y a une grande pièce pour la cuisine, la salle à manger et le salon. Il y a une chambre.

a a couple, looking for a seaside location
b a family, looking for a rural location with lots of outdoor space
c three students who don't want to do any gardening

2 Read the adverts again and answer the questions.
  a Where is property 1 situated?
  b How many floors are there in property 2?
  c What is the main room in property 3?

3 Listen to Isabelle talking about her city, Lausanne in Switzerland. Choose the *five* activities people can do there.

  a walk in the mountains
  b eat out
  c play football
  d go to museums
  e go to the lake
  f visit the castle
  g walk around the town
  h do shopping

un étage	floor, storey
le jardin	garden
la cuisine	kitchen
le salon	living room
la salle à manger	dining room
la salle de bains	bathroom
la chambre	bedroom
à la campagne	in the countryside
au bord de la mer	by the seaside
au centre-ville	in the town centre

la montagne	mountain
le restaurant	restaurant
le musée	museum
le lac	lake
le château	castle
le magasin	shop
les courses	food shopping

4 Listen again and answer the questions.
  a How big is Lausanne?
  b Where is it? Give **two** details.
  c What are there a lot of? Give **two** details.
  d Where can you walk? Mention **two** places.
  e Where can you go shopping? Give **two** details.

cent neuf 109

7.1G Le temps pendant les vacances

OBJECTIVES
- Holidays
- Adjectives ending in *-able*
- Weather expressions

1 📖 **In pairs, read aloud the weather phrases (1–8) and match them to the pictures (a–h).**

1 Il fait beau.
2 Il fait mauvais.
3 Il fait chaud.
4 Il fait froid.
5 Il pleut.
6 Il y a du soleil.
7 Il y a du vent.
8 Il y a du brouillard.

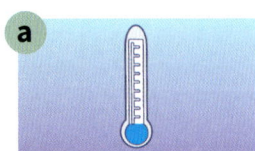

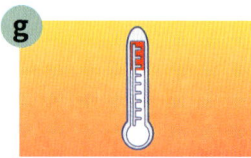

2 ✏️ **Look at the weather map and write sentences to describe the weather in each city.**

Example: À Paris, il fait mauvais.

Attention
Use the preposition *à* to say 'in' or 'to' a city.

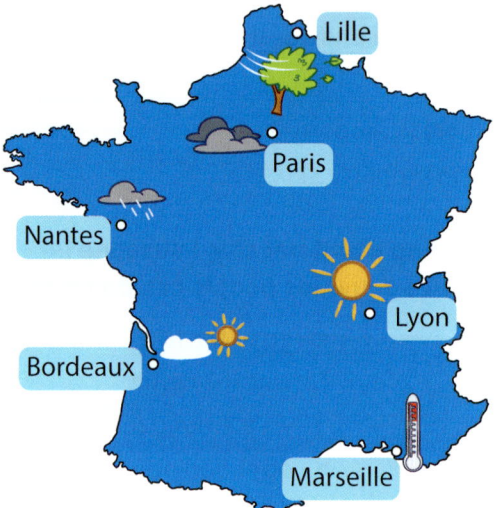

3 📖 **Match the verbs and the activities to form phrases.**

1 faire   a des gâteaux au marché
2 visiter   b des sites historiques
3 acheter   c du shopping
4 aller   d du temps dans la nature
5 regarder   e un spectacle
6 passer   f au restaurant

Les verbes

Weather expressions

To talk about the weather in French, use phrases with *il fait* + adjective, *il y a* + noun or *il* + verb.

Il fait beau / mauvais / chaud / froid.
The weather / It is nice / bad / hot / cold.

Il y a du soleil / du vent / du brouillard.
It is sunny / windy / foggy.

Il pleut. It is raining.

4 🔁 **Translate the phrases from activity 3 into English.**

5 🎧 **Listen and answer the questions.**

a Where does Léa do her shopping? Give **two** details.
b When do Léa and her sister like to go to eat out?
c What do Youssef and his family do when the weather is fine?
d Why does his dad like to cycle when it is sunny?
e What do Amirah and her family do on holiday the weather is bad?
f What do they do when the weather is good?

Travel and tourism, including places of interest 7.1G

6 🎧 Listen (1–4) and write down the sentences you hear.

7 📖 Read the blog post and find the French for the English phrases (a–h).

a for the holidays
b in our country
c we go away as a family
d we go camping
e it's pleasant
f the weather is changeable
g we spend time together
h it's preferable

8 📖 Read the text again. Choose the correct option to complete each sentence.

a For their holidays, Amélie and her family usually **stay local / go to a different country / stay at home**.
b The weather is usually **rainy / bad / good**.
c They camp **near the sea / in a national park / on a farm**.
d They like camping because it is **exciting / pleasant / cheap**.
e They visit historic sites if it **rains / is cold / is sunny**.

9 ⭐ Look at these adjectives ending in *-able* and work out their infinitive and meaning in English.

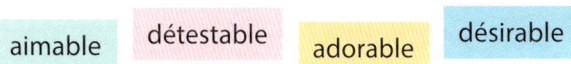

aimable   détestable   adorable   désirable

10 💬 In pairs, take turns to ask and answer the question, changing the weather phrase and holiday activity each time.

Example:
• *Qu'est-ce que tu fais quand il fait beau?*
• *Quand il fait beau, je visite des sites historiques.*

11 ✏️ Write a blog post (50 words) about a real or fictional holiday. Mention:
• where you usually go on holiday
• who you go with and for how long
• why you like this type of holiday
• what the weather is like
• what activities you do.

amelie_n

Amélie

Pour les vacances, on préfère rester dans notre pays, au Québec. Nous partons en famille, pendant une semaine. Comme il fait normalement beau et chaud, on fait du camping dans un parc national. On aime ça car c'est agréable et très pratique.

Parfois, le temps est variable. S'il pleut, on visite des sites historiques. Par contre, quand il y a du soleil, on passe du temps ensemble dans la nature – c'est préférable, c'est sain, et en plus, ça ne coûte pas cher.

Grammaire

Adjectives ending in *-able*

Some French adjectives are created by adding *-able* or *-eable* to the verb stem, where the English equivalent ends in '-able' or '-ible':

préférer	→	*préfér**able***	preferable
accepter	→	*accept**able***	acceptable
manger	→	*mang**eable***	edible

Pour les vacances,	on va je vais je reste	en	France / Espagne.
		à	la mer / la campagne / la montagne.
		chez	moi / mes grands-parents / des amis.
Je vais	avec ma famille / mes cousins.		
J'aime ces vacances	parce que	c'est agréable / relaxant / dans la nature. je joue avec mon frère / au football. je fais de la natation dans la mer. je suis avec ma famille.	
		j'aime	visiter / faire…
Il fait	souvent / parfois	beau / mauvais.	
Quand il pleut	on fait / va…		

cent onze 111

7.1F Les îles francophones

OBJECTIVES
- Places where we used to live
- Revising adjective agreement
- The imperfect tense of *être*, *avoir* and *faire*
- Phonics: è, ê, ai and a

1 Read the forum about where people used to live and match the posts (1–4) to the pictures (a–d).

| ACCUEIL | NOUVEAU | RÉPONSES | FAVORIS |

1 Quand j'étais jeune, j'habitais entre mer et montagne, sur une île située dans l'océan Indien. Il faisait souvent beau mais parfois, il y avait du vent. L'île avait une histoire intéressante. J'aimais découvrir la culture, les traditions et les religions de l'île. Par contre, la vie était chère.
Posté par **Aurélien**

3 Quand j'étais plus jeune, j'habitais sur une île, dans l'océan Indien. Il y avait beaucoup de longues plages et il faisait assez chaud toute l'année, surtout sur la côte. La vie était calme et je trouvais les gens très gentils. J'ai appris la cuisine traditionnelle et la langue de l'île. La capitale était une ville historique.
Posté par **Marinette**

2 Quand j'avais huit ans, je vivais sur une île calme située dans l'océan Atlantique. Il faisait vraiment froid, surtout en hiver, et il y avait beaucoup de neige. C'était vraiment comme l'Europe mais dans le nord de l'Amérique! On utilisait l'euro, on parlait français mais on était très près de la frontière canadienne.
Posté par **Laëtitia**

4 Quand j'avais dix ans, je vivais sur une île des Caraïbes. Il y avait deux pays sur l'île. Dans mon pays, on parlait français et dans l'autre pays, on parlait espagnol! La cuisine locale était très fraîche et on mangeait beaucoup de fruits. La vie culturelle était riche et la mer était toujours chaude.
Posté par **Adrien**

a Haïti    **b** La Réunion    **c** St Pierre et Miquelon    **d** Madagascar

2 Read the texts again. Copy and complete the sentences.

a On La Réunion, the weather was often ___ but sometimes, it was ___.
b Aurélien liked discovering the culture, ___ and religions of the island.
c In St Pierre and Miquelon, it was really ___ in winter.
d The island was very close to ___.
e In Madagascar, the beaches were ___ and life was ___.
f The ___ city was historic.
g In Haïti, the local cooking was ___ and people ate lots of ___.

Phonétique

è, ê, ai, and a

è, ê and ai all sound the same:

tr**è**s	pr**è**s	fronti**è**re	ch**è**re
f**ê**te	t**ê**te	arr**ê**ter	vous **ê**tes
vr**ai**	j'**ai**	j'**ai**mais	vr**ai**ment

Compare *ai* with *a*:

| l**a** c**a**pit**a**le | il y **a**v**ai**t |
| c**a**n**a**dienne | j'h**a**bit**ai**s |

Culture

Due to a diverse, and sometimes difficult, history, there are many francophone islands across the world. Some are overseas French territories, governed by the French government, with French as their official language. Others maintain a more distant link with France but still use French as one of their languages.

Travel and tourism, including places of interest 7.1F

3 **Copy and complete the sentences, using the correct form of *être*, *avoir* or *faire* in the imperfect tense.**

a Au nord de l'île, il y ___ une grande forêt.
b Il ___ beau tous les jours.
c L'histoire de l'île ___ intéressante.
d Quand mon frère ___ 12 ans, il habitait en Guadeloupe.
e Il ___ souvent froid, surtout en hiver.
f La cuisine locale ___ fraîche.

4 **Translate the sentences (activity 3) into English.**

5 **Listen to the podcast about Sylvain's experience of living in New Caledonia (*Nouvelle-Calédonie*), in the South Pacific. Write down the order in which the topics (a–f) are mentioned.**

a the weather
b the activities he did there
c where the island is located
d what the landscape was like
e what the people were like
f how long he lived there

7 **In the text in activity 1, find *one* example of a noun with an adjective in these forms:**

- masculine singular
- feminine singular
- masculine plural
- feminine plural.

8 **In pairs, take turns to ask and answer the questions. Use the profile cards for ideas.**

- Tu habitais où avant?
- Tu avais quel âge?
- Comment était le temps?
- La vie était comment?
- Qu'est-ce que tu faisais le week-end?

9 **Write a paragraph (90 words) using one of the profile cards.**

Example: Quand j'avais huit ans, j'habitais avec mon frère, ma mère et mon beau-père dans un village à la montagne…

Les verbes

The imperfect tense of *être*, *avoir* and *faire*

Use the imperfect tense to talk or write about what you used to do or were doing in the past. *Avoir*, *être* and *faire* are often used in the imperfect to set the scene of an action or to express feelings and opinions.

J'**avais** faim. I was hungry.
Tu **étais** jeune. You were young.
Il **faisait** du vélo. He went / used to go cycling.
Il **faisait** beau. The weather was fine.
Il y **avait** du vent. It was windy.

6 **Listen again and choose the correct option to complete each sentence.**

a Sylvain is **22** / **32** / **25**.
b He lived in New Caledonia for **5** / **10** / **15** years.
c The weather was **too hot** / **too cold** / **just right**.
d Sylvain used to go **swimming** / **horse riding** / **climbing**.
e He found that the culture was **ancient** / **varied** / **interesting**.
f He hopes to return to New Caledonia **next year** / **one day** / **next summer**.

Grammaire

Revising adjective agreement

Adjectives (describing words) must agree in gender and number with the noun they describe. For most adjectives, add an *-e* for feminine and an *-s* for plural:

un pays français   une île français**e**   des villes français**es**

Some adjectives are irregular and you need to learn their endings:

nouveau – nouvelle   gentil – gentille   blanc – blanche

Where: small town near Paris
At age: 12
Weather: quite cold in winter; sunny and nice in summer
Life: found the people nice
Activities: walks and swimming

Where: village in the mountains
At age: 8
Weather: foggy and windy in winter; very hot in summer
Life: very quiet
Activities: cycling and cooking

7.2G Mes visites de touriste

OBJECTIVES
- Tourist visits
- Prepositions for countries and modes of transport
- Revising the perfect tense

1 Read the tourist reviews and find the French for the English phrases (a–g).

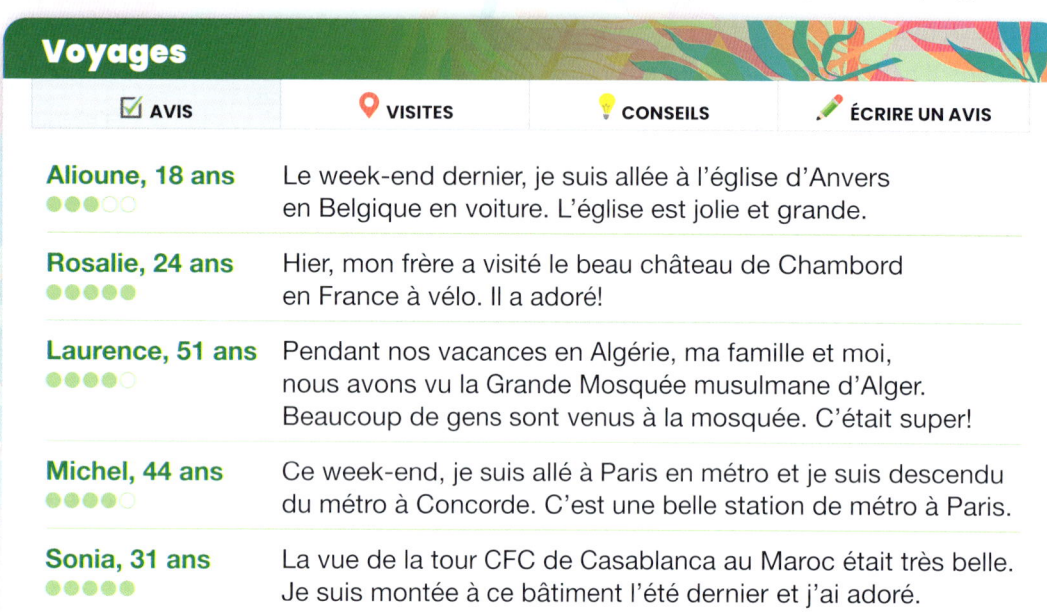

Voyages

☑ AVIS   📍 VISITES   💡 CONSEILS   ✏️ ÉCRIRE UN AVIS

Alioune, 18 ans — Le week-end dernier, je suis allée à l'église d'Anvers en Belgique en voiture. L'église est jolie et grande.

Rosalie, 24 ans — Hier, mon frère a visité le beau château de Chambord en France à vélo. Il a adoré!

Laurence, 51 ans — Pendant nos vacances en Algérie, ma famille et moi, nous avons vu la Grande Mosquée musulmane d'Alger. Beaucoup de gens sont venus à la mosquée. C'était super!

Michel, 44 ans — Ce week-end, je suis allé à Paris en métro et je suis descendu du métro à Concorde. C'est une belle station de métro à Paris.

Sonia, 31 ans — La vue de la tour CFC de Casablanca au Maroc était très belle. Je suis montée à ce bâtiment l'été dernier et j'ai adoré.

a I went
b my brother visited
c we saw
d lots of people came
e I got off the metro
f I went up
g I loved (it)

2 Read the reviews again and answer the questions in English.

a What did Alioune think of the church in Anvers? Give **two** details.
b What did Rosalie's brother visit?
c What type of building did Laurence visit?
d How did Michel travel?
e What was the high point of Sonia's visit?

Culture

Did you know?
- The *Grande Mosquée* in Algiers is the tallest in Africa and the third tallest in the world.
- The tiled letters that cover the walls and ceiling at the Concorde metro station spell out the wording of the *Déclaration des Droits de l'Homme et du Citoyen* of 1789.

Les verbes

Revising the perfect tense

The perfect tense is used to describe actions in the past. Most verbs use a part of **avoir** plus a past participle:

*j'**ai** mangé   tu **as** fini   il **a** entendu*

Some verbs have an irregular past participle (e.g. *avoir – eu, être – été, faire – fait*) and some verbs take *être* instead of *avoir*. With these verbs, the past participle agrees with the subject:

Elle est allée à l'église.   *Nous sommes descendus du train.*

When *on* is used to mean 'we' or 'people', the past participle has a plural agreement:

On est allé(e)s au restaurant.

3 Copy and complete the sentences with the correct form of *avoir* or *être*.

a L'année dernière, nous ___ allés en vacances.
b Ma famille et moi ___ visité un château historique.
c Je ___ descendue du bus et j'___ vu une église.
d Ma sœur ___ montée à la tour de la mosquée.
e Pour le déjeuner, j'___ mangé du pain.
f On ___ bu de l'eau.

Travel and tourism, including places of interest — 7.2G

4 🎧 Listen (1–3) and choose the *two* correct photos for each person.

5 🎧 Listen again and answer the questions.
- a When did Sophie go to Belgium?
- b How did she travel?
- c What sort of accommodation did Arnaud stay in?
- d What did he eat at the restaurant?
- e What did Louise visit?
- f Why did she eat ice cream?

6 Find in the reviews in activity 1:
- a **two** phrases containing modes of transport
- b **two** phrases containing *en* + a country.

7 💬 In pairs, take turns to ask and answer the questions. You can talk about a real trip you went on, or a fictional one.
- Où es-tu allé(e) en vacances récemment?
- Comment as-tu voyagé? Pourquoi?
- Où as-tu dormi?
- Qu'est-ce que tu as fait pendant ta visite?

Grammaire

Prepositions for countries and modes of transport

Use *en* to say 'to' or 'in', for a feminine country, and use *au / à l' / aux* for a masculine country:

*Je suis allé **en** Belgique. On est allés **au** Canada.*
*Nous sommes allés **aux** États-Unis.*

En and *à* are also used to say how you travelled:
*J'ai voyagé **en** train / **en** voiture / **en** bus.*
*Mon frère est allé au collège **à** vélo / **à** pied.*

8 Translate the sentences into French.
- a Last year, I went to Belgium.
- b My sister drank a cold drink.
- c My parents visited historic sites.
- d I got off the bus and I saw a castle.
- e During the holidays, we ate in a restaurant.

L'année dernière, Le mois dernier, L'été dernier, Pendant les vacances,	je suis allé(e) nous sommes allés on est allé(e)s	en	Angleterre / France. Suisse / Belgique.	
		au	Maroc / Canada.	
	j'ai visité on a visité nous avons visité	un petit village / une grande ville. Paris / la capitale.		
J'ai voyagé Nous avons voyagé	en train/bus en voiture à vélo	car	c'est	rapide. pratique.
			ce n'est pas	cher.
Je suis resté(e) On est resté(e)(s)	une semaine.			
J'ai dormi Nous avons dormi	dans un hôtel dans un camping	en ville / dans un village. au bord de la mer. à la montagne.		
Pendant la visite, Pendant les vacances,	j'ai on a nous avons	mangé	dans un restaurant.	
		bu	un café	
		visité vu	un château. des sites historiques.	
	je suis on est nous sommes	allé(e)(s) monté(e)(s)	à l'église. à la tour.	
		descendu(e)(s)	du train / du bus.	

7.2F Vacances de rêve

OBJECTIVES
- Holiday stories
- *pour* and *sans* + infinitive
- Two tenses together: perfect and imperfect
- Phonics: open *o*

1 Read the email and answer the questions in English.

eponine@monmail.fr

Chère Séverine,

L'été dernier, ma famille et moi, nous avons quitté notre maison pour aller en vacances dans le sud de la France. Nous avons pris notre voiture.

Nous sommes partis le samedi matin. Quand nous sommes arrivés dans le sud, il faisait très chaud.

Nous avons dormi dans un hôtel dans une petite ville près de Nice. L'hôtel n'était pas loin d'une synagogue. Dans le jardin, il y avait une piscine et c'était parfait pour faire de la natation et pour se relaxer.

Le lundi, comme il ne faisait pas très beau, mon père a réservé une visite de Nice en bus. C'était génial de visiter la ville sans marcher! J'ai appris l'histoire de la ville et j'ai acheté un livre pour mes parents. Plus tard, nous avons fait les courses dans des magasins sans passer trop de temps en ville.

Et toi, tu es allée en vacances récemment?

À bientôt!

Éponine

a When did Éponine go on holiday?
b When did they leave home?
c What was the weather like when they arrived?
d Where did they stay during the holiday?
e Give **two** details about the hotel.
f Why did her dad book a tour of the city?
g What did they do later?

2 Find the French for the English phrases in the email.

a we left our house to go on holiday
b the weather was very hot
c there was a swimming pool
d my dad booked a visit
e I bought a book
f we went shopping
g did you go on holiday?

Les verbes

Two tenses together: perfect and imperfect

The perfect and imperfect tenses are often used alongside each other. The **imperfect tense** is used to describe continuous actions or events in the past, settings and emotions, while the perfect tense is used for completed actions.

Il faisait beau alors <u>je suis allée</u> en ville.
It was nice so <u>I went</u> into town.

J'avais faim donc <u>j'ai mangé</u> des frites.
I was hungry so <u>I ate</u> some chips.

3 Translate the sentences into French.

a Last summer, I went on holiday.
b We left on Sunday morning.
c It was sunny every day.
d The hotel was in the countryside.
e There were lots of restaurants.

Attention

Think carefully about whether you need to use the perfect or imperfect tense.

Travel and tourism, including places of interest — 7.2F

4 ⭐ Find *five* examples of *pour* or *sans* + infinitive in activity 1 and translate them into English.

5 🎧 Listen to Josse talking about his disastrous holiday. Write down the order in which the statements (a–f) are mentioned.

a The meal was cold.
b The waiter was not nice.
c They slept on a boat.
d Josse got lost while on a walk.
e The weather was awful when they arrived.
f Josse went on holiday last year.

6 💬 In pairs, complete the role play. Take turns to ask and answer the questions.

Phonétique

open o

d**o**rmi   l**o**gement   P**o**rtugal

7 ✏️ Write an email (90 words) to your Belgian friend about your worst holiday. This can be real or fictional. Describe:

- when, where you went and with whom
- what you did and where you stayed
- something that went wrong.

Grammaire

Using *pour* and *sans* + infinitive

Use *pour* or *sans* + <u>infinitive</u> to say 'in order to' do something or 'without' doing something:

Pour <u>aller</u> *en France, j'ai pris le bus.* **In order to** <u>go</u> to France, I took the bus.

*Je suis parti **sans** <u>payer</u>.* I left **without** <u>paying</u>.

You are talking to your Canadian friend about a recent holiday.

1 *Alors, tes vacances l'année dernière?*
   Say where you went on holiday last year. (Give **one** detail.)
2 *Et le temps?*
   Say what the weather was like there. (Give **one** detail.)
3 *Et ton logement?*
   Say where you stayed. (Give **one** detail.)
4 *Et tes activités?*
   Say what you did. (Give **one** detail.)
5 Ask your friend a question about their holiday.
   Say something about your holiday.

L'année dernière, L'été dernier,	je suis allé(e) je suis parti(e)	en vacances		en France en Suisse au Portugal	avec ma famille. avec mes amis.
On est parti(e)s Je suis parti(e)	le samedi matin le dimanche après-midi		en voiture. en avion. en train.		
On a dormi J'ai dormi	dans un hôtel dans un appartement		près de la mer. à la campagne.		
Il y avait	un restaurant / une grande piscine.				
Il faisait	beau mauvais	alors donc	nous avons j'ai	fait de la natation. visité des monuments historiques.	
Malheureusement,	au restaurant, le serveur n'était pas sympa. au restaurant, le repas était froid. il faisait mauvais tous les jours.				

cent dix-sept 117

8.1G Les médias

OBJECTIVES
- All kinds of media
- Revising infinitive verbs
- Revising regular verbs in the present tense

1 📖 Match the phrases (1–5) to the photos (a–e).

1. écouter la radio
2. regarder la télé
3. utiliser Internet
4. lire des journaux
5. poster des photos sur les réseaux sociaux

2 📖 Read the online forum and decide who says each statement (a–f).

a. I buy magazines.
b. I use social media.
c. I watch films on TV.
d. I download films and music.
e. I love listening to the radio on my phone.
f. I post videos and chat with my friends.

3 🔀 Translate Rafaël and Aurélie's texts into English.

4 🎯 Note down all the regular present tense verbs in activity 2 and work out their infinitives.

5 🔀 Translate the verbs from activity 4 into English.

Rafaël — J'aime aller au cinéma. Je choisis toujours des films d'action. Parfois, je regarde aussi des films à la télé ou en streaming sur mon ordinateur.
Posté: 11:03

Soraya — J'écoute tous les jours la radio sur mon portable. J'adore connaître les événements dans le monde.
Posté: 12:23

Aurélie — J'utilise Internet plusieurs fois par jour: je recherche des informations en ligne, je lis des articles et je fais mes devoirs. Parfois, je télécharge des films et de la musique aussi. Ce n'est pas cher et c'est facile.
Posté: 14:56

Guillaume — J'achète des magazines une fois par semaine mais ma sœur aime lire des journaux en ligne, tous les jours. Je lis la vie des célébrités et je vois les influences et les blogs à la mode.
Posté: 15:29

Joseph — Je poste des vidéos sur les réseaux sociaux. J'adore utiliser Facebook pour communiquer et partager mon avis, poster des messages et chatter avec mes amis. De plus, je vends des vêtements en ligne.
Posté: 18:02

Les verbes

Revising regular verbs in the present tense

Remember to check who or what is the subject of your verb (*tu*, *il*, *elle*, etc.), to help you decide which ending to use.

-er verbs	-ir verbs	-re verbs
je jou**e**	je fin**is**	je vend**s**
tu jou**es**	tu fin**is**	tu vend**s**
il/elle/on jou**e**	il/elle/on fin**it**	il/elle/on vend
nous jou**ons**	nous fin**issons**	nous vend**ons**
vous jou**ez**	vous fin**issez**	vous vend**ez**
ils/elles jou**ent**	ils/elles fin**issent**	ils/elles vend**ent**

cent dix-huit

Media and technology 8.1G

6 🎯 **Choose the correct form of the verb to complete each sentence.**

a Pour mes devoirs, je **rechercher** / **recherche** / **recherche** des informations sur Internet.
b Ma sœur adore **vendre** / **vend** / **vendent** des vêtements en ligne.
c Mon frère **utilisent** / **utilise** / **utiliser** beaucoup son portable.
d Je déteste **poster** / **poste** / **postes** des vidéos sur les réseaux sociaux.
e Je **choisis** / **choisir** / **choisissons** toujours des photos de ma famille.

7 ⭐ **Translate the sentences into French.**

a I watch films on my phone.
b My brother loves to know about events in the world.
c I look for information for my homework.
d I download music on my computer.
e I use social media to communicate my opinion.

Grammaire

Revising infinitive verbs

Infinitives end in *-er*, *-ir* or *-re* and are translated as 'to …' or '…ing'.

utilis**er** (to use)   fin**ir** (to finish)   vend**re** (to sell)

We use an infinitive after *aimer*, *adorer* and *détester* to express likes and dislikes:

*J'adore **lire** des magazines.*
I love **to read** / **reading** magazines.

*Je n'aime pas **écouter** la radio.*
I do not like **to listen** / **listening** to the radio.

8 🎧 **Listen. Copy and complete the sentences.**

a Cécile prefers to read ___.
b Gaël likes to listen to ___.
c He listens to it ___ on his ___.
d On social media, Gaël posts ___ and sends ___.
e Cécile sends ___.
f She also downloads ___ and ___.

9 💬 **In pairs, take turns to read aloud Joseph's text (activity 2).**

10 💬 **In pairs, ask and answer the questions.**

- Comment est-ce que tu regardes des films?
- Quand est-ce que tu écoutes la radio?
- Quelle est ton opinion des réseaux sociaux?
- Tu aimes lire des journaux? Pourquoi (pas)?

11 ✏️ **Write a text message (50 words) to your friend, describing which media you use and how. Mention:**

- how you watch films
- if and how you use the internet at home
- if and how you use the internet at school
- if and how you use social media
- if you read newspapers / magazines and why (not).

Je regarde J'aime regarder	des films des séries		à la télé. sur mon portable.	
J'aime utiliser J'adore utiliser J'utilise	des outils de streaming en ligne mon ordinateur / mon portable les réseaux sociaux		pour	écouter la radio tchatter avec mes amis. télécharger de la musique.
Je vais sur Je surfe sur	Internet les réseaux sociaux		pour	chercher des informations. poster des photos. parler avec mes amis. faire mes devoirs.
Je ne lis pas	de magazines de journaux	parce que car	c'est ennuyeux. c'est cher.	
Je lis	des magazines des journaux		c'est informatif. j'adore lire la vie des célébrités.	

cent dix-neuf

8.1F Le monde avant et après Internet

OBJECTIVES
- Evolution and uses of the internet
- Present and past tenses together
- Opinion / modal verbs + infinitive
- Phonics: *au*, *eau*, closed *o* and *ô*

1 📖 Read the article and find the French for the English phrases (a–h).

Dans les années 1990, Internet est arrivé sur le marché mais tout d'abord, il n'était pas facile d'aller sur Internet. Aujourd'hui, 64,4% de la population mondiale peut aller sur Internet tous les jours.

Avant, on utilisait les smartphones pour travailler seulement, mais maintenant, beaucoup de gens utilisent leur smartphone dans la vie quotidienne.

Dans les années 2000, la technologie a fait des progrès rapides: on a développé les réseaux sociaux et aujourd'hui, on peut toujours trouver une nouvelle appli ou un nouveau site en ligne.

Internet a changé notre façon de communiquer mais aussi notre société. Cependant, avec Internet, de nouveaux dangers sont présents et nous devons faire attention.

a on the market
b at first
c it wasn't easy
d in order to work
e in daily life
f in the 2000s
g made rapid progress
h we must pay attention

2 📖 Read the article again. Choose the correct option to complete each sentence.

a The internet arrived on the market **in the 1980s** / **quickly** / **in the 1990s**.
b To start with, the internet was **easy** / **difficult** / **slow** to use.
c Smartphones were originally used **for work** / **in everyday life** / **rarely**.
d In the 2000s, **websites** / **online shops** / **social media** were developed.
e People communicate **differently** / **sometimes** / **slowly** with the internet.
f New **technologies** / **dangers** / **computers** have appeared.

3 🎯 Read the article again. Make three lists of all the verbs in the perfect, imperfect and present tense.

4 🎯 Choose the correct verb to complete each sentence.

a Aujourd'hui, les gens **utilisent** / **ont utilisé** tous les jours Internet.
b Avant, on **ne va pas** / **n'allait pas** sur Internet aussi souvent.
c Dans les années 2000, les réseaux sociaux **deviennent** / **sont devenus** plus populaires.
d Maintenant, **il y a** / **il y avait** de nouveaux dangers.
e **J'ai découvert** / **Je découvrais** Internet quand **j'avais** / **j'ai** dix ans.

Les verbes

Present and past tenses together

Use present and past tenses together to say how things have changed, or to compare what you do now with what you used to do.

Adding a time phrase makes the time frame clear.

Le week-end dernier, je **suis allé** sur Internet mais *aujourd'hui*, je **passe** moins de temps en ligne.

Avant, on **utilisait** des smartphones seulement pour le travail mais *maintenant*, beaucoup de gens **ont** un smartphone.

Attention

Use time phrases such as *aujourd'hui* (today), *maintenant* (now), and *avant* (before) to help you work out which tense to use.

120 cent vingt

Media and technology 8.1F

5 🎧 **Listen to Audrey, Sofiane and Kévin. Note the order in which the statements (a–e) are mentioned.**

a I'm reading today.
b I never used the internet when I was younger.
c I want to spend less time online.
d I have a laptop.
e I didn't have a computer before.

6 🎧 **Listen again and answer the questions.**

a How often does Audrey use the internet?
b What does she like to do on her laptop? Give **two** details.
c What did Sofiane do on his phone yesterday?
d Why does he like to go online?
e Why does Kévin use the internet every day?
f What does he prefer to do online?

7 **Read the text and find:**

a **two** phrases containing a modal verb + infinitive
b **three** phrases containing a verb of liking / disliking + infinitive.

> Aujourd'hui, on peut aller sur Internet tous les jours. Moi, je n'aime pas utiliser Internet trop souvent mais je dois faire mes devoirs en ligne. De plus, ma famille et moi adorons regarder des films en ligne car ce n'est pas cher. Par contre, je déteste jouer à des jeux vidéo. Je trouve ça très ennuyeux.

Les verbes

Opinion verbs, modal verbs + infinitive

When you use a **conjugated verb** + another verb, the second verb needs to be in the infinitive. You will often find this infinitive construction after an opinion verb or a modal verb. Be careful, as it does not always translate as an infinitive in English.

Je **peux** regarder la télé en ligne. I **can** watch TV online.
On **aime** télécharger de la musique. We **like** downloading music. / We **like** to download music.

8 🔀 **Translate the text (activity 7) into English.**

9 💬 **In pairs, look at the photo and take turns to ask and answer the questions.**
- Parle-moi de la photo.
- Comment tu utilises les ordinateurs à l'école?
- Qu'est-ce que tu as fait en ligne hier?

10 ✏️ **Write a blog entry (90 words) about how you use the internet. Describe:**
- what you usually do online
- what you did online yesterday.
- what you dislike about the internet and why.

Normalement, je / j'	regarde / fais / télécharge écris / lis discute envoie consulte télécharge / écoute joue fais recherche	des vidéos / photos / films. mes e-mails / mon blog. avec mes amis. des photos. des sites web. de la musique / des podcasts. à des jeux vidéo. mes devoirs. des informations.	
Hier, j'ai	regardé / fait / lu / joué / téléchargé / écouté…		
Je déteste Je n'aime pas	les reseaux sociaux les applis de…	parce que c'est	ennuyeux. dangereux. cher.

Phonétique

au, eau, closed o and ô

au, eau, closed o and ô all sound the same:

aujourd'hui   **au**ssi
b**eau**coup   nouv**eau**
vidé**o**   tr**o**p
h**ô**tel   dr**ô**le

8.2G Ton portable, ta vie

OBJECTIVES
- Phones and apps
- *avant de* + infinitive
- Revising *être*, *avoir*, *faire* and *aller* in the present tense

1 📖 Choose an option from each box to create translations of the English phrases (a–e).

a to discover world festivals	faire	des langues
b to learn languages	découvrir	des promenades
c to go on walks	apprendre	en vacances
d to go on holiday	avoir	les festivals du monde
e to have a healthy way of life	partir	un mode de vie sain

2 📖 Read the reviews of some apps (1–5) and match them to the photos (a–e).

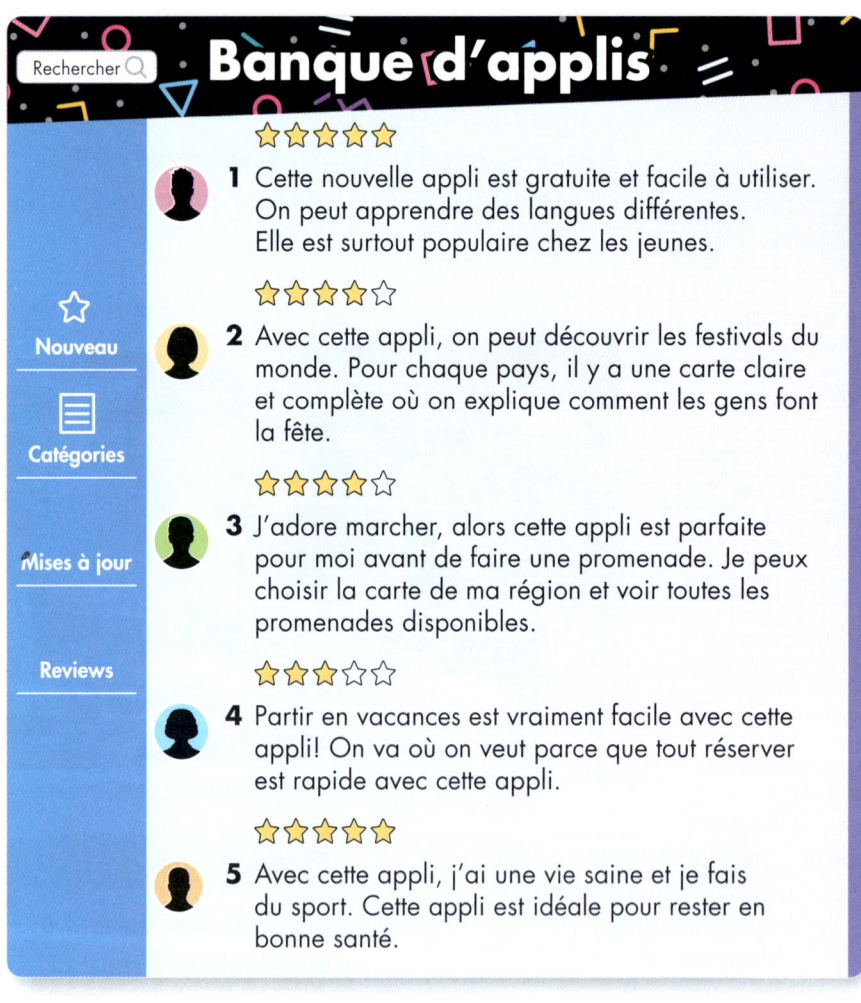

Banque d'applis

⭐⭐⭐⭐⭐
1 Cette nouvelle appli est gratuite et facile à utiliser. On peut apprendre des langues différentes. Elle est surtout populaire chez les jeunes.

⭐⭐⭐⭐☆
2 Avec cette appli, on peut découvrir les festivals du monde. Pour chaque pays, il y a une carte claire et complète où on explique comment les gens font la fête.

⭐⭐⭐⭐☆
3 J'adore marcher, alors cette appli est parfaite pour moi avant de faire une promenade. Je peux choisir la carte de ma région et voir toutes les promenades disponibles.

⭐⭐⭐☆☆
4 Partir en vacances est vraiment facile avec cette appli! On va où on veut parce que tout réserver est rapide avec cette appli.

⭐⭐⭐⭐⭐
5 Avec cette appli, j'ai une vie saine et je fais du sport. Cette appli est idéale pour rester en bonne santé.

3 📖 Read the reviews again and answer the questions.
a With which age group is app 1 popular?
b What helps users of app 2 find out where the festivals take place?
c When can app 3 be used?
d What does app 4 make easy?
e What does app 5 help you do?

122 cent vingt-deux

Media and technology 8.2G

4 **Choose the correct form of the verb to complete each sentence.**

a Le soir, je **vais** / **va** / **allons** souvent sur mon portable.
b Tu **as** / **avez** / **ai** beaucoup de photos sur ton portable.
c Nous **faisons** / **faire** / **font** nos devoirs sur notre ordinateur.
d Mon frère **a** / **avez** / **ont** un nouveau portable.
e On **allons** / **va** / **vont** tous les jours sur Internet.
f Mes sœurs **est** / **être** / **sont** souvent en ligne.

5 **Listen (1–6) and choose the correct option to complete each sentence.**

1 Before school, Sofiane plays on his phone for **20** / **30** / **40** minutes.
2 After school, he watches **films** / **videos** / **memes** on social media.
3 He often has **long** / **interesting** / **fun** conversations with his friends.
4 He downloads **music** / **TV programmes** / **films** on his devices.
5 He is now an expert on **Canadian** / **French** / **Belgian** films.
6 He stops using his phone before **having a bath** / **going to sleep** / **reading**.

6 **Listen (1–4) and write down the sentences you hear.**

7 **Translate the sentences into English.**

a J'ai un nouveau portable.
b Je fais mes devoirs.
c Je tchatte avec des copains.
d Avant d'aller au collège, je vais en ligne.
e J'aime jouer à des jeux video. C'est génial!

8 **In pairs, take turns to ask and answer the questions. Use the verbs in the box to help you.**

- Qu'est-ce que tu penses des portables?
- Qu'est-ce que tu aimes faire sur un portable?

j'ai	j'aime	je regarde	je télécharge
je suis	je joue	j'écoute	c'est
je fais	j'utilise	je trouve	

Les verbes

Revising être, avoir, faire and aller in the present tense

être (to be)	avoir (to have)
je suis	j'ai
tu es	tu as
il / elle / on est	il / elle / on a
nous sommes	nous avons
vous êtes	vous avez
ils / elles sont	ils / elles ont
faire (to do, to make)	**aller (to go)**
je fais	je vais
tu fais	tu vas
il / elle / on fait	il / elle / on va
nous faisons	nous allons
vous faites	vous allez
ils / elles font	ils / elles vont

Grammaire

avant de + infinitive

Avant de (before doing something) is always followed by an infinitive.

***Avant de** manger, je regarde des vidéos.* Before eating, I watch videos.

*Mon frère n'utilise pas son portable **avant de** dormir.* My brother doesn't use his mobile before going to sleep.

9 **Write *five* sentences to describe the photo.**

8.2F J'utilise la technologie!

OBJECTIVES
- Technology use in the past, present and future
- Adjectives beginning with *in-* or *im-*
- Three time frames
- Phonics: *en/an/em/am, on/om, ain/in/aim/im* and *un*

1  Read the email and write down the order in which the statements (a–g) are mentioned in the text.

tombeaupré18@monmail.fr

Quand j'avais dix ans, je n'avais pas de portable. Par contre, avant, on avait un ordinateur à la maison mais il était dans le salon et toute la famille l'utilisait. Sur l'ordinateur, j'écoutais parfois de la musique mais c'était presque impossible car Internet n'était pas rapide et l'ordinateur était inaccessible.

Pour mon dernier anniversaire, mes parents m'ont acheté un portable et je l'adore! **En ce moment, je télécharge beaucoup d'applis** et elles m'aident pour mes devoirs. De plus, j'envoie des messages à mes amis et j'adore prendre des photos.

Cependant, **maintenant, mes parents disent que je passe trop de temps en ligne.** C'est injuste, mais **le week-end prochain, je vais réduire mon temps en ligne. À l'avenir, je vais aussi passer plus** de temps dehors!

Thomas

a My parents bought me a mobile phone.
b My whole family used the computer.
c I use my phone for homework.
d I will spend more time outside.
e My parents think I spend too long online.
f I download apps.
g I use my phone to take photos.

2 Read the email again and answer the questions.
  a At what age did Thomas **not** have a mobile phone?
  b How did he go online instead?
  c Why was it difficult to listen to music on the computer? Give **two** details.
  d When did Thomas' parents buy him a phone?
  e Who does he send messages to?
  f What is he going to do next weekend?

3 Sort the verbs into three categories: past, present and future.
  a j'ai téléchargé
  b je n'avais pas
  c je vais utiliser
  d je découvre
  e je joue
  f j'ai recherché
  g j'étais
  h je vais réduire

Les verbes

Three time frames

It is important that you can identify which time frame or tense is being used (through verbs and time phrases) and that you can use them in your own work. Using an appropriate time phrase will help you use the correct **verb tense**.

Maintenant, **j'ai** un ordinateur dans ma chambre mais *avant*, **il était** dans le salon.

Now, **I have** a computer in my bedroom but *before*, **it was** in the living room.

Hier, **j'ai envoyé** un SMS à ma sœur mais *demain*, **je vais l'appeler**.

Yesterday, **I sent** a message to my sister but *tomorrow*, **I'm going to ring her**.

Media and technology 8.2F

4 Identify the time phrase and the tense used in the phrases in bold in the email in activity 1.

5 Copy and complete the sentences, putting the verb into the correct tense. Use the time phrases to help you decide which tense to use.

a Hier, ma sœur ___ une nouvelle chanson. (*télécharger*)
b À l'avenir, je ___ mon temps en ligne. (*réduire*)
c Maintenant, mon frère ___ son portable tous les jours. (*utiliser*)
d Mes copains et moi, on ___ tous les soirs à des jeux en ligne. (*jouer*)
e Quand j'avais dix ans, je ne ___ pas de films sur Internet. (*regarder*)

6 Listen to Lisa, Amadou and Marc talking about their use of technologies. Decide whether each one is talking about the past, present or future.

7 Listen again and answer the questions.

a What does Lisa think is a problem online?
b What does she say is important?
c How does Amadou describe his mobile phone? Give **two** adjectives.
d What has he used the new app for?
e Who does Marc say lives in Switzerland?
f Name **two** activities they will do together.

8 Copy and complete the table.

French	Noun or adjective?	+ *in-* or *im-*	English
complet			
		indifférent	
	noun		inactivity
		indépendance	

9 In pairs, take turns to ask and answer the questions.
- Comment tu as utilisé les technologies hier?
- Normalement, comment est-ce que tu utilises les technologies?
- Comment vas-tu utiliser les nouvelles technologies demain?

10 Translate the sentences into French.

a Last year, I bought a new phone.
b Now, I use my mobile every day.
c Tomorrow, I'm going to play online with my friend.
d When I was ten, I did not use the internet.
e Yesterday, my mum watched a film on TV.

Attention

The verb tense and time phrases such as *l'année dernière*, *maintenant* or *la semaine prochaine* will help you work out the time frame of a sentence.

Remember that the perfect tense is used for completed actions and the imperfect tense for ongoing actions in the past.

Phonétique

en / an / em / am, on / om, ain / in / aim / im and *un*

These groups of letter combinations all sound similar:

en / an / em / am:
pr**en**dre   av**an**t   t**em**ps   ch**am**bre

on / om:
sal**on**   c**on**tre   c**om**me   t**om**ber

ain / in / aim / im:
proch**ain**   **in**juste   f**aim**   **im**possible

un:
l**un**di   empr**un**ter

Practise reading aloud this question:
Mais cependant, comment tu passes ton temps en ce moment, maintenant?

Grammaire

Adjectives beginning with *in-* or *im-*

Some French adjectives can have *in-* or *im-* added, to give the opposite meaning or make them negative. It applies to some nouns and adverbs too. The English equivalent is *in-* or *un-*.

juste (fair) → *injuste* (unfair)

accessible (accessible) → *inaccessible* (inaccessible)

possible (possible) → *impossible* (impossible)

cent vingt-cinq 125

9.1G Tu es écolo?

OBJECTIVES
- Eco-friendly habits
- Using *a* and *à*
- Verbs + *à* / *de* + infinitive
- Phonics: *a* and *à*

1 Match the verbs (1–6) to the phrases (a–f).

1 protéger
2 éviter de
3 manger
4 faire
5 diminuer
6 utiliser

a la voiture moins souvent
b la nature
c la pollution
d du recyclage
e moins de viande
f prendre un bain

2 Match your completed phrases (1–6) to the photos (a–f).

a  b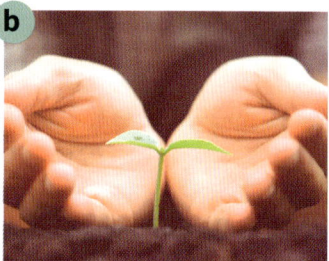

c  d  e  f

3 Read the forum posts and find the French for the English phrases (a–f).

 Agathe
J'essaye de protéger la planète car j'évite de prendre un bain et je recycle. Je ne jette pas de plastique dans la poubelle normale.

 Iman
J'ai arrêté de manger de la viande quand j'avais 10 ans et maintenant, je suis végétarien.

 Élias
J'évite d'utiliser la voiture parce que ça augmente la pollution. J'arrive à aller au collège à pied ou à vélo mais en hiver, il fait souvent trop froid.

Manon
Ma sœur protège la nature car elle arrive à utiliser les transports verts comme le bus et elle ne prend jamais l'avion.

 Guillaume
Nous devons manger local quand c'est possible. Dans ma famille, on a décidé d'acheter des produits locaux et de saison mais ils peuvent être chers.

a I try
b I avoid
c I don't throw away
d I stopped
e I manage
f we have decided

4 Read the texts again. Copy and complete the sentences.

a Agathe avoids ___ ___ and she ___.
b When he was 10, Iman stopped ___ ___ and now he is ___.
c Élias goes to school ___ ___ or ___ ___.
d Manon's sister ___ nature by never travelling by ___.
e Guillaume and his family have decided to buy ___ ___ whenever possible.

126   cent vingt-six

The environment and where people live — 9.1G

5 Find *five* examples of a verb + *à* / *de* + infinitive in activity 3 and translate them into English.

6 Translate Agathe, Élias and Manon's texts from activity 3 into English.

7 Listen to the radio headlines (1–4) and match them to the environmental issue they talk about (a–d).

a transport   b global warming   c pollution   d litter

8 Listen (1–4) and write down the sentences you hear.

9 Copy and complete the sentences with *a* or *à* (or both).
   a J'arrive ___ voyager ___ vélo.
   b Ma sœur ___ décidé de devenir végétarienne.
   c Il ___ pris l'avion hier.
   d Elle essaye de voyager ___ pied.
   e On recycle le plastique ___ la maison.
   f Je vois les conséquences de la pollution ___ la télé.

10 In pairs, take turns to make up a sentence to describe what you do to tackle each environmental problem.

la pollution   le plastique   le réchauffement

11 Write *five* sentences about the photo.

Les verbes

Verbs + *à* **/** *de* **+ infinitive**

Some verbs are followed by *à* or *de* before another verb in the infinitive. You need to learn which to use with each verb.

à: arriver à, commencer à, continuer à, s'intéresser à, réussir à

de: décider de, essayer de, accepter de, arrêter de, éviter de

J'arrive à <u>manger</u> moins de viande.
I manage <u>to eat</u> less meat.
J'ai décidé de <u>recycler</u>. **I have decided** <u>to recycle</u>.
Nous essayons de <u>manger</u> moins de viande.
We are trying <u>to eat</u> less meat.

Grammaire

Using *a* **and** *à*

a **without an accent** is the *il* / *elle* / *on* form of the present tense of *avoir*. It usually goes after a noun or pronoun.

à **with a grave accent** is a preposition which can mean 'to', 'at', 'by' or 'on'. It usually goes after a verb.

Il **a** une voiture. He **has** a car.
Il **a** voyagé en voiture. He **has** travelled by car.
Je voyage **à** pied. I travel **by** foot.
Mon copain arrive **à** recycler.
My friend manages **to** recycle.

Phonétique

Phonics: *a* **and** *à*

a and *à* sound exactly the same.
Il **a** un vélo.
Il voyage **à** vélo.
Il **a** voyagé **à** vélo.

cent vingt-sept 127

9.1F Sauvons la planète!

OBJECTIVES
- A positive impact on the planet
- Infinitives used as nouns
- *je voudrais*

1 Listen and read the texts. Choose the correct verbs to fill the gaps.

devenir   utiliser   fabriquer   voudrais   réduit
utilise   aider   coupe   fabrique   créer

Solène

On **1** ___ les arbres et ça **2** ___ l'oxygène. Ça peut **3** ___ un problème alors je **4** ___ planter des arbres et **5** ___ de nouvelles forêts pour les futures générations.

Timothée

Dans ma famille, on **6** ___ nos propres produits ménagers alors on **7** ___ moins de plastique. C'est meilleur pour la santé et pour l'environnement. Je voudrais aussi **8** ___ mon propre savon pour me laver.

Amandine

Sur la Terre, il y a des ressources naturelles, comme l'énergie du vent ou du soleil. Je voudrais **9** ___ ces ressources pour **10** ___ notre planète.

les produits ménagers	household products
le savon	soap

2 Read the texts again and answer the questions.

a What does Solène say can be a problem?
b What does she want to do? Give **two** details.
c What results does Timothée say making their own household products has? Give **three** details.
d What else would he like to make?
e What does Amandine say planet Earth has?
f What would she like to do?

3 Translate Solène and Timothée's texts into English.

4 Listen (1–4) and write down the sentences you hear.

Attention

In dictation tasks, use your knowledge of grammar to check that what you have written is correct French. Look at adjective agreements and verb endings, for example.

Les verbes

je voudrais

je voudrais (I would like) is often followed by an infinitive:

Je voudrais <u>utiliser</u> moins de plastique.
I would like <u>to use</u> less plastic.

It can also be followed by a <u>noun</u>:
Je voudrais <u>des arbres</u> dans la nature.
I would like <u>trees</u> in nature.

The environment and where people live — 9.1F

5 Read the blog post about veganism. Choose the correct heading (a–e) for each paragraph (1–5).

- a Fashion or lifestyle?
- b Life without animal-based products
- c A significant day for veganism
- d More than just food!
- e Environmental worries

Le véganisme: un nouveau mode de vie?

1 Protéger l'environnement est un souci pour tous et beaucoup de gens essayent de faire une différence.

2 Pour certains, par exemple, manger et boire des produits qui ne viennent pas des animaux est un mode de vie. Selon les experts, le véganisme encourage le respect parce qu'il n'utilise pas les animaux dans la nourriture, les vêtements et les expériences scientifiques.

3 Tu voudrais savoir si le véganisme est seulement une mode? Mais non, pour les végans, ce n'est pas une mode mais un moyen de vivre qui aide à protéger l'environnement et qui est meilleur pour la santé. Moi, je voudrais essayer de vivre de cette façon.

4 De plus en plus populaire dans un climat inquiétant, le véganisme donne des idées sur la nourriture mais aussi sur beaucoup d'autres choses. Par exemple, il est normal de fabriquer des produits ménagers sans produit animal.

5 Le 1er novembre 1994, la journée du véganisme a eu lieu pour la première fois. Chaque année, ce jour-là, on célèbre les droits des animaux. Même si c'est un choix moins populaire que le végétarisme en ce moment, deux pour cent des Français sont végans.

6 Read the text again. Find the French for the English phrases (a–i).

- a protecting the environment
- b a worry for all
- c to make a difference
- d eating and drinking
- e a way of life
- f better for your health
- g I would like to try
- h making products
- i without animal products

7 Translate the sentences into French.

- a I would like to plant trees.
- b Eating less meat is better for our health.
- c I would like to make my own products.
- d Drinking vegan products is a way of life.

8 In pairs, take turns to read aloud the problems (a–d) and say what you would do to solve each problem, using *je voudrais*…

- a couper trop d'arbres
- b utiliser toutes les ressources
- c manger trop de produits animaux
- d utiliser des produits ménagers qui ne sont pas naturels

Les verbes

Using infinitives as nouns

An infinitive can be used as a noun. It translates as a noun ending in '-ing' in English.

Couper les arbres diminue l'oxygène.
Cutting down trees decreases the oxygen.

Protéger l'environnement, c'est important.
Protecting the environment is important.

9 Write an article (90 words) for your school's newsletter. Describe:

- which environmental problems you find worrying
- what you would like to do to help
- whether you would like to become a vegan one day.

9.2G Une visite chez mon ami

OBJECTIVES
- Recent activities at home
- Revising the perfect tense with *avoir* and *être*
- *de* after a negative or expression of quantity

1 📖 Match the sentences (1–8) to a room in the house (a–h).

1. J'ai mangé dans la salle à manger.
2. Je suis allé aux toilettes.
3. J'ai joué avec un copain dans le jardin.
4. J'ai regardé la télé dans le salon.
5. On a fait un gâteau dans la cuisine.
6. J'ai discuté avec ma mère dans la chambre de ma sœur.
7. J'ai pris un bain… dans la salle de bains!
8. J'ai dormi dans ma chambre.

2 📖 Read Noémie's description of her stay at a friend's house. Write down the order in which she mentions the activities (a–h).

a. eating lunch
b. sleeping
c. not eating popcorn
d. playing football
e. having a bath
f. watching TV
g. having a barbecue
h. making a cake

> mardi, le 12 septembre
>
> Je suis arrivée chez Benjamin le vendredi soir et je suis restée jusqu'au dimanche.
> Le vendredi soir, on a joué au foot dans le jardin et le père de Benjamin a fait un barbecue. C'était super! Ils ont un beau jardin et il y a beaucoup de jolies fleurs mais il n'y a pas d'arbres. Sa maison est grande et il y a plein d'espace pour tout le monde. J'ai dormi dans la chambre de Florence, la sœur de Benjamin.
> Le samedi matin, nous avons regardé un film dans le salon. (Je n'ai pas mangé de pop-corn!) Le salon est trop petit mais je l'aime bien.
> À midi, on a mangé dans la grande cuisine et après ça, on a préparé un gâteau ensemble. On a mis trop de chocolat, mais il était bon!
> Le samedi soir, j'ai pris un bain.
> Je suis partie le dimanche matin et je suis rentrée chez moi en train.

3 📖 Find the French for the English phrases (a–f).

a. I stayed until
b. there are lots of pretty flowers
c. in the living room
d. in Florence's room
e. we made a cake together
f. we put in too much chocolate!

130   cent trente

The environment and where people live — 9.2G

4 Find the perfect tense verbs in Noémie's diary (activity 2). Write *two* lists: verbs that take *avoir* and verbs that take *être*.

5 Listen (1–4) and decide which activity (a–d) each person has done recently.

1 Lucie   2 Samuel   3 Maëlys   4 Amir

a watched TV
b read a book
c cooked a meal
d played in the garden

6 Listen again and choose the correct option to complete each statement.

a Lucie's bedroom is quite **big** / **boring** / **small**.
b Yesterday, Lucie didn't **read** / **watch TV** / **sleep**.
c Samuel's **grandma** / **aunt** / **uncle** came to visit, with his cousins.
d Samuel's kitchen is **old** / **big** / **modern**.
e There are a lot of **flowers** / **trees** / **footballs** in Maëlys's garden.
f Amir does not really like his living room because it is too **small** / **big** / **quiet**.

7 Translate the sentences into French.

a There is no dining room.
b I prepared lots of cakes.
c There is too much space in my house.
d We do not have any flowers in the garden.
e I took a bath in my bathroom.

8 In pairs, take turns to ask and answer the questions.
- Comment est ta maison?
- Quelle est ta pièce préférée? Pourquoi?
- Qu'est-ce que tu as fait chez toi récemment?

9 Write a description (90 words) of your home. Describe:
- what your home is like
- something you did at home recently
- an activity you will do at home soon.

Les verbes

Revising the perfect tense with *avoir* and *être*

For the perfect tense, use part of *avoir* or *être* + the past participle of the verb.

-er verbs: j'ai jou**é**, je suis all**é(e)**
-ir verbs: tu as fin**i**, tu es part**i(e)**
-re verbs: il a attend**u**, il est descend**u**

Some past participles are irregular. For example:

faire: **fait**   prendre: **pris**
mettre: **mis**   venir: **venu**

Remember, for verbs that take *être*, the past participle adds -*e*, -*s* or -*es* to agree with the subject.

Grammaire

de after a negative or an expression of quantity

Where a positive statement uses *un* / *une* / *des* + noun, its matching negative statement needs *de* instead:

*Elle a **un** jardin.*
She has **a** garden.

*Il n'a pas **de** jardin.*
He does **not** have **a** garden.

With expressions of quantity that use *de*, the word *de* stays unchanged, whatever the gender and number of the noun that follows.

*Nous avons beaucoup **de** fleurs dans le jardin.*
We have a lot of flowers in the garden.

Ma maison Mon appartement	est	(assez) grand(e) / petit(e) en ville / à la montagne / à la campagne.
Il y a	un grand une petite deux / des	salon / jardin salle de bains / salle à manger / cuisine. chambres / toilettes.
J'aime / J'adore		ma chambre parce que…
Hier / La semaine dernière,	j'ai	lu un livre / regardé la télé.
Demain,	je vais	faire mes devoirs / regarder un film.

cent trente et un 131

9.2F Un guide de ma ville

OBJECTIVES
- Describing your town
- *si* and *quand*
- Modal verbs in the present tense
- Phonics: *h*

1 📖 Read the review of Sarlat and choose a heading (a–d) for each paragraph (1–4).

Sarlat (Dordogne)

Accueil | **Lieux** | Hôtels | Transport | Restaurants | Météo

1 J'habite à Sarlat, en Dordogne, dans le sud-ouest de la France. Je sais qu'aujourd'hui il y a environ 10 000 habitants à Sarlat. La Dordogne est une région qui reçoit beaucoup de touristes.

2 C'est une très jolie ville médiévale, avec beaucoup de vieilles maisons et de bâtiments historiques. Dans le centre-ville, il n'y a pas beaucoup de voitures et on peut faire du shopping au marché et dans les petits magasins indépendants.

3 J'adore ma ville parce qu'il y a beaucoup à faire, pour les jeunes et pour les familles. Cependant, en juillet et août, il y a vraiment trop de gens et à mon avis, on doit réduire le nombre de visiteurs.

4 Les touristes peuvent visiter les églises, les petites rues, les places et les jardins. Ils peuvent aussi manger dans les restaurants locaux car la cuisine de la région est délicieuse. Quand il fait beau, ils peuvent faire de la natation dans la rivière. Et quand il pleut, ils peuvent aller au cinéma.

a Sarlat, a historic town
b Location
c What's offered for tourists
d My opinion

2 📖 Read the review again. Copy and complete the sentences.

a Sarlat is situated in the ___ of France.
b The Dordogne attracts many ___.
c It is a very ___ town, with lots of ___ houses.
d There are not many ___ in the town centre.
e There are too many ___ in Sarlat in the summer.
f Tourists can visit the ___ and they can also try the ___.

Culture

La Dordogne in the south-west of France is one of the most popular tourist regions in France. It is famous for its rivers, castles and picturesque villages. The region also boasts rich cuisine and a warm climate.

Les verbes

Modal verbs in the present tense

Devoir, pouvoir, savoir and *vouloir* are irregular modal verbs. They are often followed by an infinitive.

On **peut** faire du shopping dans le centre-ville.
We **can** go shopping in the city centre.

Je **sais** qu'il y a 5 000 habitants dans ma ville.
I **know** there are 5,000 inhabitants in my city.

devoir (to have to / must)	
je dois	nous devons
tu dois	vous devez
il / elle / on doit	ils / elles doivent

pouvoir (to be able to / can)	
je peux	nous pouvons
tu peux	vous pouvez
il / elle / on peut	ils / elles peuvent

vouloir (to want)	
je veux	nous voulons
tu veux	vous voulez
il / elle / on veut	ils / elles veulent

savoir (to know)	
je sais	nous savons
tu sais	vous savez
il / elle / on sait	ils / elles savent

The environment and where people live — 9.2F

3 **Choose the correct option to complete each sentence.**
a Je **dois** / **doit** / **devoir** aller en ville à pied.
b Mon frère **peux** / **peut** / **pouvons** visiter le château.
c On **voulez** / **veux** / **veut** essayer les restaurants locaux.
d Si on **sait** / **savons** / **savoir** faire du vélo, il y a un parc pas loin.
e Je **veut** / **veux** / **voulez** faire du shopping dans les magasins.

4 **Translate the sentences (activity 3) into English.**

5 **Listen (1–5) and decide whether Aurélie's opinions are positive (P), negative (N) or positive and negative (P+N).**

6 **Listen (1–6) and answer the questions.**
1 What does Aurélie say about the weather in the mountains?
2 How does Aurélie describe the houses?
3 What does Aurélie say are expensive? Give **two** details.
4 Why is the shopping not good for young people? Give **two** details.
5 What is the problem when it's cold?
6 Which **two** cultural places do Aurélie's parents go to?

7 **Listen (1–4) and write down the sentences you hear.**

8 **Translate the sentences into French.**
a There are lots of restaurants.
b We can visit the church.
c I know that my town is historic.
d When it is cold, I can go to the shopping centre.
e If you (*tu*) want to see a film, you can go to the cinema.

Grammaire

si and *quand*
Si on aime l'histoire, on peut visiter le château.
If you like history, you can visit the castle.

Quand il fait froid, il n'y a rien à faire.
When it is cold, there is nothing to do.

9 **In pairs, take turns to read aloud paragraph 2 of the review (activity 1).**

10 **In pairs, ask and answer the questions.**
- Comment s'appelle ta ville? C'est où?
- Qu'est-ce qu'il y a pour les jeunes?
- Qu'est-ce qu'il y a pour les touristes?
- Tu aimes ta ville? Pourquoi (pas)?

Phonétique
h
hôtel   à l'**h**ôtel
historique j'**h**abite

11 **Write an article (90 words) for a tourist website where you live.**
Describe:
- what your town / city / village is like
- what there is to see and do there
- something you have done there recently.

Example: Ma ville s'appelle… C'est dans le nord de… Il y a beaucoup de… Il n'y a pas de… On peut visiter… et aller… Le week-end dernier, j'ai…

cent trente-trois 133

Theme 3 — Culture: Cannes, la ville des médias

1 **Read the fact file about the Cannes festival and copy and complete the sentences in English.**

a The Cannes Festival takes place in ___ every ___ .
b It is an ___ film festival.
c Cannes is on the Mediterranean ___ in the ___ of France.
d It was ___ in 1946.
e The ___ film wins a Palme d'or.

Nom:	Le Festival de Cannes
Date:	au mois de mai tous les ans
Où:	Cannes, sur la côte de la mer Méditerranée dans le sud-est de la France
Quoi:	un festival international du film
Création:	1946
Prix pour le meilleur film:	La Palme d'Or

2 **Read the summary of this francophone film which won a *Palme d'Or* at the Cannes Festival and answer the questions.**

a What genre of film is *Les Parapluies de Cherbourg*?
b Who made it and when?
c Who is the main actress?
d Who is Guy in the film?
e Why does he leave Geneviève?
f Give **two** opinions about the film from the final paragraph.

Les Parapluies de Cherbourg est une comédie romantique et musicale réalisée par Jacques Demy en 1964. L'actrice principale s'appelle Catherine Deneuve. Après ce film, elle est devenue très populaire en France. Le film raconte l'histoire de Geneviève, qui tombe amoureuse de Guy, un beau mécanicien. Malheureusement, Guy doit partir faire son service militaire en Algérie et alors Geneviève doit se marier avec un autre homme, Roland.

Le film a gagné la Palme d'Or en 1964. La mise en scène est très bien faite, les couleurs sont vives, les chansons sont très belles et les acteurs chantent très bien.

devenir	to become
tomber amoureux	to fall in love
le service militaire	military service
la mise en scène	set design

Theme 3

3 Read the summary again and find the French for the English words and phrases.

  a made / created
  b she became
  c the film tells the story
  d unfortunately
  e the film won

Culture
The Cannes festival is probably the most famous film festival in France. Do you know of any film festivals in the UK? Discuss the similarities and differences with a partner.

4 Research another award-winning film at the Cannes Festival or at another festival that you know of. In pairs, take turns to give the following details about the film:
   - title and genre of the film
   - filmmaker and year of making
   - main actor(s)
   - the plot
   - opinions.

5 Listen and write down the correct words to complete the text.

> Le Festival … des Jeux se déroule en … à Cannes. C'est un … qui célèbre les … pour les petits et les … Le festival a … dans une immense arène de jeux. Il y a des jeux … et des jeux … Le festival accueille 80 000 …

Culture
Le Festival International des Jeux is another festival that takes place in Cannes but this one celebrates games in all their forms.

6 Decide whether each statement refers to the film (*film*) or the games (*jeux*) festival.

  a Ce festival a lieu tous les ans en mai.
  b Ce festival est pour les adultes et les enfants.
  c Ce festival accueille 80 000 visiteurs.
  d La Palme d'Or est le prix pour le gagnant.
  e Ce festival a lieu dans une arène de jeux.
  f Le premier festival a eu lieu en 1946.

7 Research the *Festival international du film d'animation* and create a factfile like the one in activity 1.

Nom:
Date:
Quoi:
Création:

Theme 3 — Grammar practice

Weather expressions

1 Copy and complete the sentences with the correct phrase: *il fait*, *il y a* or *il*.

a ___ chaud dans ce pays.
b ___ tout le temps du vent ici.
c ___ froid dans le nord de la France.
d Quand ___ pleut, on reste chez nous.
e Je vais à la plage s'___ du soleil.
f J'aime aller en ville quand ___ beau.

The imperfect tense

2 Copy and complete the sentences with the imperfect tense of the verb given in brackets. Then translate the sentences into English.

a L'année dernière, il ___ beau quand on est allés en vacances. (*faire*)
b Il y ___ beaucoup de magasins en ville. (*avoir*)
c Au café, j'ai bu de l'eau. Elle ___ froide! (*être*)
d Nous avons voyagé en avion mais c'___ cher. (*être*)
e Il y ___ beaucoup de touristes quand nous avons visité la capitale. (*avoir*)
f Mon frère ___ du vélo dans le jardin quand il ___ cinq ans. (*faire*, *avoir*)

Adjective agreements

3 Choose the correct adjective to complete each sentence.

a C'est une **grand** / **grande** / **grandes** île située dans l'océan Atlantique.
b Il y a de **nouvelles** / **nouveaux** / **nouvelle** rues (*f*) dans mon village.
c Dans ma région, on peut faire de **longues** / **longs** / **longue** promenades (*f*).
d Le temps est **idéale** / **idéals** / **idéal** pour faire de la natation.
e Les sites (*m*) **culturels** / **culturelles** / **culturel** de ma ville sont **intéressantes** / **intéressante** / **intéressants**.

Grammaire

Adjectives need to agree in gender and number with the noun they describe.

The perfect tense

4 Choose the correct form of the auxiliary verb (*avoir* or *être*) to complete each sentence.

a L'année dernière, **je suis** / **j'ai** allé en vacances au Québec.
b Nous **sommes** / **avons** pris l'avion.
c Hier soir, mon frère **a** / **est** téléchargé de la musique.
d Mes parents **ont** / **sont** partis au cinéma.
e On **a** / **est** regardé la télé dans le salon.
f **Je suis** / **J'ai** restée dans ma chambre.

Les verbes

Most verbs take *avoir* in the perfect tense, but a few (mainly verbs of movement) take *être*.

The past participle of verbs that take *être* needs to agree in number and gender with the subject of the verb.

Communication and the world around us — Theme 3

The perfect and imperfect tenses

5 Copy and complete the sentences, putting the verbs in the perfect or imperfect tense.

a Nous ___ tôt en voiture. (*partir*)
b Il y ___ une piscine dans le jardin. (*avoir*)
c La viande ___ froide. (*être*)
d Les films ___ ennuyeux. (*être*)
e Mes parents ___ des musées. (*visiter*)
f Mon frère ___ des films en ligne. (*regarder*)

Les verbes

The **perfect tense** is used to present completed actions in the past, while the **imperfect tense** is used to describe continuous actions or events, and settings and emotions, all in the past.

pour and sans + infinitive

6 Copy and complete the sentences with *pour* (for / to) or *sans* (without).

a Je ne peux pas vivre ___ avoir un portable.
b ___ aller en vacances, nous préférons prendre le train.
c ___ visiter les sites historiques, on n'apprend pas la culture d'une région.
d On utilise les réseaux sociaux ___ communiquer avec notre famille.
e ___ faire mes devoirs, je vais sur Internet.
f Je ne peux pas dormir ___ regarder la télé avant.

Attention

Think about the meaning of each sentence to work out whether *sans* or *pour* makes most sense.

The present tense

7 Choose the correct form of the present tense to complete each sentence.

a J'**écoute** / **écoutes** / **écoutons** de la musique.
b On **visites** / **visitez** / **visite** des sites historiques.
c Ma sœur **apprends** / **apprenez** / **apprend** l'espagnol.
d Nous **choisis** / **choisissons** / **choisit** un camping proche de la mer.
e Mes parents n'**utilisent** / **utilise** / **utilisez** jamais les réseaux sociaux.
f Tu **regardons** / **regardes** / **regardent** souvent des films?

The present, perfect and imperfect tenses

8 Choose the correct tense of the verb to complete each sentence.

a Dans les années 1990, Internet n'**est** / **était** pas très rapide.
b Tout le monde **a** / **avait** un portable maintenant.
c L'année dernière, on **est allés** / **va** en France.
d Maintenant, mon frère **a habité** / **habite** en Algérie.
e Quand j'étais au Maroc, il **fait** / **faisait** trop chaud.
f Dans le passé, on **utilisait** / **utilise** plus de plastique mais aujourd'hui, on **a préféré** / **préfère** les sacs qui ne sont pas en plastique.

Attention

Use the adverbs of time and the meaning of the sentence to help you decide which tense to use.

cent trente-sept 137

Theme 3 — Grammar practice

Verbs + infinitive

9 Rewrite the sentences in the correct order. Then translate them into English.

a regarder   J'adore   en ligne   des films   .

b aimes   en vacances   Tu   aller   ?

c écouter   préfère   de la musique   Elle   .

d n'aime pas   à mes amis   Je   en ligne   parler   .

e peux   Je   suivre   sur l'appli   mes progrès   .

f en ville   peuvent   les musées   visiter   Mes parents   .

Les verbes

After a conjugated opinion verb or modal verb, the second verb needs to be an infinitive.

The present tense of *avoir*, *être*, *faire* and *aller*

10 Copy and complete the sentences with the present tense of the verb given in brackets.

a Je ___ du recyclage tous les jours. (*faire*)
b Nous ___ souvent au cinéma. (*aller*)
c On ___ un nouvel ordinateur dans le salon. (*avoir*)
d Tu ___ végétarien ou tu manges de la viande? (*être*)
e Ma sœur ___ un mode de vie sain. (*avoir*)
f Vous ___ vos devoirs à l'école? (*faire*)

avant de + infinitive

11 Copy and complete the sentences with *avant de* + an infinitive.

a J'écoute de la musique ___ . (*before sleeping*)
b ___ , je regarde la télé. (*before going to school*)
c ___ , elle a appris la langue. (*before visiting the country*)
d On a fait des recherches ___ . (*before buying a mobile*)

Grammaire

Avant de (before doing something) is always followed by another verb in the infinitive.

Remember that *de* changes to *d'* if the infinitive that follows starts with a vowel.

Verbs + *à* / *de* + infinitive

12 Copy and complete the sentences with the correct preposition: *à* or *de* / *d'*. Then translate the sentences into English.

a J'essaye ___ utiliser Internet seulement le soir.
b Mon frère a arrêté ___ prendre le train car c'est trop cher.
c Nous avons décidé ___ faire nos propres produits.
d On arrive ___ manger moins de viande.
e Ma sœur a commencé ___ apprendre une langue étrangère.
f Pour aider la planète, j'évite ___ prendre un bain.

Les verbes

Some verbs are always followed by *à* or *de* and the infinitive. These include:

arriver à, commencer à, continuer à, réussir à

décider de, essayer de, arrêter de, éviter de

Remember that *de* will become *d'* before a verb that starts with a vowel.

Communication and the world around us — Theme 3

a and à

13 Copy and complete the sentences with *a* or *à*.

a La nouvelle appli est facile ___ utiliser.
b Mon frère ___ un nouveau portable.
c Sur Internet, il y ___ des dangers.
d ___ l'école, on utilise moins de plastique.
e Mon meilleur ami ___ une maison en ville.
f J'aime regarder des films ___ la télé.

Grammaire

a is the *il/elle/on* form of *avoir* in the present tense. It often follows a noun or pronoun.

à is a preposition meaning 'to', 'at', 'by' or 'on'. It usually comes after a verb.

Modal verbs

14 Copy and complete the sentences with the present tense of the verb given in brackets.

a Je ___ réduire mon temps sur Internet. (*devoir*)
b Mon frère ___ utiliser moins de plastique. (*pouvoir*)
c Nous ___ comment protéger la planète. (*savoir*)
d Les touristes ___ essayer le nouveau restaurant. (*vouloir*)
e Cette année, on ___ aller en vacances. (*vouloir*)
f Je ___ prendre l'avion moins souvent. (*pouvoir*)

si and quand

15 Copy the sentences, adding *si* or *quand* to make them match the English translations.

a ___ il fait chaud, on va à la plage.
   (*If it is hot, we go to the beach.*)
b Je fabrique mes propres produits ___ j'ai le temps.
   (*I make my own products when I have time.*)
c ___ il pleut, ma sœur prend le bus.
   (*If it rains, my sister takes the bus.*)
d ___ ils vont à Sarlat, les touristes visitent le château.
   (*When they go to Sarlat, tourists visit the castle.*)

Grammaire

Remember that *si* becomes *s'* before a word that starts with a vowel.

cent trente-neuf

Theme 3 — Vocabulary

Words that are highlighted in grey in this list are words that may be useful, but you won't need to know them for the exam.

Introductory vocabulary

- à pied on foot
- adorer to love
- aider to help
- aimer to like
- aller to go
- l' ami(e) (m./f.) friend
- l'/les animal/animaux (m. pl.) animal(s)
- l' appartement (m.) flat
- s' appeler to be called
- assez quite, enough
- au bord de la mer by the sea
- au restaurant at, in a restaurant
- aussi also
- avec with
- l' avion (m.) plane
- avoir le mal de mer to be sea sick
- le bain bath
- le bateau boat
- beaucoup (de) a lot (of), lots of
- le bus bus
- la caisse checkout
- la campagne countryside
- car because
- le centre-ville city centre
- la chambre bedroom
- chaque each, every
- chez at someone's place/house
- le collège (secondary) school
- la cuisine kitchen, cooking
- dangereux/dangereuse dangerous
- dans in
- de plus en plus more and more
- dehors outside
- détester to hate
- les devoirs (m. pl.) homework
- dormir to sleep
- écouter to listen (to)
- l' émission (f.) TV programme
- en in, by, to
- en ligne online
- en Suisse in/to Switzerland
- en vacances on holiday
- ennuyeux/ennuyeuse boring
- et and
- l' étage (m.) floor
- être to be
- faire to do, make
- faire de la natation to go swimming
- faire du camping to go camping
- faire du shopping to go shopping
- faire du vélo to go cycling
- faire les courses to go (grocery) shopping
- la famille family
- le frère brother
- le fruit fruit
- grand(e) big, large
- habiter to live
- l' heure (f.) hour, time, o'clock
- historique historical
- l' hôtel (m.) hotel
- ici here
- il fait beau it is fine weather
- il fait chaud it is hot
- il fait froid it is cold
- il y a there is/are
- il y a du soleil it is sunny
- l' information (f.) information
- Internet (m.) internet
- jamais never
- le jardin garden
- jeter to throw away
- jouer to play
- le/les journal/journaux (m. pl.) newspaper(s)
- le jour day
- le lac lake
- le légume vegetable
- lire to read
- le magasin shop
- la maison house
- manger to eat
- la manifestation demonstration, event
- le marché market
- marcher to walk
- mauvais pour l'environnement (m.) bad for the environment
- la mer sea
- le message message
- moi me
- moins (de) less (of), fewer (of)
- les montagnes (f. pl.) mountains
- le musée museum
- la musique music
- la nature nature
- ne … pas not
- normalement normally
- on we, one
- l' ordinateur (m.) computer
- parce que because
- parler (de) to speak, to talk (about)
- partager to share
- partir to leave
- passer (du temps) to spend (time)
- pas cher cheap
- la photo photo
- la pièce room
- la plage beach
- la planète planet
- le plastique plastic
- pleuvoir to rain
- plus (de) more (of)
- la pollution pollution
- poster to post
- la poubelle bin
- pour for, in order to
- pouvoir to be able to
- pratique practical
- préférer to prefer
- prendre to take
- près de near
- le problème problem
- protéger to protect
- quand when
- la radio radio
- rapide fast
- le réchauffement du climat global warming
- rechercher to search (for)
- le recyclage recycling
- regarder to watch
- le repas meal
- les réseaux sociaux (m. pl.) social networks/media
- le restaurant restaurant
- rester to stay
- la rue street
- la salle à manger dining room
- la salle de bains bathroom
- le salon lounge, living room
- si if
- le site site
- situer to situate, to locate
- le soir evening
- surtout especially
- la télé TV
- télécharger to download
- le temps time, weather
- le train train
- le transport public public transport
- trois three
- trop (de) too much, many (of)
- l' usine (f.) factory
- utiliser to use
- les vacances (f. pl.) holiday
- le vélo bike
- la viande meat
- la ville town, city
- visiter to visit (place)
- la voiture car
- vouloir to want
- voyager to travel

7.1G Le temps pendant les vacances

- à l'étranger abroad
- acceptable acceptable
- acheter to buy
- agréable pleasant, nice
- aller en vacances to go on holidays
- au marché at the market
- au musée at the museum
- c'est it is
- changeable changeable
- comme such as, like, since
- coûter to cost
- dans la nature in nature
- en famille as a family
- en général in general
- en plus in addition
- ensemble together
- idéal(e) ideal

Theme 3

il fait mauvais it is bad weather
il pleut it is raining
il y a du brouillard it is foggy
il y a du vent it is windy
ma sœur my sister
mangeable edible
le *manque (de)* lack (of)
non not
notre/nos our
ou or
par contre on the other hand
le *parc national* national park
parfois sometimes
le *pays* country
pendant during
pendant les vacances during the holiday
penser que to think that
le *père* father
pour les vacances for the holidays
préférable preferable
le *Québec* Quebec
sain(e) healthy
la *semaine* week
les *sites historiques (m. pl.)* historical sites
les *toilettes (f. pl.)* toilet
très very
variable varied
voir to see
vraiment really

7.1F Les îles francophones

l' *âge (m.)* age
l' *an (m.)/année (f.)* year
apprendre to learn, to teach
aujourd'hui today
autre (adj.) other
bien good, well
bonjour good morning, afternoon
calme (adj.) calm, quiet
les *Caraïbes (f. pl.)* Caribbean
ce/cet/cette/ces this, these
chaud(e) hot, warm
cher/chère expensive
comment how
la *Corse* Corsica
la *côte* coast

la *culture* culture
culturel(le) cultural
différent(e) (de) different (from)
dix ten
en hiver in winter
entre between
espérer que to hope that
être situé(e) to be situated
l' *euro (m.)* euro
l' *expérience (f.)* experience
faire des promenades to go for walks
la *forêt* forest, wood
frais/fraîche fresh
la *frontière* border
le *gâteau* cake
l' *histoire (f.)* history, story
l' *hiver (m.)* winter
il faisait froid it was cold
il faisait beau it was nice weather
il y avait there was, there were
il y avait du vent it was windy
l' *île (f.)* island
intéressant(e) interesting
l' *invitation (f.)* invitation
le/la *jeune (n.)* young person
jeune (adj.) young
là there
là-bas over there
la *langue* language
le/la/l'/les the
local(e)(s)/locaux local
long(ue) long
la *mer Méditerranée* Mediterranean sea
le *nord* North
nouveau/nouvelle (adj.) new
la *Nouvelle-Calédonie* New Caledonia
l' *océan Atlantique (m.)* Atlantic ocean
l' *océan Indien (m.)* Indian ocean
l' *océan Pacifique (m.)* Pacific ocean
le *parc naturel* natural park
parfait(e) perfect
plusieurs several
le *podcast* podcast
populaire popular

préparer to prepare
qu'est-ce que what
quel(le) what, which
raconter to tell
la *religion* religion
retourner to go back
souvent often
traditionnel(le) traditional
trouver to find
venir (de) to come (from)
vivre to live
vrai(e) true

7.2G Mes visites de touriste

à at, to
Alger Algiers
l' *Algérie (f.)* Algeria
amusant(e) amusing, fun, funny, enjoyable
l' *année dernière (f.)* last year
au at the, to the
le *bâtiment* building
beau/belle beautiful
la *Belgique* Belgium
boire to drink
la *boisson* drink
c'est it is
le *café* coffee, coffee shop
le *camping* camping, campsite
le *château* castle
de of, from
dernier/dernière last
descendre to go down, descend, get off
du/de la/des/de l' some, of the
l' *église (f.)* church
l' *été (m.)* summer
faire beau to be nice (weather)
la *France* France
les *frites (f. pl.)* chips
la *gare* train station
les *gens (m. pl.)* people
hier yesterday
joli(e) pretty
le *métro* underground (train)
le *mois* month
mon/ma/mes my
monter to go up
la *mosquée* mosque
musulman(e) Muslim

la *place* square
quelque(s) a few
la *station* station
la *tour* tower
traverser to cross
venir to come
la *vue* view
le *week-end* weekend

7.2F Vacances de rêve

à bientôt see you soon
arriver to arrive
le *brouillard* fog
l' *Espagne (f.)* Spain
faire chaud to be hot
froid(e) cold
génial(e) great, super
il faisait mauvais it was bad weather
jusque until
le *livre* book
le *logement* accommodation
loin far
(le) *lundi* Monday
(le) *mardi* Tuesday
le *matin* morning
oublier to forget
le/les *parent(s) (m. pl.)* parents
le *portable* mobile phone
propre clean, own
quitter to leave
récemment recently
réserver to book
le *rêve* dream
sans without
sortir to go out
le *sud* south
sympa nice
la *synagogue* synagogue
tard late
tous les jours every day
vite quick

8.1G Les médias

à la mode in fashion, fashionable
l' *article (m.)* article
l' *avis (m.)* opinion
la *célébrité* celebrity
chatter to chat
choisir to choose
le *cinéma* cinema

cent quarante et un 141

Theme 3 — Vocabulary

communiquer to communicate
connaître to know (person, place)
le copain friend, boyfriend
la copine friend, girlfriend
de plus in addition
de temps en temps from time to time
l' e-mail (m.) e-mail
en streaming streamed
envoyer to send
l' événement (m.) event
facile easy
le film d'action action film
… fois par … … time per …
l' influence (f.) influence
informatif informative
le magazine magazine
le monde world
l' opinion (f.) opinion
l' outil (m.) tool
par by
toujours always
vendre to sell
le(s) vêtement(s) (m.) (pl.) clothes
le vidéo video

8.1F Le monde avant et après Internet

l' appli (f.) app
content(e) happy, glad, pleased
le danger danger
devoir to have to, must
la façon way, manner
faire attention à to be careful of, to pay attention to
faire des progrès to make progress
le jeu vidéo video game
leur(s) their
maintenant now
mais but
mondial(e) global
ne … jamais never
l' ordinateur portable (m.) laptop
présent(e) (adj.) present
seulement only
le smartphone smartphone
la société society
la technologie technology

le téléphone phone
tout d'abord first of all
travailler to work
la vie quotidienne daily life

8.2G Ton portable, ta vie

avant (de) before
clair(e) clear
complet / complète complete
découvrir to discover
disponible available
l' école (f.) school
elles they (female)
en bonne santé in good health
expliquer to explain
faire la fête to party, celebrate
faire mes devoirs to do my homework
faire une promenade to go for a walk
le festival festival
gratuit(e) free
ils they (male)
la mode de vie way of life, lifestyle
penser to think
les recherches (f. pl.) research
recycler to recycle
la région region
le sport sport
la tablette tablet (computer)
tchatter to chat
tout(e)(s) all

8.2F J'utilise la technologie!

à l'avenir in the future
l' anniversaire (m.) birthday
appeler to call
cependant however
changer to change
la chanson song
le contenu content
cool cool
la dépendance addiction
en ce moment at the moment
enregistrer to record
impossible impossible
inaccessible inaccessible

l' inactivité (f.) inactivity
incomplet / incomplète incomplete
l' indépendance (f.) independence
indifférent(e) indifferent
injuste unfair
le jeu game
moderne modern
presque almost
prochain(e) next
réduire to reduce
savoir to know
la sécurité safety, security

9.1G Tu es écolo?

arrêter de to stop
arriver à to manage
augmenter to increase
la conséquence consequence, result
décider de to decide
diminuer to decrease
l' environnement (m.) environment
éviter (de) to avoid
faire du recyclage to do recycling, to recycle
le jambon ham
menacer to threaten
le niveau level
polluer to pollute
possible possible
prendre un bain to take a bath
le produit product
le réchauffement warming
le transport transport
la trottinette scooter
végétarien(ne) vegetarian
vert(e) green, eco-friendly

9.1F Sauvons la planète!

animal (adj.) from, of animals
alors so, well, then
l' arbre (m.) tree
certain(e)(s) some
le choix choice
la chose thing
le climat climate
couper to cut

créer to create
la date date
devenir to become
donner to give
la douche shower
le droit right
l' énergie (f.) energy
encourager to encourage
l' expert(e) expert
fabriquer to make
faire une différence to make a difference
le futur future
la génération generation
inquiétant(e) worrying
la journée day
se laver to wash
même si even if
la mode fashion
le moyen de vivre way of living
naturel(le) natural
novembre November
l' oxygène (m.) oxygen
par exemple for example
planter to plant
le/la premier/première first
le produit ménager household product
le respect respect
la ressource resource
le savon soap
scientifique (adj.) scientific
selon according to
le soleil sun
le souci worry
la Terre Earth
végan(e) vegan
le véganisme veganism
le végétarisme vegetarianism
le vent wind

9.2G Une visite chez mon ami

l' après-midi (m.) afternoon
au(x) to the
le barbecue barbecue, BBQ
bon(ne) good
(le) dimanche Sunday
discuter to discuss, talk
l' espace (m.) space
faire un gâteau to bake, make a cake
fatigué(e) tired

la fleur flower
le foot football
   il n'y a pas de there is, are no
le lit bed
la mère mother
   mettre to put (on)
le midi midday
le popcorn popcorn
   préféré(e) favourite
   puis then
   rentrer to go back, to go home
   son/sa/ses his/her
(le) vendredi Friday
le week-end dernier last weekend

9.2F Un guide de ma ville

   août August
   avoir faim to be hungry
   avoir le temps to have time
   beaucoup à faire a lot to do
   bien sûr of course
le centre commercial shopping centre
la citadelle citadel
   confortable comfortable
la couleur colour
   croire que to believe that
   délicieux/délicieuse delicious
la Dordogne Dordogne
   en été in summer
   environ about, thereabouts
   faire froid to be cold
   faire les magasins to go shopping
   juillet July
   médiéval(e) medieval
le nombre number
   penser de to think of
la/les personne(s) person/people
le port port
   quatorzième fourteenth
   qui who, which
   recevoir to receive
   recommander to recommend
   rien à faire nothing to do

le/la seul(e) … the only …
le sud-ouest South-West
le théâtre theatre
   vieux/vieil/vieille old

Culture

   accueillir to welcome
l' adulte (m./f.) adult
l' arène (f.) arena
   autre other
   avoir lieu to take place
   bien fait(e) well done
la comédie comedy
la création creation
se dérouler to take place
   février February
le/la gagnant(e) winner
les grands grown-ups
   immense huge
   international(e)/internationaux international
   mai May
   malheureusement unfortunately
le/la mécanicien(ne) mechanic
la Méditerranée the Mediterranean
le/la/les meilleur(e)(s) best
la mise en scène set design
   musical(e) (adj.) musical
l' or (m.) gold
   où where
les petits children
   principal(e) main
le prix prize, price
   quoi what
   réaliser to make (a film)
   romantique romantic
le service militaire military service
   sur on (top of)
   tomber amoureux/amoureuse to fall in love
   très bien very well
le visiteur visitor
   vif/vive bright, vivid

Theme 3 — Test and revise: Foundation Listening

1 You hear some Belgian students talking about holidays. What opinion do they give on the following aspects (1–4)?

Write **P** for a **positive** opinion
N for a **negative** opinion
P+N for a **positive** and **negative** opinion.

1 Transport
2 Accommodation
3 Weather
4 Holiday activities

4 marks

Conseil

Listen out for positive and negative opinions and adjectives. Listen also for words such as *mais*, *cependant* and *malheureusement* which can indicate a contrasting opinion.

2 Your French friends have sent you some messages. What did each person do?

Write the correct letter for each person (1–4).

A	cooked
B	played
C	watched a film
D	slept
E	washed
F	ate

4 marks

Conseil

Think about the types of words you might hear. For example, for 'slept', you might expect to hear words such as *dormir*, *chambre* or *fatigué*. Listen to each extract carefully, so you don't get confused by distractors.

3 You hear this conversation between Ryad and his grandma, Mélanie.

Answer the following questions in **English**.

1 What are Ryad's biggest worries about the environment? Give **two** details in English.

2 marks

2 What does Ryad's grandma suggest he could do? Write the **two** correct letters.

2 marks

A	Use public transport
B	Stop taking baths
C	Recycle
D	Eat less meat

Conseil

Always check how many marks are available for each question. This will help you work out how many elements to include in your answer.

4 You hear this advert about Algiers, the capital of Algeria.

Which aspects of the city are mentioned?

Write the **two** correct letters for each section (1–2).

A	Size
B	Climate
C	Restaurants
D	Activities
E	Location
F	Age

4 marks

Conseil

Listen out for any key words related to the six aspects to help you identify the correct answers.

Theme 3

5 You hear this podcast about uses of technology.

Complete the sentences in **English**.

1. a Young people use the internet to… **1 mark**
   b They also like… **1 mark**
2. a Yesterday morning, Khalid… **1 mark**
   b After that, he… **1 mark**

Conseil

Use the sentence starters to help you locate the answers on the recording. Make sure your English answers fit within the context of the sentence.

6 You hear this online item about young people and why good weather is so important for their holidays.

What **two** reasons does each person (1–2) give?

Write the correct letters.

A	Camping
B	Relaxing
C	Swimming
D	Eating outside
E	Walking
F	Boating

4 marks

Conseil

In this type of task, remember that you need to identify **two** reasons for each section that you hear.

Dictation A

You will now hear **four** short sentences.

Listen carefully and, using your knowledge of French sounds, write down in French exactly what you hear for each sentence.

You will hear each sentence **three** times: the first time as a full sentence, the second time in short sections and the third time again as a full sentence.

Use your knowledge of French sounds and grammar to make sure that what you have written makes sense. Check carefully that your spelling is accurate.

8 marks

Dictation B

You will now hear **four** more sentences.

Write down in French exactly what you hear for each sentence.

8 marks

cent quarante-cinq

Theme 3 — Test and revise: Foundation Speaking

Role play

You are talking to your Swiss friend.

Your teacher will play the part of your friend and will speak first.

You should address your friend as *tu*.

When you see this – ? – you will have to ask a question.

> In order to score full marks, you must include a verb in your response to each task.
>
> 1 Describe your home. (Give **one** detail.)
>
> 2 Say what you do in your home. (Give **one** detail.)
>
> 3 Say what you like best about your home. (Give **one** detail.)
>
> 4 Give **one** opinion of your local area.
>
> ? 5 Ask your friend a question about their home.

10 marks

Conseil

In order to complete the role play successfully, read the instructions and bullet points carefully so you know exactly what you need to say. Make sure that you include an opinion if the bullet point asks for one, and ask a question where instructed to.

Reading aloud

When your teacher asks you, read aloud the following text **in French**.

> J'utilise tous les jours Internet.
>
> Je pense que c'est très pratique.
>
> J'aime beaucoup regarder des films d'action.
>
> Je télécharge souvent de la musique sur mon portable.
>
> Je trouve les nouvelles technologies très utiles dans ma vie quotidienne.

You will then be asked four questions **in French** that relate to the topic of **Media and technology**. Make sure you **answer all four questions as fully as you can**.

15 marks

Conseil

Remember the pronunciation rules you have learnt and take your time! Pay particular attention to the pronunciation of cognates.

Theme 3

Photo card

- During your preparation time, look at the two photos. You may make as many notes as you wish and use these notes during the test.
- Your teacher will ask you to talk about the content of these photos. The recommended time is approximately **one minute**. You must **say at least one thing about each photo**.
- After you have spoken about the content of the photos, your teacher will then ask you questions related to **any** of the topics within the theme of **Communication and the world around us**.

25 marks

Conseil

Make sure you say at least one thing about each photo and give as much information as you can, using accurate language.

Try to extend your answers to the follow-up questions as much as possible. Give opinions with reasons, and use a variety of tenses, adjectives, adverbs, pronouns and intensifiers.

Photo 1

Photo 2

cent quarante-sept | **147**

Theme 3 — Test and revise: Foundation Reading

1 These French students are saying what they do to help the environment. What does each person mention? Write the correct letter.

1 Amadou
Je prends le bus pour aller au collège.

2 Alizée
Je ne voyage jamais en avion pour aller en vacances.

3 Fabien
Je fais souvent du recyclage.

4 Édith
Je ne mange plus de viande.

A	Diet
B	Saving water
C	Daily travel
D	Recycling
E	Plant trees
F	Holiday travel

4 marks

Conseil
Look for words related to the options in the grid. For example, for 'diet', you might expect to see *manger*, *boire* or items of food and drink.

2 You receive some messages from your friends. They describe their usual holidays. Match the correct person with each of the following questions (a–f).

Write **L** for **Louane**
C for **Christophe**
N for **Nolwen**.

Amis

Louane
Je préfère aller en vacances là où il fait beau car j'adore le soleil. Quand il fait chaud, je fais de la natation dans la mer avec mon frère, c'est très amusant.

Christophe
Quand je pars en vacances avec ma famille, nous voyageons toujours en camping-car parce que c'est meilleur pour l'environnement. Comme nous adorons passer du temps dans la nature, c'est très pratique.

Nolwen
J'adore voyager à l'étranger! J'essaye toujours d'apprendre quelques mots dans la langue du pays et je découvre la culture et les traditions. Par contre, je déteste ça quand il pleut.

Conseil
Read the texts carefully and work out the gist (overall meaning) before looking at the questions. Once you have worked out the main ideas, you should find it easier to decide who says what.

a Who likes going abroad?
b Who prefers warm weather?
c Who considers the environment when they travel?
d Who likes being outdoors?
e Who enjoys an activity with their brother?
f Who speaks different languages?

6 marks

Theme 3

3 You read this email that Molly sent to her friend in France.

She describes where she lives.

Answer the following questions in **English**.

Bonjour,

J'habite dans une petite ville située dans l'ouest de l'Angleterre. Notre appartement est assez grand car il y a trois chambres. J'ai ma propre chambre mais ma petite sœur et mon petit frère doivent partager. Chez moi, on aime regarder la télé ensemble dans le salon mais moi, je lis souvent des livres dans ma chambre.

Ma ville n'est pas historique parce qu'il n'y a pas de châteaux ou de vieux bâtiments. Malgré ça, les jeunes aiment la ville parce qu'ils peuvent faire du shopping au centre commercial et manger dans de bons restaurants.

Molly

a Give **two** details about Molly's flat. **2 marks**

b What does Molly's family like to do at home? **1 marks**

c Why does she describe her town as 'not historic'? Give **two** details. **2 marks**

d Why do young people like her town? Give **two** details. **2 marks**

Conseil

Don't be overwhelmed by longer texts. Take your time and focus on what you understand. Use the questions to identify the parts of the text you need to answer them. For example, in question a, you are looking for details about Molly's flat, so the information you need is likely to follow shortly after the cognate *appartement*.

4 Translate these sentences into English.

a Pour mes vacances, je vais à l'étranger.

b Mon frère prend tous les jours le bus.

c Nous allons télécharger un nouveau film en ligne.

d Hier soir, j'ai dormi dans mon nouveau lit dans ma chambre.

e Ma maison est située à la campagne près d'une vieille église.

10 marks

5 Translate these sentences into English.

a On écoute souvent de la musique à la radio.

b Vous faites beaucoup de recyclage?

c Les touristes peuvent visiter des sites historiques.

d Je vais aller en France pour travailler dans une usine.

e J'ai décidé de manger moins de viande

10 marks

Conseil

Read the French sentences carefully and use the time markers to help you use the correct tense in your English translation. Make sure you have accounted for every word in your translation, but remember that French sometimes uses small words when English does not.

Theme 3 — Test and revise: Foundation Writing

1 **You have received this photo on WhatsApp from your friend.**
What is in this photo? Write **five** sentences in **French**.

> **Conseil**
> Keep your sentences short and simple but make sure you include a verb in each one.

10 marks

2 **Your French friend has asked about where you live.**
Write a short description for your friend.

Write approximately **50** words in **French**.

You must write something about each bullet point.

Mention:
- your home
- your town, village or city
- what you do at home
- your local area
- what you do with your friends.

> **Conseil**
> Make sure you address all five bullet points and write in full sentences.

10 marks

Theme 3

3 Using your knowledge of grammar, complete the following sentences in French.

Choose the correct French word from the three options in the grid.

Write the correct word, as shown in the example.

Example: *L'été, dans le sud de la France, il __fait__ chaud.*

| fait | est | a |

a Quand j'___ petit, j'habitais en Belgique.

| suis | était | étais |

1 mark

b La cuisine locale est ___.

| bon | bonne | bonnes |

1 mark

c Nous avons ___ des musées.

| visiter | visité | visités |

1 mark

d Mes parents ___ de la musique à la radio.

| écoute | écouter | écoutent |

1 mark

e J'aime ___ de la musique en ligne.

| télécharger | téléchargé | téléchargés |

1 mark

Conseil

Use the whole sentence to help you decide which option to choose. There will be clues before or after the missing word to help you decide.

4 Translate the following sentences into French.

   a It is cold in winter.
   a I watch TV every day.
   c In my town, we can go swimming.
   d Yesterday, my sister listened to music.
   e To help the planet, I like to do recycling.

10 marks

Conseil

Look at the time phrases carefully as they will help you decide which tense to use.

Either question 5.1 or question 5.2

5.1 You are emailing your Canadian friend about holidays.

Write approximately **90** words in **French**.

You must write something about each bullet point.

Describe:
- what sort of holidays you like
- a recent holiday
- what you will do during your summer holiday.

15 marks

5.2 You are writing an article about the environment.

Write approximately **90** words in **French**.

You must write something about each bullet point.

Describe:
- the main environmental problems in your region
- what you did recently to help the environment
- a habit you will change to protect the planet.

15 marks

Conseil

Make sure you read the bullet points carefully and write something about each one. Your verbs and time phrases need to match what each bullet point is asking you.

cent cinquante et un **151**

All themes — Test and revise: Foundation Listening

1. **You hear some Belgian students talking about their school life. What is their opinion on the following aspects?**

    Write P for a **positive** opinion

    N for a **negative** opinion

    P+N for a **positive** and **negative** opinion.

    1 Break time

    2 Journey to school

    3 Other students

    4 Homework

    4 marks

    ### Conseil
    In this type of task, a negative expression doesn't always indicate a negative opinion. Listen carefully to understand the context of each expression.

2. **Your Canadian friend has sent you some voice messages (1–4).**

    What is each message about?

    Write the correct letter.

A	Family
B	Bedroom
C	Meals
D	Home
E	Town
F	Friends

    4 marks

    ### Conseil
    Before listening, look at the list of options (A–F) and think of some corresponding French words you might hear.

3. **You hear this conversation about a French holiday resort. For each section (1–2), which two aspects of the resort are mentioned?**

    Write the **two** correct letters for each section.

A	The number of people
B	The children's activities
C	The shops
D	The distance to the beach
E	The quality of the accommodation
F	The weather

    4 marks

    ### Conseil
    Make sure that you listen out for **two** separate points in each section of the recording. They may or may not be in the same order as the printed options.

4. **You hear some young people talking about a festival in Switzerland. Which aspect of the festival is each person (1–4) talking about?**

    Write the correct letter.

A	Camping
B	Food
C	Toilet facilities
D	Entertainment
E	Transport
F	Cost

    4 marks

    ### Conseil
    Listen to the whole of each section before deciding on your answer. Remember that you may not hear the exact French equivalent of the English options (A–F).

All themes

5 You hear two Swiss students talking about technology.

Complete the sentences in **English**.

1. a Yesterday, Sophie bought… **1 mark**
    b Afterwards, she… **1 mark**
2. a This morning, Khalid looked for… **1 mark**
    b This evening, he will… **1 mark**
3. a Sophie thinks that social media networks are… **1 mark**
    b Last week, Sophie… **1 mark**

Conseil

When completing sentences, make sure that what you write fits correctly with the sentence opening. For example, in this task, question 1a already has a verb ('bought') but question 1b does not.

6 You hear this interview with a French influencer.

Answer the questions in **English**.

1. a What idea did the influencer's friend give her? **1 mark**
    b What happened after one year? **1 mark**
2. How **exactly** does the influencer explain her success? Give **two** details. **2 marks**

Conseil

In this task, there are two marks for each section, with either two separate questions or one two-mark question. Be aware of this before you start listening.

Dictation A

You will now hear **four** short sentences.

- Listen carefully and, using your knowledge of French sounds, write down in **French** exactly what you hear for each sentence.
- You will hear each sentence **three** times: the first time as a full sentence, the second time in short sections and the third time again as a full sentence.
- Use your knowledge of French sounds and grammar to make sure that what you have written makes sense. Check carefully that your spelling is accurate.

8 marks

Dictation B

You will now hear **four** more sentences.

Write down in French exactly what you hear for each sentence.

8 marks

cent cinquante-trois **153**

All themes — Test and revise: Foundation Speaking

Role play

You are talking to a new friend from Québec.

Your teacher will play the part of your friend and will speak first.

You should address your friend as *tu*.

When you see this – ? – you will have to ask a question.

> In order to score full marks, you must include a verb in your response to each task.
>
> 1 Give your name and your age.
>
> 2 Describe your personality. (Give **one** detail.)
>
> 3 Say what your best friend is like. (Give **one** detail.)
>
> 4 Give **one** opinion about sport.
>
> ? 5 Ask your friend a question about free-time activities.

10 marks

Conseil

Remember that you are allowed to take notes for all tasks in the speaking exam. You can refer to these at any point during the test. Use this to help you!

Conseil

The role play should usually last one to one and half minutes. There are two marks for each task (1–5) on the role play card. Try to make sure you use a conjugated verb in each response, give an opinion if the task asks for one, and ask a question where required.

Reading aloud

When your teacher asks you, read aloud the following text **in French**.

> Je suis toujours travailleur.
>
> Je préfère le cinéma français mais je déteste le football.
>
> Je m'entends très bien avec ma cousine.
>
> On se voit souvent pour faire la fête en famille.
>
> C'est toujours sympa parce qu'elle est très drôle.

You will then be asked four questions **in French** that relate to the topic of **Identity and relationships with others**. Make sure you **answer all four questions as fully as you can**.

15 marks

Conseil

The reading aloud task and follow-up questions should usually last two to two and half minutes in total.

When reading the text aloud, focus carefully on your pronunciation, particularly verb and noun endings. You may lose marks if your pronunciation affects communication.

For the follow-up questions, try to develop your answers but stick to language you know and avoid making errors by using unfamiliar complicated structures.

All themes

Photo card

- During your preparation time, look at the two photos. You may make as many notes as you wish and use these notes during the test.
- Your teacher will ask you to talk about the content of these photos. The recommended time is approximately **one minute**. You must **say at least one thing about each photo**.
- After you have spoken about the content of the photos, your teacher will then ask you questions related to **any** of the topics within the theme of **People and lifestyle**.

25 marks

Conseil

Your description of the two photos should last about one minute and you need to say something about both photos. The follow-up conversation should last three to four minutes.

Use familiar language that you learnt when studying the topic. Keep your sentences short and avoid any complicated structures that you're not sure of.

Photo 1

Photo 2

All themes — Test and revise: Foundation Reading

1 You see an online forum. Some French students are talking about their towns. Match the correct person with each of the following questions (a–e).

Write **M** for **Moussa**
       L for **Loane**
       E for **Édouard**

Moussa
J'habite à la campagne. C'est très calme et les gens sont sympas, mais il y a peu de choses pour les jeunes.

Loane
Ici, il n'y a pas de grands magasins mais il y a un joli château qui est très vieux. Je le visite souvent avec mes amis. Il n'y a pas de piscine.

Édouard
Quand il fait beau, je vais dans le parc et quand il pleut, je vais au centre sportif où il y a une grande piscine. J'adore la natation. Il y a toujours quelque chose à faire dans ma ville.

a	Who visits the castle?	1 mark
b	Who goes swimming?	1 mark
c	Who thinks there is **not** a lot for young people to do?	1 mark
d	Who spends time outside when the weather is nice?	1 mark
e	Who lives in the countryside?	1 mark

Conseil

Make sure you read the whole text before answering the questions, rather than just looking for key words. Question b, for example, mentions swimming, but both Louane and Édouard use the word *piscine*. Look carefully at what each person says before deciding on your answers.

2 These French students are talking about their school. What do they think about their school?

Write **P** for a **positive** opinion
      N for a **negative** opinion
      P+N for a **positive** and **negative** opinion.

 Mégane
Les profs sont gentils et pas trop stricts. Ils ne donnent pas beaucoup de devoirs – c'est très bien! Les leçons sont claires et j'ai de bons amis.

 Anthony
À l'école, je fais beaucoup de sport et notre équipe de foot gagne souvent – c'est génial! Cependant, je n'aime pas les devoirs.

 Patrice
Dans mon collège, les bâtiments sont vieux et les salles de classes sont sales. On ne mange pas bien car il n'y a pas assez de choix. J'espère changer de collège bientôt.

 Ahmad
Mes profs ne nous aident pas beaucoup quand on trouve les leçons difficiles. C'est dommage parce que dans l'ensemble, j'aime mon école.

 Louise
Je suis dans le même collège que mon meilleur ami. Tous les deux, on pense que c'est le meilleur collège de la région. Ce n'est pas trop strict mais on apprend bien.

5 marks

Conseil

Here, you only really need to work out the gist (overall meaning) of each text, focusing on clues that tell you whether each person's opinion is positive or negative. Look out for words such as *mais* or *cependant*, which can change the meaning of a sentence from positive to negative or the other way round.

All themes

3 You see an article written by Léa, describing her recent trip to Chad.

Answer the following questions in **English**.

L'année dernière, j'ai passé trois semaines au Tchad, un pays situé au centre de l'Afrique. En premier, nous sommes allés à N'Djamena et nous avons visité de jolis petits villages et des marchés traditionnels dans la région. Ensuite, nous avons fait du camping dans le nord du pays. Dans la journée, il faisait très chaud mais la nuit, il faisait vraiment froid. Le soir, on faisait du feu pour avoir un peu plus chaud et on mangeait de la nourriture traditionnelle. C'était trop bien! L'année prochaine, nous voulons visiter un autre endroit au Tchad. Je pense que c'est devenu mon pays préféré!

a What did they visit in N'Djamena?
    (Give **two** details.) **2 marks**

b What was the problem at night? **1 mark**

c What did they do in the evenings?
    (Give **two** details.) **2 marks**

d What does she want to do next year? **1 mark**

Conseil

Make sure you check the words in **bold** and give the required number of details for each question.

4 In his blog, Benoît talks about his free time. What does Benoît say about his hobbies (a–e)?

Write **P** for a hobby he did **in the past**
       N for a hobby he does **now**
       F for a hobby he wants to do **in the future**.

Je suis un ado qui adore lire! Je lis au moins un roman par semaine et cette semaine, je lis un nouveau roman policier très intéressant. J'aime aussi la musique et récemment, je suis allé au concert de Taylor Swift. C'est ma chanteuse préférée. Elle est très populaire car elle a beaucoup de talent.
Je joue d'un instrument de musique et je fais ça une fois par semaine avec mon amie. Avec des copains, on va bientôt créer un groupe.
Quand j'étais plus jeune, je jouais au football mais maintenant j'ai arrêté. L'été prochain, je voudrais essayer de faire plus de vélo car un jour, je voudrais participer à des courses.

a Reading   d Cycling
b Going to a concert   e Football
c Playing an instrument   **5 marks**

5 Translate these sentences into English.

a Ma sœur est moins amusante que mon frère.
b J'envoie souvent des messages à mes amis.
c L'année prochaine, je vais étudier l'allemand.
d Quand j'étais petit, je passais mes vacances au Canada.
e On doit réduire le nombre de touristes dans ma ville.

10 marks

6 Translate these sentences into English.

a La pollution sur Terre est inquiétante.
b Au collège, mon ami n'a pas trop de devoirs.
c On va faire une promenade au soleil.
d Son blog parle de mode.
e Vendredi dernier, j'ai travaillé dans un bureau.

10 marks

cent cinquante-sept

All themes — Test and revise: Foundation Writing

1 **You are sharing photos with a friend on Snapchat.**

What is in this photo?

Write **five** sentences in **French**.

Conseil

For this task, you must describe what you see on the photo and not refer to what is **not** on it. You won't lose marks for using the same grammatical structure for each sentence (e.g. *Il y a…* or *Je vois…*). You can use the present tense throughout, though other tenses will also be accepted. Make sure each sentence contains a conjugated verb. Each sentence is worth two marks.

10 marks

2 **You are writing to your Belgian friend.**
Write a short description of life at school.

Write approximately **50** words in **French**.

You must write something about each bullet point.

Mention:
- your subjects
- your teachers
- the rules at your school
- breaktime at school
- your friends at school.

10 marks

Conseil

Write something about all five bullet points, and make sure it is relevant to the bullet point. You can make up the facts if that helps you use language that you know. Focus on clear communication and try to use a range of language. You can stick to the present tense if you don't want to use other tenses.

All themes

3 Using your knowledge of grammar, complete the following sentences in French.

Choose the correct French word from the three options in the grid.

Write the correct word, as shown in the example.

Example: *Le garçon __part__ en vacances.*

partent	part	pars

a Nous ___ tous les jours du sport.

faisons	fais	font

1 mark

b Cette influenceuse est très ___.

fiers	fière	fier

1 mark

c Samedi prochain, ___ vont visiter le château.

je	elle	ils

1 mark

d Mon frère ___ très bavard.

es	est	suis

1 mark

e À l'avenir, il va ___ dans une école.

travaille	travailler	travaillé

1 mark

Conseil

Check each sentence carefully. Use any time indicators to help you with tenses, and use nouns and pronouns to help you with verbs and adjectives. Make sure you copy the word exactly as it is written in the grid, including any accents.

4 Translate the following sentences into French.

a My brother is chatty and happy.

a I have a new mobile phone.

c I am a volunteer in my town and it's great.

d We often go to music festivals with our family.

e Yesterday, I went to the cinema.

10 marks

Conseil

You need to convey the message in each sentence clearly. Make sure you use the correct pronoun and verb form. Try not to leave any gaps – use a synonym if you don't know the exact word.

Either question 5.1 or question 5.2

5.1 You are emailing your French friend about holidays.

Write approximately **90** words in **French**.

You must write something about each bullet point.

Describe:

- what you usually do for the holidays
- the activities you did during a recent holiday
- your dream holiday.

15 marks

5.2 You are writing a blog about free time for your Canadian partner school.

Write approximately **90** words in **French**.

You must write something about each bullet point.

Describe:

- your favourite hobbies
- what you did recently at the weekend
- a new hobby you would like to try in future.

15 marks

Conseil

Make sure you write something about all the bullet points, but you don't need to cover them equally. Give information that is relevant to the bullet points and that conveys your message accurately. You should try to use varied vocabulary and grammar, refer to all three time frames and give opinions with reasons.

Grammar

Contents

Glossary of terms	**161**

1 Nouns — 161
- Masculine and feminine nouns
- Singular and plural forms

2 Articles — 162
- Definite articles: *le, la, les* – the
- Indefinite articles: *un, une, des, de* – a, an, some
- Partitive articles: *du, de la, de l', des* – some, any

3 Adjectives — 163
- Feminine and masculine, singular and plural adjectives
- The position of adjectives
- Comparative adjectives
- Demonstrative adjectives: *ce, cet, cette, ces* – this, that, these, those
- Indefinite adjectives
- Possessive adjectives, one 'owner'
- Possessive adjectives, several 'owners'
- Interrogative adjectives: *quel, quelle, quels, quelles*

4 Adverbs — 165
- Comparative adverbs

5 Pronouns — 165
- Subject pronouns: *je, tu, il, elle, on, nous, vous, ils, elles*
- Direct object pronouns: *me, te, vous, le, la*
- Indirect object pronouns: *me, te, lui*
- Reflexive pronouns: *me, te, se*
- Emphatic pronouns: *moi, toi*
- Possessive pronouns
- Relative pronouns: *qui*

6 Verbs — 167
- The infinitive
- The present tense
- The perfect tense
- The imperfect tense
- The near future
- The imperative
- The conditional
- *en* + present participle
- Useful verbs
- Modal verbs: *devoir, pouvoir, vouloir*
- Impersonal verbs: *il pleut, il faut, il y a*

7 Negatives — 171
- Negatives in the perfect tense

8 Questions — 171

9 Prepositions — 172
- *à, au, à la, à l', aux, de*
- *en, au, aux* + countries
- More prepositions

10 Ordinal Numbers — 173
- *premier, deuxième*, etc.

11 Morphology — 173

Prefixes

Adding *in-* or *im-* to adjectives, adverbs, and nouns

Suffixes

Adjectives created by adding *-able* or *-eable* to the verb stem

Adverbs created by dropping *-ant(e) / -ent(e)* from an adjective and adding *-amment / -emment*

Nouns created by adding *-ion* or *-ation* to the verb stem

Agent nouns created by adding *-eur* or *-ateur* to a verb stem

Verb tables — 174

Grammar

Glossary of terms

Adjectives *les adjectifs*
Words that describe somebody or something:
petit small   *timide* shy

Adverbs *les adverbes*
Words that complement (add meaning to) verbs, adjectives or other adverbs:
très very   *lentement* slowly

Articles *les articles*
Short words used before nouns:
un / une a, an   *des* some, any   *le / la / les* the

The infinitive *l'infinitif*
The verb form given in the dictionary:
aller to go   *avoir* to have

Nouns *les noms*
Words that identify a person, a place or a thing:
mère mother   *maison* house

Prepositions *les prépositions*
Words used in front of nouns to give information about when, how, where, etc.:
à at   *avec* with   *de* of, from   *en* in

Pronouns *les pronoms*
Short words used to replace nouns:
je I   *tu* you   *il* he   *elle* she   *moi* me   *toi* you

Verbs *les verbes*
Words used to express an action or a state:
je parle I speak   *il est* he is

1 Nouns

Masculine and feminine nouns

All French nouns are either masculine or feminine. In the singular, masculine nouns are introduced with *le*, *l'* or *un*:

le père	**the** father	*un livre*	**a** book
l'hôtel	**the** hotel		

Feminine nouns are introduced with *la*, *l'* or *une*:

la mère	**the** mother	*une table*	**a** table
l'eau	**the** water		

Some nouns have two different forms, masculine and feminine:

un écrivain	a male writer
une écrivaine	a female writer
un serveur	a male waiter
une serveuse	a female waiter
un facteur	a postman
une factrice	a postwoman
un physicien	a male physicist
une physicienne	a female physicist
un policier	a male police officer
une policière	a female police officer

Some nouns stay the same for masculine and feminine:

le prof	the male teacher
la prof	the female teacher
un enfant	a male child
une enfant	a female child

Singular and plural forms

As in English, French nouns can be either singular (one) or plural (more than one).

Most plural nouns end in -s. Unlike English, the added -s is usually not pronounced.

un chien, deux chiens   one dog, two dogs

As in English, there are some exceptions.

- With most nouns ending in -al, you change the ending to -aux in the plural:
  un animal, des animaux   an animal, animals

- With many nouns ending in -au or -eu, you add an -x:
  un gâteau, des gâteaux   a cake, cakes
  un jeu, des jeux   a game, games

- Words already ending in -s, or in -x or -z, do not change:
  le bras, les bras   arm, arms
  le prix, les prix   prize, prizes

- A few nouns change completely:
  un œil, des yeux   an eye, eyes

cent soixante et un **161**

Grammar

2 Articles

Definite articles: *le, la, les* – the

The word for 'the' depends on whether the noun it goes with is masculine (m), feminine (f), singular or plural.

m singular	f singular	m + f plural
le	la	les

le beau-père — the step-father
la belle-mère — the step-mother
les parents — the parents

When a singular noun starts with a vowel or a silent *h*, *le* and *la* are shortened to *l'*:
*l'*ami — the friend
*l'*histoire — the story

In French, you often need to use *le*, *la* and *les* even when we wouldn't say 'the' in English:
- when talking about likes and dislikes:
  J'adore *le* fromage. — I love cheese.
  Elle déteste *les* maths. — She hates maths.
- when referring to abstract things:
  La musique est très importante. — Music is very important.

As in English, definite articles can be used before an adjective to form a noun:
seul — only (m.) — *le* seul — **the** only
anglaise — English (f.) — *l'*Anglaise — **the** English (girl/woman)

Indefinite articles: *un, une, des, de* – a, an, some

Like the words for 'the' (*le/la/les*), the words for 'a/an' and 'some' depend on whether the noun they go with is masculine or feminine, singular or plural.

m singular	f singular	m + f plural
un	une	des

un vélo — a bike
une ville — a town
des voitures — (some) cars

When talking about jobs, *un* and *une* are not used in French where 'a' or 'an' is used in English.
Il est professeur. — He is **a** teacher.

In negative constructions, *de* replaces *un*, *une* or *des* after *pas*:
J'ai un frère. – Je n'ai **pas de** frère.*
I don't have **any** brothers.

Il y a une piscine. – Il n'y a **pas de** piscine.
There is **no** swimming pool.

J'ai des sœurs. – Je n'ai **pas de** sœur.*
I don't have **any** sisters.

* Note that in French you use a singular noun after a negative construction, unlike in English.

Change *de* to *d'* in front of a vowel or a silent *h*:
Je n'ai pas **d'**animal. — I don't have any pets.

Partitive articles: *du, de la, de l', des* – some, any

masculine	feminine	words beginning with a vowel or silent *h*	plural
de + le = du	de + la = de la	de + l' = de l'	de + les = des

du café — (some) coffee
de la nourriture — (some) food
*de l'*eau — (some) water
des frites — (some) chips

- *du* always replaces *de + le*
- *des* always replaces *de + les*

Use *du, de la, de l', des* to mean 'some' or 'any':
Je voudrais *du* pain. — I'd like **some** bread.
Elle prend *de la* glace. — She's having (**some**) ice cream.
Elle boit *de l'*eau. — She's drinking (**some**) water.
Avez-vous *des* croissants? — Do you have **any** croissants?

Also use *du, de la, de l', des* to talk about activities someone is doing or musical instruments someone is playing:
Je fais *du* judo. — I do judo.
Elle joue *de la* guitare. — She is playing the guitar.
Il fait *de l'*équitation. — He goes horse riding.
Ils font *des* voyages. — They go on trips.

After a negative, *de* or *d'* (before a vowel) replaces these forms:
Je ne fais pas **de** judo. — I don't do judo.

Grammar

3 Adjectives

Feminine and masculine, singular and plural adjectives

In French, adjectives have different endings depending on whether they describe masculine, feminine, singular or plural nouns.

- The masculine singular form has no extra ending:
  Mon frère est petit.   My brother is small.

- Add -*e* if the noun is feminine singular:
  Ma sœur est petite.   My sister is small.

- Add -*s* to the masculine singular form if the noun is masculine plural:
  Mes frères sont petits.   My brothers are small.

- Add -*s* to the feminine singular form if the noun is feminine plural:
  Mes sœurs sont petites.   My sisters are small.

- When an adjective describes a group of masculine and feminine people or things, it has to be the masculine plural form:
  Mes parents sont grands.   My parents are tall.

There are many exceptions in the feminine forms.

- With adjectives that already end in -*e*, don't add another -*e* in the feminine:
  un vélo rouge   a red bike
  une fleur rouge   a red flower

- But with adjectives that end in -*é*, do add another -*e* in the feminine:
  mon film préféré   my favourite film
  ma chanson préférée   my favourite song

- With some adjectives, you double the final consonant before the -*e* in the feminine:
  Il est canadien.   He is Canadian.
  Elle est canadienne.   She is Canadian.
  Un parc naturel.   A natural park.
  Une plage naturelle.   A natural beach.

- Adjective endings -*x* change to -*se* in the feminine:
  un garçon paresseux   a lazy boy
  une fille paresseuse   a lazy girl

- The adjective ending -*f* changes to -*ve* in the feminine:
  un copain sportif   a sporty (boy)friend
  une copine sportive   a sporty (girl)friend

- The feminine of *gentil* is *gentille*:
  Ma sœur est gentille.   My sister is kind.

There are also some exceptions in the plural forms.

- Adjective endings -*al* and -*eau* change to -*aux* or -*eaux* in the masculine plural:
  J'ai des poissons nouveaux.   I have got some new fish.

- With adjectives that end in -*s* or -*x*, don't add an -*s* in the masculine plural:
  Mes frères sont paresseux.   My brothers are lazy.
  Les murs sont gris.   The walls are grey.

The position of adjectives

Most adjectives follow the noun they describe:
     *un prof **sympa***   a nice teacher
     *une copine **intelligente***   an intelligent friend
     *des idées **intéressantes***   interesting ideas

However, a few adjectives, such as *petit, grand, bon, mauvais, joli, beau, jeune* and *vieux*, usually come in front of the noun:
     *un **petit** garçon*   a small boy
     *une **jolie** ville*   a pretty town

A few adjectives that come in front of the noun have a special masculine form before a vowel or a silent *h*:
     *un **bel** endroit*   a beautiful place
     *un **vieil** homme*   an old man
     *un **nouvel** ami*   a new friend

Comparative adjectives

To make comparisons, use:

- *plus … que*   more … than / …er than
  *La Loire est **plus** longue **que** la Tamise.*
  The Loire is long**er than** the Thames.

- *moins … que* less … than
  *Les vélos sont **moins** rapides **que** les trains.*
  Bicycles are **less** fast **than** trains.

- *aussi … que*   as … as
  *Les fruits sont **aussi** chères **que** les légumes.*
  Fruits are **as** expensive **as** vegetables.

cent soixante-trois

Grammar

Demonstrative adjectives: ce, cet, cette, ces – this, that, these, those

The French for 'this' or 'that' is *ce*, *cet* or *cette* and for 'these' or 'those' is *ces*.

masculine	feminine	masculine and feminine plural
ce	cette	ces

ce magasin	**this** / **that** shop
cette maison	**this** / **that** house
ces bâtiments	**these** / **those** buildings

But *ce* changes to *cet* when the noun after it is masculine and begins with a vowel or a silent *h*:

cet ami	**this** / **that** friend
cet hôtel	**this** / **that** hotel

Indefinite adjectives

The most common indefinite adjectives are:

autre(s)	other
chaque	each
même(s)	same
plusieurs	several
quelque(s)	some
tout / toute / tous / toutes	all

Chaque is always singular and *plusieurs* is always plural:
  Il y a une télévision dans **chaque chambre**.
  There is a television in **each room**.
  Il a **plusieurs voitures**.   He has **several cars**.

Possessive adjectives, one 'owner'

mon / ma / mes	my
ton / ta / tes	your
son / sa / ses	his / her / its

There are three different ways of saying 'my' in French, as it depends on whether the noun is masculine or feminine, singular or plural. It is the same for 'your' and 'his' / 'her' / 'its'.

masculine singular	feminine singular	masculine and feminine plural
mon, ton, son	ma, ta, sa	mes, tes, ces

mon père	**my** father
ma mère	**my** mother
ton* père	**your** father
ta* mère	**your** mother
son pied	**his** / **her** / **its** foot
sa porte	**his** / **her** / **its** door

mes parents	**my** parents
tes* parents	**your** parents
ses fenêtres	**his** / **her** / **its** windows

* to someone you normally say *tu* to

French doesn't have three different words for 'his', 'her' and 'its'. The word changes according to whether the noun it is used with is masculine, feminine, singular or plural.

Possessive adjectives, several 'owners'

notre / nos	our
votre / vos	your
leur / leurs	their

masculine and feminine singular	masculine and feminine plural
notre, votre, leur	nos, vos, leurs

notre père	**our** father
notre mère	**our** mother
votre* père	**your** father
votre* mère	**your** mother
leur frère	**their** brother
leur sœur	**their** sister
nos parents	**our** parents
vos* copains	**your** friends
leurs profs	**their** teachers

* to several people **or** to someone you normally say *vous* to

Interrogative adjectives: quel, quelle, quels, quelles

Quel (meaning 'which' or 'what') agrees with the noun it refers to.

m singular	f singular	m plural	f plural
quel	quelle	quels	quelles

C'est **quel** cinéma?   **Which** cinema is it?
Quelle heure est-il?   **What** time is it?
Quelles sont tes matières préférées?
What are your favourite subjects?

4 Adverbs

Adverbs are used with a verb, an adjective or another adverb to express how, when, where or to what extent something happens.

Many French adverbs are formed by adding -ment (the equivalent of '-ly' in English) to the feminine form of the adjective.

m adjective	f adjective	adverb
final	finale	finalement – finally
heureux	heureuse	heureusement – fortunately
probable	probable	probablement – probably

Comparative adverbs

As with adjectives, you can make comparisons using *plus*, *moins* and *aussi … que*:

*Tu parles **plus** lentement **que** moi.*
You speak **more** slowly **than** me.

*Je mange **moins** vite **que** ma sœur.*
I eat **less** quickly than **my** sister.

*Elle joue **aussi** bien **que** Paul.*
She plays **as** well **as** Paul.

5 Pronouns

Subject pronouns: je, tu, il, elle, on, nous, vous, ils, elles

Subject pronouns usually come before the verb and express who or what performs the action.

singular	plural
je – I	nous – we
tu – you	vous – you
il – he / it	ils – they (m)
elle – she / it	elles – they (f)
on – we / you / they	

Je parle français.	**I** speak French.
Tu as quel âge?	How old are **you**?
Il s'appelle Théo.	**He** is called Théo.
Elle s'appelle Aïcha.	**She** is called Aïcha.
On se retrouve où?	Where shall **we** meet?
Nous habitons en ville.	**We** live in town.
Vous avez une chambre?	Do **you** have a room?
Ils s'appellent Do et Mi.	**They** are called Do and Mi.
Elles sont amusantes.	**They** are fun.

There are two French words for 'you': *tu* and *vous*.
- Use *tu* when talking to someone (one person) of your own age or someone in your family.
- Use *vous* when talking to an adult not in your family (e.g. your teacher). For example:
  Vous avez …   **You** have …
  Que voudriez-**vous** … ?   What would **you** like … ?
- Also use *vous* when talking to more than one person – whatever their age and whether you know them well or not.

Il and *elle* can both also mean 'it', depending on the gender of the noun they replace.

L'hôtel est bien?   Is the hotel good?
  Oui, **il** est très moderne.   Yes, **it** is very modern.
Je déteste ma chambre: I hate my bedroom: **it** is too
  elle est trop petite.   small.

On can mean 'we', 'you' or 'they', depending on the context:

On s'entend bien.   **We** get on well.
Comment dit-**on** «pencil»   How do **you** say 'pencil' in
  en français?   French?
On parle français au   **They** speak French in
  Canada.   Canada.

There are two French words for 'they': *ils* and *elles*.
- Use ils when all the people / things you are talking about are male, or it is a mixed group of males and females:
  J'ai un frère et une sœur; **ils** *s'appellent Nicolas et Aurélie.*
  I have a brother and a sister; **they** are called Nicolas and Aurélie.
- Use elles when all the people / things you are talking about are female:
  J'ai deux copines espagnoles; **elles** *habitent à Madrid.*
  I have two Spanish friends; **they** live in Madrid.

Direct object pronouns: me, te, vous, le, la

Direct object pronouns replace a noun that is not the subject of the verb.

me / m' – me
te / t' – you
vous – you (formal)
le / l' – him / it (m.)
la / l' – her / it (f.)

cent soixante-cinq **165**

Grammar

Direct object pronouns come in front of the verb, unlike in English:

> Je **le** prends. I'll take **it**.
> Je peux **vous** aider? Can I help **you**?

Le and la are shortened to l' in front of a vowel or a silent h:

> Mon petit frère a deux ans. Je **l'**adore! My little brother is two. I love **him**!

Indirect object pronouns: *me, te, vous, lui*

Indirect object pronouns are used to replace a noun that would be introduced with the preposition *à*.

| me / m' – (to) me |
| te / t' – (to) you |
| vous – (to) you (formal) |
| lui – (to) him / her / it |

Je donne du café à mon père.
Je lui donne du café.   I give him some coffee.

Je parle à ma mère.
Je lui parle.   I speak to her.

Reflexive pronouns: *me, te, se*

Reflexive pronouns are an extra pronoun used in front of a reflexive verb:

me	me je **me** réveille	I wake up
te	tu **te** lèves	you get up
se	il / elle **s'**appelle	he / she is called
	on **se** lave	we (have a) wash

Note that *me, te* and *se* are shortened to *m', t'* and *s'* in front of a vowel or a silent *h*.

Some common reflexive verbs that you will need to use reflexive pronouns with:

se changer	to get changed
se preparer	to get ready
s'appeler	to be called
se laver	to have a wash
se disputer	to argue
se lever	to get up
se coucher	to go to bed
se passer	to happen
se trouver	to be situated
se perdre	to get lost
s'excuser	to apologise
se relaxer	to relax

Emphatic pronouns: *moi, toi*

Emphatic pronouns are also called disjunctive pronouns. Use them:

- for emphasis:
  Moi, j'adore les fraises.   **I** love strawberries.
  Toi, tu as quel âge?   How old are **you**?

- after *c'est*:
  C'est **moi**.   It's **me**.

- after a preposition:
  avec **moi**   with **me**
  pour **toi**   for **you**

- after a comparative:
  Elle est plus sympa que **toi**.   She is nicer than **you**.

- with *à*, to express possession:
  Il est **à toi**, ce livre?   Does this book **belong to you**?

Relative pronouns: *qui*

Relative pronouns are used to link phrases together.

Use *qui* as the subject of the relative clause. It can refer to people and things, and means 'who', 'that' or 'which':

> le copain **qui** habite à Lyon   the friend **who** lives in Lyon
> le livre **qui** est sur la chaise   the book **that** is on the table
> J'ai trouvé un travail **qui** me va.   I have found a job **that** suits me.

Grammar

6 Verbs

French verbs have different endings depending on who is doing the action and whether the action takes place in the past, the present or the future. The verb tables on pages 174–179 set out the patterns of endings for several useful verbs.

When using a name or a singular noun, use the same form of the verb as for *il / elle*:

| *Martin **parle** espagnol.* | Martin **speaks** Spanish. |

When using two names or a plural noun, use the same form of the verb as for *ils / elles*:

| *Thomas et Lola **jouent** au basket.* | Thomas and Lola **are playing** basketball. |
| *Mes frères **écoutent** de la musique.* | My brothers **are listening** to music. |

The infinitive

The infinitive is the form of the verb you find in a dictionary, e.g. *jouer, finir, être*. It never changes.

- Modal verbs *vouloir, pouvoir* and *devoir* and the verb *savoir* are also followed by the infinitive:

*Tu veux **aller** au cinéma?*	Do you want **to go** to the cinema?
*On peut **faire** du shopping.*	You can **go** shopping.
*Je dois **faire** mes devoirs.*	I must **do** my homework.
*Je sais **conduire**.*	I know how to **drive**.

The infinitive is used after *avant de* to mean 'before doing something':

| *Je me lave les mains avant de **manger**.* | I wash my hands before **eating**. |

The present tense

Use the present tense to describe:

- something that is taking place now:
  J'écoute de la musique.   I **am listening** to music.
- something that happens regularly:
  J'ai maths le lundi.   I **have** maths on Mondays.

Present tense verb endings change depending on who is doing the action:

| *Je parle à ma mère.* | I **speak** to my mother. |
| *Nous lavons la voiture.* | We **wash** the car. |

You can also use the present tense with adverbs of time to talk about actions in the past or future:

| *Mon ami arrive **demain**.* | My friend **arrives tomorrow**. |

Most verbs follow a regular pattern.

Regular -er verbs

To form the present tense of *-er* verbs, remove the *-er* from the infinitive to form the stem, e.g. *parl-* from *parler*. Then add the endings shown below.

parler – to speak / to talk	
je parl**e**	nous parl**ons**
tu parl**es**	vous parl**ez**
il / elle / on parl**e**	ils / elles parl**ent**

Some other regular *-er* verbs:

adorer	to love	habiter	to live
aimer	to like	jouer	to play
détester	to hate	regarder	to watch
écouter	to listen	rester	to stay

Regular -ir verbs

To form the present tense of *-ir* verbs, remove the *-ir* from the infinitive to form the stem, e.g. *chois-* from *choisir*. Then add the endings shown below.

choisir – to choose	
je chois**is**	nous chois**issons**
tu chois**is**	vous chois**issez**
il / elle / on chois**it**	ils / elles chois**issent**

partir – to leave	
je par**s**	nous part**ons**
tu par**s**	vous part**ez**
il / elle / on par**t**	ils / elles part**ent**

venir – to come	
je vien**s**	nous venons
tu vien**s**	vous venez
il / elle / on vien**t**	ils / elles viennent

ouvrir – to open	
j'ouvr**e**	nous ouvr**ons**
tu ouvr**es**	vous ouvr**ez**
il / elle / on ouvr**e**	ils / elles ouvr**ent**

Grammar

Other regular -ir verbs:
- *choisir* — to choose
- *remplir* — to fill
- *réussir* — to succeed

Regular -re verbs

To form the present tense of -re verbs, remove the -re from the infinitive to form the stem, e.g. *attend-* from *attendre*. Then add the endings shown below.

attendre – to wait	
j'attend**s**	nous attend**ons**
tu attend**s**	vous attend**ez**
il / elle / on attend	ils / elles attend**ent**

Other regular -re verbs:
- *descendre* — to go down
- *répondre* — to reply
- *vendre* — to sell

Irregular verbs

Some verbs are irregular and do not follow these patterns. See pages 175–179 for details of the most common ones.

The perfect tense

Use the perfect tense to talk about what somebody did or has done.

*Il **a mangé** un sandwich.*
He **ate** a sandwich. / He **has eaten** a sandwich.

To make the perfect tense of most verbs, use the present tense of *avoir* + past participle:

parler – to speak / to talk	
j'ai parlé	nous avons parlé
tu as parlé	vous avez parlé
il / elle / on a parlé	ils / elles ont parlé

Some verbs use the present tense of *être* instead of *avoir*:

aller – to go	
je suis allé(e)	nous sommes allé(e)s
tu es allé(e)	vous êtes allé(e)(s)
il est allé	ils sont allés
elle est allée	elles sont allées
on est allé(e)(s)	

Verbs that use *être* to form the perfect tense include:

aller	to go
arriver	to arrive
descendre	to go down
entrer	to enter
monter	to go up
mourir	to die
naître	to be born
partir	to leave
rentrer	to come back
rester	to stay
retourner	to return / to go back
sortir	to go out
tomber	to fall
venir	to come

All reflexive verbs use *être* to form the perfect tense. Don't forget the extra pronoun that comes before the part of *être*:

se lever – to get up
je **me** suis levé(e)
tu **t'**es levé(e)
il **s'**est levé
elle **s'**est levée
on **s'**est levé(e)(s)

When using *être*:

- add *-e* to the past participle if the subject is female:
  *Elle est parti**e** en Écosse.*   She went off to Scotland.

- add *-s* to the past participle if the subject is masculine plural:
  *Ils sont arrivé**s** en retard.*   They arrived late.

- add *-es* to the past participle if the subject is feminine plural:
  *Elles sont arrivé**es** en retard.*   They arrived late.

When making a negative statement in the perfect tense, *ne* comes before *avoir / être* and *pas* comes after it:
*Je **n'**ai **pas** mangé.*   I haven't eaten.
*Elle **n'**est **pas** sortie.*   She didn't go out.

Grammar

Past participles

The past participle of *-er* verbs ends in *-é*:
- *aller – allé* — gone
- *donner – donné* — given
- *parler – parlé* — spoken

The past participle of regular *-ir* verbs ends in *-i*:
- *choisir – choisi* — chosen
- *finir – fini* — finished

The past participle of regular *-re* verbs ends in *-u*:
- *attendre – attendu* — waited
- *vendre – vendu* — sold

Many common verbs have an irregular past participle:
- *avoir – eu* — had
- *être – été* — been
- *faire – fait* — done / made

The imperfect tense

Use the imperfect tense:
- to say what was happening at a certain time in the past:
  Je regardais la télé quand il a téléphoné.
  I **was watching** TV when he rang.
- describe something that used to happen regularly in the past:
  Je faisais de la natation tous les matins.
  I **used to swim** every morning.

To form the imperfect tense, take the nous form of the verb in the present tense, remove *-ons* to form the stem, then add the correct endings:

finir – to finish (present tense: *nous finissons*)
je finiss**ais**
tu finiss**ais**
il / elle / on finiss**ait**

Perfect or imperfect?

To help you decide between the perfect and the imperfect, remember that:
- the perfect tense usually describes single events in the past:
  *Hier, je **me suis levée** à six heures.*
  Yesterday, I **got up** at six.
- the imperfect describes what used to happen:
  *Je **me levais** à huit heures.*
  I **used to get up** at eight.

The near future

Use the present tense of *aller* followed by an infinitive to say what you are going to do or what is going to happen:
- *je **vais danser*** — I am going to dance
- *nous **allons manger*** — we are going to eat
- *tu **vas partir*** — you are going to leave
- *vous **allez boire*** — you are going to drink
- *elle **va chanter*** — she is going to sing
- *ils **vont dormir*** — they are going to sleep

The imperative

Use the imperative to give advice or instructions. Use the *tu* form with a person your own age or a person you know very well:

- **Continue** *tout droit.* — **Go** straight on.
- **Prends** *la première rue.* — **Take** the first street.
- **Tourne** *à gauche.* — **Turn** left.
- **Fais** *vos devoirs!* — **Do** your homework!

Use the *vous* form with a person you don't know very well or to more than one person:

- **Continuez** *tout droit.* — **Go** straight on.
- **Prenez** *la première rue.* — **Take** the first street.
- **Tournez** *à gauche.* — **Turn** left.
- **Allez, Allez!** — **Go, go, go!**

The imperative is the same as the *tu* or the *vous* form of the present tense, but without using a word for 'you' first. In the case of *-er* verbs, you miss off the *-s* of the *tu* form:

- **Va** *au lit!* — **Go** to bed!
- **Achète** *des pommes.* — **Buy** some apples.

Note that all vous form imperatives end in *-ez* except for *faire*:

- **Faites** *vos devoirs!* — **Do** your homework!

cent soixante-neuf

Grammar

The conditional

The conditional is used in French where we say 'would' in English. It is useful for talking about what you would like or would do.

The conditional has the same stem as the future tense and the same endings as the imperfect:

vouloir – to want
je voudr**ais**
tu voudr**ais**
il / elle / on voudr**ait**

en + present participle

The English present participle ends in '-ing', and the French present participle ends in -ant. Take the nous form of the present tense, remove -ons and replace it with -ant:

arriver → arrivons → arrivant.

En + present participle can be used when two actions happen together:

Il fait ses devoirs **en chantant**.
He does his homework while singing.
En travaillant le soir, je gagne de l'argent.
By working in the evening, I earn money.

Useful verbs

avoir – to have

Some useful expressions with avoir:

avoir chaud	to be hot
avoir faim	to be hungry
avoir froid	to be cold
avoir mal	to hurt
avoir peur	to be afraid
avoir raison	to be right
avoir soif	to be thirsty
avoir tort	to be wrong

faire – to do

This verb is also used with il to talk about the weather:

Il **fait** beau. The weather is nice.
Il **fait** mauvais. The weather is bad.

Modal verbs: *devoir, pouvoir, vouloir, savoir*

Modal verbs are usually followed by an infinitive.

Use *devoir* (to have to) + infinitive to say what you must / mustn't do:

Je **dois porter** un uniforme.
I **have to wear** a uniform.
On **ne doit pas jeter** de papiers par terre.
You **mustn't drop** litter on the ground.

devoir – to have to	
je dois	nous devons
tu dois	vous devez
il / elle / on doit	ils / elles doivent

Use *pouvoir* (to be able to) + infinitive to say what you can / can't do:

On **peut faire** des promenades.
You **can go** hiking.
Elle **ne peut pas sortir** pendant la semaine.
She **can't go** out during the week.

pouvoir – to be able to	
je peux	nous pouvons
tu peux	vous pouvez
il / elle / on peut	ils / elles peuvent

Use *vouloir* (to want to) + infinitive to say what you want and don't want to do. Adding *bien* changes the meaning:

Je **veux partir**. I **want to leave**.
Je **veux bien partir**. I **am happy to leave**.

vouloir – to want	
je veux	nous voulons
tu veux	vous voulez
il / elle / on veut	ils / elles veulent

Use *savoir* (to know (how to), can) + infinitive to say what you know how to do.

Je **sais** parler anglais. I **can** speak English.
Elle **sait** jouer au foot. She **knows how** to play football.

savoir – to know	
je sais	nous savons
tu sais	vous savez
il / elle / on sait	ils / elles savent

Impersonal verbs: *il pleut, il faut, il y a*

This verb is only used with *il*:
Il pleut. **It**'s raining.

Il faut can be used with an infinitive to say what is is necessary or what must be done:
Il faut boire beaucoup d'eau.
You must drink a lot of water.
Il ne faut pas fumer.
You mustn't smoke.

Il est can be used for telling the time:
Il est huit heures. It is eight o'clock.

Il y a means there is or there are:
Il y a une banque. There is a bank.
Il y a beaucoup de cafés. There are lots of cafés.

Il y avait means there was, there were or there used to be:
Il y avait une banque. There was a bank.
Il y avait beaucoup de cafés. There were lots of cafés.

Il y aura means there is going to be, there are going to be or there will be:
Il y aura une banque. There is going to be a bank.
Il y aura beaucoup de cafés. There are going to be lots of cafés.

7 Negatives

To make a sentence negative, you normally put *ne* before the verb and *pas* after it:
Je parle espagnol.. → *Je ne parle pas espagnol.*
I don't speak Spanish.

Shorten *ne* to *n'* if the word that follows begins with *h* or a vowel:
C'est difficile.. → *Ce n'est pas difficile.*
It's **not** difficult.

In negative sentences, use *de* instead of *un, une* or *des*:
Il y a un cinéma. → *Il n'y a pas de cinéma.*
There is no cinema.
J'ai des frères. → *Je n'ai pas de frère.*
I don't have any brothers.

Other common negative phrases:
ne … jamais – never   *Je ne fume jamais.* I **never** smoke.
ne … rien – nothing / not anything   *Il ne fait rien.* He **doesn't** do **anything**.
ne … personne – not anybody   *Je ne vois personne.* I **don't** see **anybody**.

Negatives in the perfect tense

In most negative phrases in the perfect tense, the phrase goes around the part of *avoir* or *être*.
Je n'ai pas dormi. I **didn't** sleep.

Direct and indirect object pronouns are included within the negative phrase:
Je ne l'ai pas vu. I didn't see **it**.
Il ne me parle plus. He no longer speaks to **me**.

With reflexive verbs, the *ne* goes before the reflexive pronoun (*me*, *te*, etc.):
Il ne s'est pas lavé. He **didn't** have a wash.

8 Questions

You can turn statements into questions by adding a question mark and making your voice go up at the end:
Tu joues au tennis. → *Tu joues au tennis?*
Do you play tennis?

You can also add *est-ce que …* at the beginning of the question:
Je peux vous aider. → *Est-ce que je peux vous aider?*
Can I help you?

In more formal situations, you can change the word order so that the verb comes first:
Vous pouvez m'aider. → *Pouvez-vous m'aider?*
Can you help me?

In the perfect tense, the auxiliary verb comes first:
Vous avez aidé la dame. → *Avez-vous aidé la dame?*
Did you help the lady?

Many questions start with *qu'est-ce que …*
***Qu'est-ce que** c'est?* **What** is it?
***Qu'est-ce qu'**il y a à manger?* **What** is there to eat?
***Qu'est-ce que** vous avez comme journaux?*
What kind of newspapers do you have?

Grammar

Other question words

These can also be combined with *est-ce que*:

combien (de)	how much / how many	Tu as **combien de** chiens? **Combien de** chiens as-tu? **Combien de** chiens est-ce que tu as? **How many** dogs do you have?
comment	how	C'est arrivé **comment**? How did that happen? **Comment** vas-tu? **How** are you? **Comment** est-ce que je peux vous aider? **How** can I help you?
où	where	Tu habites **où**? **Où** habites-tu? **Où** est-ce que tu habites? **Where** do you live?
pourquoi	why	Tu n'aimes pas ça **pourquoi**? **Pourquoi** est-ce que tu n'aimes pas ça? **Pourquoi** n'aimes-tu pas ça? **Why** don't you like it?
quand	when	Il vient **quand**? **When** is he coming? **Quand** a-t-il commencé? **When** did he start? **Quand** est-ce que il arrive? **When** is he arriving?
que / qu'	what	Tu veux **quoi**? **Que** veux-tu? **Qu'**est-ce que tu veux? **What** do you want?
qui	who	C'est **qui**? **Who** is it? **Qui** est là? **Who** is there? **Qui** est-ce que tu vois? **Who** do you see?
quoi	what	Elle fait **quoi**? **What** is she doing? De **quoi** est-ce que tu parles? **What** are you talking about?

9 Prepositions

à, au, à la, à l', aux

À can mean:

in	J'habite **à** Nice.	I live **in** Nice.
at	Je me lève **à** sept heures.	I get up **at** seven.
to	Je vais **à** l'école.	I go **to** school.

To say 'at the' or 'to the', you need to pay attention to the gender of the noun that follows:

masculine	feminine	nouns which start with a vowel or silent *h*	plural
au (à + le)	à la	à l'	aux

    au théâtre   **at** / **to the** theatre
    à la piscine   **at** / **to the** pool
    à l'hôtel   **at** / **to the** hotel
    aux États-Unis   **in** / **to the** USA

de

De is shortened to *d'* before a vowel or a silent *h*.
De can mean 'of':
    la mère **de** ma copine (the mother of my friend)
    my friend**'s** mother

Note that the word order can be different from English:
    la maison **de** mes grands-parents
    my grandparent**s'** house

en, au, aux + countries

En is used to introduce most names of countries. It means both 'to' and 'in':
    Je vais **en** Allemagne.   I am going **to** Germany.
    Il habite **en** France.   He lives **in** France.
    Elle part **en** Angleterre.   She's going **to** England.

A few names of countries are masculine. These are introduced with *au* or *aux*:
    Il va **au** Portugal.   He's going **to** Portugal.
    Elle habite **au** pays de Galles.   She lives **in** Wales.
    Nous partons **aux** États-Unis.   We're going **to** the USA.

More prepositions

pour	for	C'est super pour les jeunes. It's great **for** young people.
sans	without	sans mes copains **without** my friends

Grammar

10 Ordinal Numbers

premier, deuxième, etc.

To write 'second', 'third', etc., simply add *-ième* to the original number:

deuxième	second
troisième	third

To write 'fifth', add a *u* before *-ième*:

cinquième	fifth

For 'ninth', change the *f* of *neuf* to a *v*:

neuvième	ninth

If the original number ends with an *-e*, drop the *-e* before adding *-ième*:

quatrième	fourth
onzième	eleventh

To revise how numbers are used in dates and telling the time, see the Useful language section, pages 10–11.

11 Morphology

Prefixes

You can reverse the meaning of some adjectives, adverbs and nous by adding *in-* or *im-* at the beginning of the word:

- *également* → *inégalement*
- *sécurité* → *insécurité*
- *possible* → *impossible*

Suffixes

Adjectives can sometimes be created by adding *-able* or *-eable* to a verb stem:

- *porter* → *portable*
- *changer* → *changeable*

Similarly, adverbs can sometimes created by dropping *-ant(e)* / *-ent(e)* from an adjective and adding *-amment* / *-emment*:

- *courant* → *couramment*
- *patient* → *patiemment*

Nouns can sometimes be created by adding *-ion* or *-ation* to a verb stem:

- *progresser* → *progression*
- *préparer* → *preparation*

Agent nouns (a noun describing a person or object doing a verb) can be created by adding *-eur* or *-ateur* to a verb stem:

- *porter* → *porteur*
- *consommer* → *consommateur*

Verb tables

Regular -er verbs

infinitive	present	perfect	imperfect
parler to speak	je parle tu parles il / elle / on parle nous parlons vous parlez ils / elles parlent	j'ai parlé tu as parlé il / elle / on a parlé nous avons parlé vous avez parlé ils / elles ont parlé	je parlais tu parlais il / elle / on parlait nous parlions* vous parliez* ils / elles parlaient*

Regular -ir verbs

infinitive	present	perfect	imperfect
choisir to choose	je choisis tu choisis il / elle / on choisit nous choisissons vous choisissez ils / elles choisissent	j'ai choisi tu as choisi il / elle / on a choisi nous avons choisi vous avez choisi ils / elles ont choisi	je choisissais tu choisissais il / elle / on choisissait nous choisissions* vous choisissiez* ils / elles choisissaient*

Regular -re verbs

infinitive	present	perfect	imperfect
entendre to hear	j'entends tu entends il / elle / on entend nous entendons vous entendez ils / elles entendent	j'ai entendu tu as entendu il / elle / on a entendu nous avons entendu vous avez entendu ils / elles ont entendu	j'entendais tu entendais il / elle / on entendait nous entendions* vous entendiez* ils / elles entendaient*

Reflexive verbs

infinitive	present	perfect	imperfect
se laver to (have a) wash	je me lave tu te laves il se lave elle se lave on se lave nous nous lavons vous vous lavez ils se lavent elles se lavent	je me suis lavé(e) tu t'es lavé(e) il s'est lavé elle s'est lavée on s'est lavé(e)(s) nous nous sommes lavé(e)s vous vous êtes lavé(e)(s) ils se sont lavés elles se sont lavées	je me lavais tu te lavais il se lavait elle se lavait on se lavait nous nous lavions vous vous laviez ils se lavaient elles se lavaient

Verb tables

infinitive	present	perfect	imperfect
aller to go	je vais tu vas il va elle va on va nous allons vous allez ils / elles vont	je suis allé(e) tu es allé(e) il est allé elle est allée on est allé(e)(s) nous sommes allé(e)s vous êtes allé(e)(s) ils /elles sont allés	j'allais* tu allais* il allait* elle allait* on allait* nous allions* vous alliez* ils / elles allaient*
avoir to have	j'ai tu as il / elle / on a nous avons vous avez ils / elles ont	j'ai eu tu as eu il / elle / on a eu nous avons eu vous avez eu ils / elles ont eu	j'avais tu avais il / elle / on avait nous avions* vous aviez* ils / elles avaient*
boire to drink	je bois tu bois il / elle / on boit nous buvons vous buvez ils / elles boivent	j'ai bu tu as bu il / elle / on a bu nous avons bu vous avez bu ils / elles ont bu	je buvais* tu buvais* il / elle / on buvait* nous buvions* vous buviez* ils / elles buvaient*
connaître to know	je connais tu connais il / elle / on connaît nous connaissons vous connaissez ils / elles connaissent	j'ai connu tu as connu il / elle / on a connu nous avons connu vous avez connu ils / elles ont connu	je connaissais* tu connaissais* il / elle / on connaissait* nous connaissions* vous connaissiez* ils / elles connaissaient*
courir to run	je cours tu cours il / elle / on court nous courons vous vous courez ils / elles courent	j'ai couru tu as couru il / elle / on a couru nous avons couru vous avez couru ils / elles ont couru	je courais* tu courais* il / elle / on courait* nous courions* vous couriez* ils / elles couraient*
croire to believe	je crois tu crois il / elle / on croit nous croyons vous croyez ils / elles croient	j'ai cru tu as cru il / elle / on a cru nous avons cru vous avez cru ils / elles ont cru	je croyais* tu croyais* il / elle / on croyait* nous croyions* vous croyiez* ils / elles croyaient*

*Higher Tier only

Verb tables

infinitive	present	perfect	imperfect
devoir to have to	je dois tu dois il / elle / on doit nous devons vous devez ils / elles doivent	j'ai dû tu as dû il / elle / on a dû nous avons dû vous avez dû ils / elles ont dû	je devais* tu devais* il / elle / on devait* nous devions* vous deviez* ils / elles devaient*
écrire to write	j'écris tu écris il / elle / on écrit nous écrivons vous écrivez ils / elles écrivent	j'ai écrit tu as écrit il / elle / on a écrit nous avons écrit vous avez écrit ils / elles ont écrit	j'écrivais* tu écrivais* il / elle / on écrivait* nous écrivions* vous écriviez* ils / elles écrivaient*
être to be	je suis tu es il / elle / on est nous sommes vous êtes ils / elles sont	j'ai été tu as été il / elle / on a été nous avons été vous avez été ils / elles ont été	j'étais tu étais il / elle / on était nous étions* vous étiez* ils / elles étaient*
faire to do / to make	je fais tu fais il / elle / on fait nous faisons vous faites ils / elles font	j'ai fait tu as fait il / elle / on a fait nous avons fait vous avez fait ils / elles ont fait	je faisais tu faisais il / elle / on faisait nous faisions* vous faisiez* ils / elles faisaient*
lire to read	je lis tu lis il / elle / on lit nous lisons vous lisez ils / elles lisent	j'ai lu tu as lu il / elle / on a lu nous avons lu vous avez lu ils / elles ont lu	je lisais* tu lisais* il / elle / on lisait* nous lisions* vous lisiez* ils / elles lisaient*
ouvrir to open	j'ouvre tu ouvres il / elle / on ouvre nous ouvrons vous ouvrez ils / elles ouvrent	j'ai ouvert tu as ouvert il / elle / on a ouvert nous avons ouvert vous avez ouvert ils / elles ont ouvert	j'ouvrais* tu ouvrais* il / elle / on ouvrait* nous ouvrions* vous ouvriez* ils / elles ouvraient*

Verb tables

infinitive	present	perfect	imperfect
partir to leave	je pars tu pars il part elle part on part nous partons vous partez ils / elles partent	je suis parti(e) tu es parti(e) il est parti elle est partie on est parti(e)(s) nous sommes parti(e)s vous êtes parti(e)(s) Ils /elles sont partis	je partais* tu partais* il partait* elle partait* on partait* nous partions* vous partiez* ils /elles partaient*
pouvoir to be able to	je peux tu peux il / elle / on peut nous pouvons vous pouvez ils / elles peuvent	j'ai pu tu as pu il / elle / on a pu nous avons pu vous avez pu ils / elles ont pu	je pouvais* tu pouvais* il / elle / on pouvait* nous pouvions* vous pouviez* ils / elles pouvaient*
prendre to take	je prends tu prends il / elle / on prend nous prenons vous prenez ils / elles prennent	j'ai pris tu as pris il / elle / on a pris nous avons pris vous avez pris ils / elles ont pris	je prenais* tu prenais* il / elle / on prenait* nous prenions* vous preniez* ils / elles prenaient*
recevoir to receive	je reçois tu reçois il / elle / on reçoit nous recevons vous recevez ils / elles reçoivent	j'ai reçu tu as reçu il / elle / on a reçu nous avons reçu vous avez reçu ils / elles ont reçu	je recevais* tu recevais* il / elle / on recevait* nous recevions* vous receviez* ils / elles recevaient*
rire to laugh	je ris tu ris il / elle / on rit nous rions vous riez ils / elles rient	j'ai ri tu as ri il / elle / on a ri nous avons ri vous avez ri ils / elles ont ri	je riais* tu riais* il / elle / on riait* nous riions* vous riiez* ils / elles riaient*
savoir to know	je sais tu sais il / elle / on sait nous savons vous savez ils / elles savent	j'ai su tu as su il / elle / on a su nous avons su vous avez su ils / elles ont su	je savais* tu savais* il / elle / on savait* nous savions* vous saviez* ils / elles savaient*

*Higher Tier only

Verb tables

infinitive	present	perfect	imperfect
sortir to go out	je sors tu sors il sort elle sort on sort nous sortons vous sortez ils / elles sortent	je suis sorti(e) tu es sorti(e) il est sorti elle est sortie on est sorti(e)(s) nous sommes sorti(e)s vous êtes sorti(e)(s) ils / elles sont sortis	je sortais* tu sortais* il sortait* elle sortait* on sortait* nous sortions* vous sortiez* ils / elles sortaient*
suivre to follow	je suis tu suis il / elle / on suit nous suivons vous suivez ils / elles suivent	j'ai suivi tu as suivi il / elle / on a suivi nous avons suivi vous avez suivi ils / elles ont suivi	je suivais* tu suivais* il / elle / on suivait* nous suivions* vous suiviez* ils / elles suivaient*
traduire to translate	je traduis tu traduis il / elle / on tu traduit nous traduisons vous traduisez ils / elles traduisent	j'ai traduit tu as traduit il / elle / on a traduit nous avons traduit vous avez traduit ils / elles ont traduit	je traduisais* tu traduisais* il / elle / on traduisait* nous traduisions* vous traduisiez* ils / elles traduisaient*
venir to come	je viens tu viens il vient elle vient on vient nous venons vous venez ils / elles viennent	je suis venu(e) tu es venu(e) il est venu elle est venue on est venu(e)(s) nous sommes venu(e)s vous êtes venu(e)(s) ils / elles sont venus	je venais* tu venais* il venait* elle venait* on venait* nous venions* vous veniez* ils / elles venaient*
vivre to live	je vis tu vis il / elle / on vit nous vivons vous vivez ils / elles vivent	j'ai vécu tu as vécu il / elle / on a vécu nous avons vécu vous avez vécu ils / elles ont vécu	je vivais* tu vivais* il / elle / on vivait* nous vivions* vous viviez* ils / elles vivaient*
voir to see	je vois tu vois il / elle / on voit nous voyons vous voyez ils / elles voient	j'ai vu tu as vu il / elle / on a vu nous avons vu vous avez vu ils / elles ont vu	je voyais* tu voyais* il / elle / on voyait* nous voyions* vous voyiez* ils / elles voyaient*

Verb tables

infinitive	present	perfect	imperfect
vouloir	je veux	j'ai voulu	je voulais*
to want	tu veux	tu as voulu	tu voulais*
	il / elle / on veut	il / elle / on a voulu	il / elle / on voulait*
	nous voulons	nous avons voulu	nous voulions*
	vous voulez	vous avez voulu	vous vouliez*
	ils / elles veulent	ils / elles ont voulu	ils / elles voulaient*

*Higher Tier only

Glossary

Words that are highlighted in grey in this list are words that may be useful, but you won't need to know them for the exam.

à at, to
à bientôt see you soon
à l'âge de at the age of
à l'avenir in the future
à l'étranger abroad
à la mode in fashion, fashionable
à l'avenir in the future
à pied on foot
acceptable acceptable
accepter to accept
accessible accessible
l' accident (m.) accident
accueillir to welcome
acheter to buy
l' acteur/actrice actor, actress
actif/active active
l' action (f.) action
l' activité (f.) activity
actuel(le) current
adopté(e) adopted
adorer to love
l' adresse (f.) address
l' adulte (m./f.) adult
l' âge (m.) age
âgé(e) old, older
agréable pleasant, nice
l' agronomie (f.) agronomy
l' aidant/aidante carer
Aïd-el-Fitr Eid al-Fitr
aider to help
aimer to like
aimer mieux to prefer
l' alcool (m.) alcohol
Alger Algiers
l' Algérie (f.) Algeria
l' allemand (n.) (m.) German (language)
aller to go
aller en vacances to go on holidays
alors so, well, then

les Alpes (f. pl.) Alps
améliorer to improve
américain(e) (adj.) American
l' Amérique (f.) America
l' ami(e) (m./f.) friend
l' amoureux/amoureuse lover
amusant(e) amusing, fun, funny, enjoyable
amuser to entertain
l' an (m.) year
l' anglais (n.) (m.) English (language)
anglais(e) (adj.) English
animal (adj.) from, of animals
l'/les animal/animaux (m. pl.) animal(s)
l' année (f.) year
l' année dernière (f.) last year
l' anniversaire (m.) birthday
août August
l' appartement (m.) flat
s' appeler to be called
appeler to call
l' appli (f.) app
apporter to bring
apprendre to learn, to teach
l' apprentissage (m.) apprenticeship
après after
l' après-midi (m.) afternoon
l' arbre (m.) tree
l' arène (f.) arena
l' argent (m.) money
arrêter (de) to stop
arriver to arrive
arriver à to manage
l' article (m.) article
l' artiste (m./f.) artist
assez (de) quite, enough
l' athlète (m./f.) athlete
l' athlétisme (m.) athletics
attendre to wait
Attention! Watch out!
au at the, to the
au bord de la mer by the sea

au chômage unemployed
au marché at the market
au musée at the museum
au restaurant at, in a restaurant
au revoir goodbye
au(x) to the
augmenter to increase
aujourd'hui today
aussi also
aussi … que as … as
l' auteur/autrice author
l' automne (m.) autumn
autre other
autre (adj.) other
autre chose anything else
les autres (m./f. pl.) others
avant (de) before
l' avantage (m.) advantage
avec with
l' avion (m.) plane
l' avis (m.) opinion
avoir to have
avoir faim to be hungry
avoir le mal de mer to be sea sick
avoir le temps to have time
avoir lieu to take place
avoir mal to hurt
avoir peur to be scared
avril April
le bain bath
le barbecue barbecue, BBQ
le basket basketball
le bateau boat
le bâtiment building
bavard(e) chatty
beau/belle beautiful, handsome
beaucoup (de) a lot (of), lots of
beaucoup à faire a lot to do
le beau-père stepfather, father-in-law
la Belgique Belgium
la belle-mère stepmother, mother-in-law

Glossary

le/la	bénévole	volunteer
le	beurre persillé à l'ail	parsley and garlic butter
la	bibliothèque	library
	bien	good, well
	bien fait(e)	well done
	bien sûr	of course
	bientôt	soon
le	billet	ticket
	blanc	white
	bleu(e)	blue
le	blog	blog
	boire	to drink
la	boisson	drink
	bon(ne)	good
	bonjour	good morning, afternoon
	bonne chance	good luck
le	bord	edge
la	bouche	mouth
le	bras	arm
	britannique	British
le	brouillard	fog
	brun(e)	brown
le	bureau	desk, office
le	bus	bus
le	but	goal
	c'est	it is
	ça	it, that
le	cadeau	present
le	café	coffee, coffee shop
la	caisse	checkout
le	calcium	calcium
	calme (adj.)	calm, quiet
le	Cameroun	Cameroon
la	campagne	countryside
le	camping	camping, campsite
le	Canada	Canada
	canadien(ne)	Canadian
la	capitale	capital city
	car	because
les	Caraïbes (f. pl.)	Caribbean
la	carrière	career
la	carte	card/map
la	catastrophe	catastrophe
	ce/cet/cette/ces	this, these

	cela	that, it
la	célébration	celebration
	célèbre	famous
	célébrer	to celebrate
la	célébrité	celebrity
le	centre	centre
le	centre commercial	shopping centre
le	centre-ville	city centre
	cependant	however
	certain(e)(s)	some, certain
	c'est	it is
la	chambre	bedroom
le/la	champion(ne)	champion
la	chance	luck, opportunity
	changeable	changeable
	changer	to change
la	chanson	song
	chanter	to sing
le/la	chanteur/chanteuse	singer
	chaque	each, every
le	château	castle
	chatter	to chat
	chaud(e)	hot, warm
le/la	chef (de cuisine)	chef
le/la	chef/cheffe	chef, boss
	cher/chère	expensive
	chercher	to research, to look for
les	cheveux (m. pl.)	hair
	chez	at someone's place/house
	chez moi	at my place, at mine
	chez nous	at/to our place
le	chien	dog
le	chocolat	chocolate
le	chocolatier	chocolatier
	choisir	to choose
le	choix	choice
le	chômage	unemployment
la	chose	thing
	chrétien(ne) (adj.)	Christian
la	cigarette	cigarette
le	cinéma	cinema
	cinq	five
la	cinquième	fifth, Year 8
la	citadelle	citadel
	clair(e)	clear

la	classe	class, classroom, year group
	classé(e)	classified
	classique (adj.)	classical
la	clé	key
le	climat	climate
le	cola	coke
la	collecte	collection
le	collège	(secondary) school
	combien	how many
la	comédie	comedy
	comme	such as, like, since
	commencer	to start
	comment	how
	commercial(e) (adj.)	commercial
la	communication	communication
	communiquer	to communicate
la	compétence	skill
la	compétition	competition
	complet/complète	complete
	complètement	completely
	complexe	complex
	comprendre	to understand
le	concert	concert
le	concours	competition
	confortable	comfortable
	connaître	to know (person, place)
	connu(e)	famous, known
le	conseil	a piece of advice
la	conséquence	consequence, result
la	construction	construction
	content(e)	glad, pleased, happy
le	contenu	content
le	continent	continent
	continuer	to continue
	cool	cool
le	copain	friend, boyfriend
la	copine	friend, girlfriend
le	corps	body
la	Corse	Corsica
la	côte	coast
la	Côte d'Ivoire	Ivory Coast
se	couche	to go to bed
la	couleur	colour

Glossary

	couper to cut
le	couple couple
	couramment fluently
	courir to run
le	courrier post
le	cours lesson
les	courses (f. pl.) (grocery) shopping
	court(e) short
le/la	cousin(e) cousin
	coûter to cost
	créatif/créative creative
la	création creation
la	créativité creativity
	créer to create
	croire (que) to believe (that)
la	cuisine kitchen, cooking
	cultivable arable
la	culture culture
	culturel(le) cultural
le	cyclisme cycling
	d'abord first of all
	d'accord ok, agreed
	d'habitude usually
	d'abord first of all
la	dame lady
le	danger danger
	dangereux/dangereuse dangerous
	dans in
	dans la nature in nature
la	danse dancing
	danser to dance
le/la	danseur/danseuse dancer
la	date date
	de of, from
	de plus in addition, besides, moreover
	de plus en plus more and more
	de temps en temps from time to time
	décembre December
	décider de to decide
la	décision decision
	découvrir to discover
le	défi challenge
le	défilé parade

	dehors outside
	déjà already
le	déjeuner lunch
	délicieux/délicieuse delicious
	demain tomorrow
	demander to ask
le	demi-frère half-brother
la	demi-sœur half-sister
	démocratique democratic
la	dépendance addiction
	dernier/dernière last
se	dérouler to take place
	descendre to go down, descend, get off
la	détermination determination
	détester to hate
	deux two
	devant in front of
	développer to develop
	devenir to become
	devoir to have to, must
les	devoirs (m. pl.) homework
	différent(e) (de) different (from)
	difficile difficult
(le)	dimanche Sunday
	diminuer to decrease
le	dîner dinner
	dîner (v.) to have dinner
	dire say, tell
le/la	directeur/directrice (company) director, headteacher
	discuter to discuss, talk
	disponible available
se	disputer to argue
	distribuer to distribute
la	diversité diversity
	divorcé(e) divorced
	dix ten
	donc so
	donner to give
la	Dordogne Dordogne
	dormir to sleep
le	dos back
	double double
la	douche shower
	douze twelve

la	drogue drug
le	droit right
	drôle funny
	du/de la/des/de l' some, of the
	du tout at all
	dur(e) hard
	durer to last
l'	eau (f.) water
l'	école (f.) school
	écouter to listen (to)
	écrire to write
l'	écrivain(e) (m./f.) writer
l'	éducation (f.) education
l'	effort (m.) effort
l'	église (f.) church
l'	élève (m./f.) pupil, student
	elle she
	elles they (female)
l'	e-mail (m.) e-mail
	embêtant(e) annoying
l'	émission (f.) TV programme
	en in, by, to
	en bonne santé in good health
	en ce moment at the moment
	en été in summer
	en fait in fact, in reality
	en famille as a family
	en général in general
	en hiver in winter
	en ligne online
	en plus in addition
	en premier first of all, firstly
	en retard late
	en streaming streamed
	en Suisse in/to Switzerland
	en vacances on holiday
	encore again, still, yet
	encourager to encourage
l'	endroit (m.) place
l'	énergie (f.) energy
l'	enfant (m./f.) child
	enfin finally
	ennuyeux/ennuyeuse boring
	énormément hugely
	enregistrer to record
	ensemble together

Glossary

ensuite then
entendre to hear
s' entendre avec to get on with
entre between
l' entrée (f.) entrance
entrer (dans) to go into
l' entretien (m.) interview
environ about, thereabouts
l' environnement (m.) environment
envoyer to send
équilibré(e) balanced
l' équipe (f.) team
l' équitation (f.) horse riding
l' escalade en salle (f.) climbing (on a climbing wall)
l' escargot (m.) snail
l' espace (m.) space
l' Espagne (f.) Spain
l' espagnol (n.) (m.) Spanish (language)
espagnol(e) (adj.) Spanish
espérer (que) to hope (that)
essayer to try
et and
l' étage (m.) floor
les États-Unis (m. pl.) United States
l' été (m.) summer
être to be
être situé(e) to be situated
l' étude (f.) study
étudier to study
l' euro (m.) euro
l' Europe (f.) Europe
européen(ne) European
l' événement (m.) event
éviter (de) to avoid
examiner to examine
excellent(e) excellent
s' excuser to apologise
l' exemple (m.) example
l' exercice (m.) exercise
l' expérience (f.) experience
l' expert(e) (m./f.) expert
expliquer to explain
exprimer to express

extraordinaire extraordinary
fabriquer to make
facile easy
facilement easily
la façon way, manner
le/la facteur/factrice postman/postwoman
la faim hunger
faire to do, to make
faire attention (à) to be careful (of), to pay attention (to)
faire beau to be nice (weather)
faire chaud to be hot
faire de la natation to go swimming
faire des progrès to make progress
faire des promenades to go for walks
faire du camping to go camping
faire du recyclage to do recycling, to recycle
faire du shopping to go shopping
faire du vélo to go cycling
faire froid to be cold
faire la fête to party, celebrate
faire les courses to go (grocery) shopping
faire les magasins to go shopping
faire mauvais to be bad (weather)
faire mes devoirs to do my homework
faire un gâteau to bake, make a cake
faire une différence to make a difference
faire une promenade to go for a walk
familial(e) (adj.) family
la famille family
le fan fan
fantastique fantastic
la farine flour
le fast-food fast food
fatigué(e) tired
la femme woman, wife

la femme politique politician (female)
la ferme farm
le festival festival
la fête party, celebration
le feu d'artifice firework display
février February
fier/fière proud
la fille girl, daughter
le film film
le film d'action action film
le fils son
la fin end
finir to finish
la fleur flower
la flûte flute
… fois par … … time(s) per …
la fois time, occasion
le foot(ball) football
le/la footballeur/footballeuse footballer
la forêt forest, wood
fort(e) strong
frais/fraîche fresh
le français (n.) French (language)
français(e) (adj.) French
la France France
francophone French-language
le frère brother
le frigo fridge
les frites (f. pl.) chips
froid(e) cold
le fromage cheese
la frontière border
le fruit fruit
fumer to smoke
le futur future
le/la gagnant(e) winner
gagner to win, earn
la gare train station
le gâteau cake
gauche left
généralement generally
la génération generation
génial(e) great, super
les gens (m. pl.) people

cent quatre-vingt-trois 183

Glossary

	gentil(le)	kind
la	géographie	geography
la	girafe	giraffe
la	glace	ice, ice cream
la	gorge	throat
le	goût	taste
le	gouvernement	government
	grand(e)	big, large, tall
	grandir	to grow (up)
la	grand-mère	grandmother
la	grand-mère	grandma
les	grand-parents (m. pl.)	grandparents
le	grand-père	grandfather
les	grands	grown-ups
les	grands-parents (m. pl.)	grandparents
	gratuit(e)	free
	grave	serious
la	grève	strike
le	groupe	group, band
la	guitare	guitar
	habiter	to live
l'	habitude (f.)	habit
le	hamburger	hamburger
	handicapé(e) (adj.)	disabled
	Hanouka	Hanukkah
	haut	high
l'	héliciculteur / hélicicultrice	snail farmer
l'	héroïne	(female) hero
le	héros	(male) hero
l'	heure (f.)	hour, time, o'clock
	heureux / heureuse	happy
	hier	yesterday
le	hip-hop	hip-hop
l'	histoire (f.)	history, story
	historique	historical
l'	hiver (m.)	winter
le	hockey sur glace	ice hockey
l'	homme politique	politician (male)
l'	hôpital (m.)	hospital
l'	hôtel (m.)	hotel
l'	humoriste (m./f.)	humorist, comedian
l'	humour (m.)	humour
	ici	here
	idéal(e)	ideal
l'	idée (f.)	idea
	il	he
	il faisait beau	it was nice weather
	il faisait froid	it was cold
	il faisait mauvais	it was bad weather
	il fait beau	it is fine weather
	il fait chaud	it is hot
	il fait froid	it is cold
	il fait mauvais	it is bad weather
	il faut (falloir)	it is necessary, must
	il n'y a pas de	there is, are no
	il pleut	it is raining
	il y a	there is / are
	il y a du brouillard	it is foggy
	il y a du soleil	it is sunny
	il y a du vent	it is windy
	il y avait	there was, there were
	il y avait du vent	it was windy
l'	île (f.)	island
	ils	they (male)
	immédiatement	immediately
	immense	huge
	important(e)	important
	impossible	impossible
	inaccessible	inaccessible
l'	inactivité (f.)	inactivity
	incomplet / incomplète	incomplete
l'	indépendance (f.)	independence
	indépendant(e)	independent
	indifférent(e)	indifferent
l'	influence (f.)	influence
l'	influence (f.)	influence
	influencer	to influence
l'	influenceur / influenceuse (m./f.)	influencer
	informatif	informative
l'	information (f.)	information
l'	informatique (f.)	IT, computer science
l'	Ingénieur(e) agronome	agronomist
	injuste	unfair
	inquiet / inquiète	worried
	inquiétant(e)	worrying
	intelligent(e)	intelligent
	intéressant(e)	interesting
	intéresser	to interest
s'	intéresser à	to be interested in
	international(e) / internationaux	international
	Internet (m.)	internet
l'	invitation (f.)	invitation
	inviter	to invite
	jamais	never
la	jambe	leg
le	jambon	ham
	janvier	January
le	jardin	garden
le	jazz	jazz
	je voudrais (vouloir)	I would like
	je / j'	I
	jeter	to throw away
le	jeu	game
le	jeu de société	board game
le	jeu vidéo	video game
(le)	jeudi	Thursday
	jeune	young
	jeune (adj.)	young
le/la	jeune (n.)	young person
le/la	jeune (n.)	young person
	joli(e)	pretty
	jouer	to play
	jouer	to play
le/la	joueur / joueuse	player
le	jour	day
le	jour de l'An	New Year's Day
le	jour férié	public holiday
le/les	journal / journaux (m. pl.)	newspaper(s)
la	journée	day
le	judo	judo
	juif / juive (adj.)	Jewish
	juillet	July
	jusque	until
le	kilomètre	kilometre

Glossary

	là there	
	là-bas over there	
le	laboratoire laboratory	
le	lac lake	
le	lait milk	
la	langue language	
se	laver to wash (yourself)	
	le/la/l'/les the	
la	lecture reading	
le	légume vegetable	
	lentement slowly	
la	lettre letter	
	leur(s) their	
	lever to raise	
se	lever to get up	
	libre free	
le	lieu place	
	lire to read	
le	lit bed	
le	livre book	
	local(e)(s)/locaux local	
le	logement accommodation	
	loin far	
	Londres London	
	long(ue) long	
	lui (to) him, (to) her	
la	lumière light	
(le)	lundi Monday	
la	lutte wrestling	
le	lycée school, 6th form	
	ma sœur my sister	
la	machine machine, equipment	
	madame Mrs, Ms	
le	magasin shop	
le	magazine magazine	
	mai May	
	maintenant now	
	mais but	
la	maison house	
le	mal ache	
	malade ill, sick	
	malgré despite	
	malheureusement unfortunately	
	mangeable edible	
	manger to eat	

la	manifestation demonstration, event	
le	manque (de) lack (of)	
le	marché market	
	marcher to walk	
(le)	mardi Tuesday	
le	mari husband	
le	mariage marriage	
se	marier to get married	
le	Maroc Morocco	
	mars March	
le	match match	
les	maths (f. pl.) maths	
la	matière subject	
le	matin morning	
	mauvais pour l'environnement (m.) bad for the environment	
	mauvais(e) bad	
le/la	mécanicien(ne) mechanic	
	méchant(e) naughty, nasty	
la	médaille medal	
le	médecin doctor	
la	médecine medicine (field, profession)	
le	médicament medication	
	médiéval(e) medieval	
la	Méditerranée the Mediterranean	
	meilleur(e) best, better	
le/la	meilleur(e) ami(e) best friend	
	meilleur(e) que better than	
le/la/les	meilleur(e)(s) best	
le	membre member	
	même same	
	même si even if	
	menacer to threaten	
la	mer sea	
la	mer Méditerranée Mediterranean sea	
	merci thank you	
(le)	mercredi Wednesday	
la	mère mother	
le	message message	
le	métier job	
le	métro underground (train)	
	mettre to put (on)	
le	midi midday	

	militaire (adj.) military	
les	milliers (m. pl.) thousands	
le	million million	
	minuit midnight	
la	mise en scène set design	
la	mission mission	
la	mode fashion	
la	mode de vie way of life, lifestyle	
	moderne modern	
	moi me	
	moins (de) less (of), fewer (of)	
	moins … que less than	
le	mois month	
	mon/ma/mes my	
la	monarchie monarchy	
le	monde world	
	mondial(e) global, universal, international	
la	montagne mountain(s)	
	monter to go up	
	montrer to show	
la	mosquée mosque	
	mourir to die	
le	moyen de vivre way of living	
le	musée museum	
	musical(e) (adj.) musical	
le/la	musicien(ne) musician	
la	musique music	
	musulman(e) (adj.) Muslim	
	naître to be born	
la	natation swimming	
	national(e)(s)/nationaux national	
la	nature nature	
	naturel(le) natural	
	ne … jamais never	
	ne … pas not	
	né(e) born	
la	neige snow	
	neuf/neuve new	
le	nez nose	
le	niveau level	
	Noël Christmas	
	noir(e) black	
le	nombre number	
	non not, no	

cent quatre-vingt-cinq

Glossary

	non-binaire	non-binary
	non seulement	not only
le	nord	North
	normal	normal
	normalement	normally
la	note	grade, mark
	notre/nos	our
la	nourriture	food
	nous	we
	nouveau/nouvelle (adj.)	new
la	Nouvelle-Calédonie	New Caledonia
	novembre	November
(le)	nucléaire	nuclear
la	nuit	night
	nul(le)	rubbish
l'	occasion (f.)	occasion, chance, opportunity
l'	océan Atlantique (m.)	Atlantic ocean
l'	océan Indien (m.)	Indian ocean
l'	océan Pacifique (m.)	Pacific ocean
	octobre	October
l'	offre (f.)	offer
	on	we, one
l'	oncle (m.)	uncle
	onze	eleven
l'	opinion (f.)	opinion
l'	or (m.)	gold
l'	ordinateur (m.)	computer
l'	ordinateur portable (m.)	laptop
l'	oreille (f.)	ear
l'	organisation (f.)	organisation
l'	organisation caritative	charity
	organisé(e)	organised
	organiser	to organise
	ou	or
	où	where
	oublier	to forget
	oui	yes
l'	outil (m.)	tool
	ouvert(e)	open
	ouvrir	to open
l'	oxygène (m.)	oxygen
le	pain	bread
le	pantalon	trousers
le	papier	paper
	Pâques	Easter
le	paquet	parcel
	par	by
	par contre	on the other hand
	par exemple	for example
le	parc	park
le	parc national	national park
le	parc naturel	natural park
	parce que	because
le/les	parent(s) (m. pl.)	parents
	paresseux/paresseuse	lazy
	parfait(e)	perfect
	parfois	sometimes
le	parfum	perfume, scent
	Paris	Paris
	parler (de)	to speak, to talk (about)
les	paroles	words, lyrics
	partager	to share
le/la	partenaire	partner
le/la	participant(e)	participant
la	participation	contribution
	participer (à)	to participate, take part (in)
la	partie	part, round of (game)
la	partie (de foot)	(football) match, game
	partir	to leave
	partout	everywhere
	pas cher	cheap
le	passé	past
	passer	to spend (time), to pass
se	passer	to happen, go (well/badly)
le	passe-temps	pastime
la	passion	passion
	passionnant(e)	exciting
la	patience	patience
	patient(e) (adj.)	patient
le	patrimoine mondial	worldwide heritage
	payé(e)	paid
	payer	to pay
le	pays	country
	pendant	during
	pendant les vacances	during the holiday
	penser (de/que)	to think (of/that)
	perdre	to lose
le	père	father
le	personnage	character
la	personnalité	personality
	personne	nobody
la/les	personne(s)	person/people
	personnel	personal
le	petit copain	boyfriend
	petit(e)	small, little, short
le	petit-déjeuner	breakfast
la	petite copine	girlfriend
les	petits	children
	peut-être	maybe
la	photo	photo
la	photographie	photography
le/la	physicien(ne)	physicist
la	pièce	room
la	pièce (de théâtre)	play (theatre)
le	pied	foot
	pire que	worse than
la	piscine	swimming pool
la	place	place, square, spot
la	plage	beach
la	planète	planet
la	plantation de cacao	cocoa farm
	planter	to plant
le	plastique	plastic
	plein(e)	full
	pleuvoir	to rain
	plus (de)	more (of)
	plus … que	more than
	plusieurs	several
le	podcast	podcast
le	poisson	fish
le	poisson-frites	fish and chips
le/la	policier/policière	policeman/policewoman
la	politique	politics
	polluer	to pollute
la	pollution	pollution
le	popcorn	popcorn
	populaire	popular

Glossary

le	port	port
le	portable	mobile phone
	porter	to wear, to carry
	poser	to ask
	positif/positive	positive
	possible	possible
	poster	to post
la	poubelle	bin
	pour	for, in order to
	pour les vacances	for the holidays
	pourquoi	why
	pouvoir	to be able to
	pratique	practical
	préférable	preferable
	préféré(e)	favourite
	préférer	to prefer
(le/la)	premier/première	first
la	première	first, Year 12
	prendre	to take
	prendre un bain	to take a bath
le	prénom	first name
	préparer	to prepare
	près de	near
	présent(e) (adj.)	present
le/la	président/présidente	president
	presque	almost
	prêt(e)	ready
	principal(e)	main
le	printemps	spring
le	prix	prize, price
le	problème	problem
	prochain(e)	next
le	produit	product
le	produit ménager	household product
le	professeur/professeure, prof	teacher
le	programme	schedule
le	progrès	progress
	progresser	to progress
la	promenade	walk, stroll
	promouvoir	to promote
la	proposition	proposition
	propre	clean, own
	protéger	to protect
le	public	audience
	puis	then
les	Pyrénées (f. pl.)	Pyrenees
la	qualité	quality
	quand	when
le	quartier	neighbourhood
	quatorzième	fourteenth
la	quatrième	fourth, Year 9
	que	that
le	Québec	Quebec
	quel(le)	what, which
	quelque	some
	quelque chose	something
	quelque(s)	a few, some, several
	quelqu'un	someone
	qu'est-ce que	what
la	question	question
	qui	who, which
	quitter	to leave
	quoi	what
	quotidien(ne)	daily
	raconter	to tell
la	radio	radio
la	raison	reason
	ramasser	to collect
	rapide	fast
	rapidement	quickly
le/la	rappeur/rappeuse	rapper
	rarement	rarely
	réaliser	to make (a film)
	récemment	recently
la	recette	recipe
	recevoir	to receive
le	réchauffement	warming
le	réchauffement du climat	global warming
la	recherche	research
	rechercher	to search (for)
les	recherches (f. pl.)	research
	recommander	to recommend
la	récréation	breaktime
le	recyclage	recycling
	recycler	to recycle
	réduire	to reduce
	regarder	to look, to watch
la	région	region
la	règle	rule, ruler
se	relaxer	to relax
la	religion	religion
	remplir	to fill up
la	rencontre	meeting
	rencontrer	to meet
le	rendez-vous	rendez-vous, appointment
	rentrer	to go back, to go home
le	repas	meal
	répondre	to answer
	répondre	to answer
la	réponse	answer
	représenter	to represent
la	reproduction	reproduction
	République démocratique du Congo	Democratic Republic of the Congo
le	réseau	network
les	réseaux sociaux (m. pl.)	social networks/media
	réserver	to book
le	respect	respect
	ressembler	to look like
la	ressource	resource
le	restaurant	restaurant
	rester	to stay
	retourner	to go back, to return
la	Réunion	Reunion (island)
	réunir	to gather
	réussir	to succeed
le	rêve	dream
	rêver	to dream
	riche	rich
	rien	nothing
	rien à faire	nothing to do
	rire	to laugh
le	riz	rice
le	rôle	role, part
le	roman	novel
	romantique	romantic
	rouge	red
la	Roumanie	Romania
la	route	road
la	rue	street
le	sac	bag
	sain(e)	healthy

cent quatre-vingt-sept

Glossary

le	salaire	salary
la	salle	room
la	salle à manger	dining room
la	salle de bains	bathroom
le	salon	lounge, living room
	salut	hi, hello
(le)	samedi	Saturday
la	sandwicherie	sandwich bar
	sans	without
la	santé	health
	savoir	to know
le	savon	soap
les	sciences (f. pl.)	sciences
le/la	scientifique	scientist
	scientifique (adj.)	scientific
la	sculpture	sculpture
la	seconde	second, Year 11
la	sécurité	safety, security
	selon	according to
la	semaine	week
le	Sénégal	Senegal
	sénégalais(e) (adj.)	Senegalese
se	séparer	to split up, separate
	séparé	separated
	septembre	September
	sérieux/sérieuse	serious
le/la	serveur/serveuse	waiter/waitress
le	service militaire	military service
	seul(e)	alone
le/la	seul(e) …	the only …
	seulement	only
	si	if
le	siècle	century
le	site	(tourist) site
le	site web	website
les	sites historiques (m. pl.)	historical sites
la	situation	situation
	situer	to situate, to locate
la	sixième	sixth, Year 7
le	smartphone	smartphone
le	SMS	text message
	social	social
la	société	society
la	sœur	sister
la	soif	thirst
le	soir	evening
la	soirée	evening
le	soleil	sun
la	solution	solution
	son/sa/ses	his/her
	sorte	sort, kind
	sortir	to go out
le	souci	worry
la	soupe	soup
	sourire	to smile
le	souvenir	souvenir
se	souvenir (de)	to remember
	souvent	often
	spécial(e)	special
le	spectacle	show
le	sport	sport
	sportif/sportive	sporty, athletic
le/la	sportif, sportive (n.)	sportsman/sportswoman
le	stade	stadium
la	star	star, celebrity
la	station	station
	strict(e)	strict
le	studio	studio
le	style	style
le	stylo	pen
le	succès	success
le	sud	south
le	sud-ouest	South-West
la	Suisse	Switzerland
	suivre	to follow
	super	great, super
	sur	on (top of)
	sûr(e)	safe, secure
le	surf	surf, surfing
la	surprise	surprise
	surtout	especially
le	symbole	symbol
	sympa	nice
la	synagogue	synagogue
la	table	table
la	tablette	tablet (computer)
la	tante	aunt
	tard	late
	tchatter	to chat
	te/t'	(to) you
les	techniques agricoles (f. pl.)	agricultural techniques
la	technologie	technology
le	tee-shirt	T-shirt
la	télé(vision)	TV, television
	télécharger	to download
le	téléphone	phone
la	télé-réalité	reality TV
le	temps	time, weather
le	tennis de table	table tennis
la	terminale	last, Year 13
la	terre	earth, soil
la	Terre	Earth
	terrible	terrible
la	tête	head
le	thé	tea
le	théâtre	drama, theatre
le	thème	theme
	timide	timid, shy
	toi	you (singular)
les	toilettes (f. pl.)	toilet
	tolérant(e)	tolerant
	tomber	to fall
	tomber amoureux/amoureuse	to fall in love
	ton/ta/tes	your (singular)
	tôt	early
	toujours	always
la	tour	tower
le	Tour de France	Tour de France
	tous	all, every
	tous les jours	every day
	tout	all
	tout d'abord	first of all
	tout le monde	everyone
	tout le temps	all the time
	tout(e)(s)	all, every
la	tradition	tradition
	traditionnel(le)	traditional
le	train	train
	transgenre	transgender
le	transport	transport
le	transport public	public transport
le	travail	work

Glossary

	travailler	to work
	travailleur/travailleuse	hard-working
	traverser	to cross
	très	very
	très bien	very well
	triste	sad
	trois	three
la	*troisième*	third, Year 10
	trop (de)	too much, many (of)
la	*trottinette*	scooter
	trouver	to find
le	*t-shirt*	t-shirt
	tu	you (singular)
	tuer	to kill
l'	*ultra-marathon (m.)*	ultramarathon
	un peu	a little
	un(e)	a
l'	*uniforme (m.)*	uniform
l'	*univers (m.)*	universe
l'	*université (f.)*	university
l'	*urgence (f.)*	emergency
l'	*usine (f.)*	factory
	utiliser	to use
les	*vacances (f. pl.)*	holidays
	vapoter	to vape
	variable	varied
	végan(e)	vegan
le	*véganisme*	veganism
	végétarien(ne)	vegetarian
le	*végétarisme*	vegetarianism
le	*vélo*	bike
	vendre	to sell
(le)	*vendredi*	Friday
	venir (de)	to come (from)
le	*vent*	wind
	vers	towards
	vert(e)	green, eco-friendly
les	*vêtements (m. pl.)*	clothes
la	*viande*	meat
la	*vidéo*	video
la	*vie*	life
la	*vie quotidienne*	daily life
le	*Vietnam*	Vietnam
	vieux/vieil/vieille	old
	vif/vive	bright, vivid
le	*village*	village
la	*ville*	town, city
le	*vin*	wine
le	*vin chaud*	mulled wine
la	*visite*	visit
	visiter	to visit (place)
le	*visiteur*	visitor
	vite	quick
	vivre	to live
	voici	here is
	voir	to see
le/la	*voisin(e)*	neighbour
la	*voiture*	car
	vouloir	to want
	vous	(to) you (polite, plural)
le	*voyage*	journey
	voyager	to travel
	vrai(e)	real, true
	vraiment	really
la	*vue*	view
le	*week-end*	weekend
le	*week-end dernier*	last weekend
	y compris	including
les	*yeux (m. pl.)*	eyes
le	*yoga*	yoga

Acknowledgements

The publisher and authors would like to thank the following for permission to use photographs and other copyright material:

Cover: Sua Balac

Artist: Andrew Painter, Gina Stephens, John Batten, Martyn Cain, Matt Ward, Mauro Marchesi, Mo Choy and Phil Garner.

Photos: p14(t), 68: LightField Studios / Shutterstock; **p14(b), 17(d), 27, 36, 38(h), 55(b), 76(t), 148(a):** Monkey Business Images / Shutterstock; **p16(t):** Alpheton / Shutterstock; **p16(d):** M_Videous / Shutterstock; **p17(a), 41:** DC Studio / Shutterstock; **p17(b), 20(l), 108(m):** fizkes / Shutterstock; **p17(c), 38(g):** Victor Velter / Shutterstock; **p17(e), 38(a), 78(a):** Drazen Zigic / Shutterstock; **p17(f):** Odua Images / Shutterstock; **p19:** Mix and Match Studio / Shutterstock; **p20(m):** cheapbooks / Shutterstock; **p20(r):** PinkCoffee Studio / Shutterstock; **p23:** PictureLux / The Hollywood Archive / Alamy Stock Photo; **p24, 122(l):** WarmWorld / Shutterstock; **p28:** Drawlab19 / Shutterstock; **p29(l):** Sergio Arjona / Shutterstock; **p29(m):** VN_KK / Shutterstock; **p29(r):** aire images / Getty; **p31:** Antonio Guillem / Shutterstock; **p32(t), 82(m):** Pixel-Shot / Shutterstock; **p32(b):** Chekyravaa / Shutterstock; **p34(a):** michaeljung / Shutterstock; **p34(b):** Slatan / Shutterstock; **p34(c):** GaudiLab / Shutterstock; **p34(d):** Andrey_Popov / Shutterstock; **p34(e):** WPixz / Shutterstock; **p34(f):** Rawpixel.com / Shutterstock.com; **p37(l):** Philippe Turpin / Getty; **p37(r):** Lucky Business / Shutterstock; **p38(b), 108(b), 126(d):** Africa Studio / Shutterstock; **p38(c):** wavebreakmedia / Shutterstock; **p38(d), 58:** Gorodenkoff / Shutterstock; **p38(e), 60(b), 66(r), 102(b), 108(t), 148(f), 148(g), 156(t):** Krakenimages.com / Shutterstock; **p38(f), 42(mr):** Elnur / Shutterstock; **p38(i):** alinabuphoto / Shutterstock; **p40(l):** Roman Samborskyi / Shutterstock; **p40(m):** Vadym Pastukh / Shutterstock; **p40(r), 87:** Frame Stock Footage / Shutterstock; **p42(t), 43(t):** NStafeeva / Shutterstock; **p42(b):** vic josh / Shutterstock; **p42(ml):** nimito / Shutterstock; **p43(t):** RossHelen / Shutterstock; **p43(b):** YARUNIV Studio / Shutterstock; **p55(t):** George Rudy / Shutterstock; **p60(t):** dwphotos / Shutterstock; **p63(a), 101(t):** Ground Picture / Shutterstock; **p63(b), 126(c):** New Africa / Shutterstock; **p63(c):** Microgen / Shutterstock; **p63(d):** sirtravelalot / Shutterstock; **p63(e):** SeventyFour / Shutterstock; **p63(f), 65, 66(l):** Jacob Lund / Shutterstock; **p66(m):** paulaphoto / Shutterstock; **p67(t):** BearFotos / Shutterstock; **p67(b):** catwalker / Shutterstock; **p69, 86:** PeopleImages.com - Yuri A / Shutterstock; **p70(a):** ohrim / Shutterstock; **p70(b):** SusaImages / Shutterstock; **p70(c):** dotshock / Shutterstock; **p70(d):** YKD / Shutterstock; **p71(b):** Iriskana / Shutterstock; **p73:** Cosmo Condina North America / Alamy Stock Photo; **p74(l):** VH-studio / Shutterstock; **p74(r):** jakkapan / Shutterstock; **p76(b):** Belga News Agency / Alamy Stock Photo; **p78(b):** Yapasphoto StefClement / Shutterstock; **p78(c):** Jerome LABOUYRIE / Shutterstock; **p78(d):** Nina Mikryukova / Shutterstock; **p79:** Grisha Bruev / Shutterstock; **p80(a):** True Touch Lifestyle / Shutterstock; **p80(b):** Master1305 / Shutterstock; **p80(c):** chaoss / Shutterstock; **p80(d):** Lionel Wotton / Alamy Stock Photo; **p80(e):** Olena Yakobchuk / Shutterstock; **p81:** Victoria Will / Associated Press / Alamy Stock Photo; **p82(l):** BrunoRosa / Shutterstock; **p82(r):** Tobias Schenk / Shutterstock; **p83:** PA Images / Alamy Stock Photo; **p84(a):** Craig Mercer / Alamy Stock Photo; **p84(b):** Franklin Sheard Jr / Shutterstock; **p84(c):** Everett Collection Inc / Alamy Stock Photo; **p84(d):** Jo Bouroch / Shutterstock; **p84(e):** NurPhoto SRL / Alamy Stock Photo; **p88(t), 89(t):** Juice Dash / Shutterstock; **p88(m), 88(b), 89(b): Abaca Press / Alamy Stock Photo; p89(inset):** BestOne01 / Shutterstock; **p101(b), 155(t):** Prostock-studio / Shutterstock; **p102(a):** Daisy Daisy / Shutterstock; **p102(c):** FotoLabRitratto / Shutterstock; **p102(d):** asife / Shutterstock; **p104:** YAKOBCHUK VIACHESLAV / Shutterstock; **p106(t):** A_B_C / Shutterstock; **p106(b):** nickfz / Shutterstock; **p109:** Samuel Borges Photography / Shutterstock; **p111:** DariaGa / Shutterstock; **p112(a):** Kolpakova Svetlana / Shutterstock; **p112(b):** andrmoel / Shutterstock; **p112(c):** Gregory Bergman / Alamy Stock Photo; **p112(d):** Pierre-Yves Babelon / Shutterstock; **p114(l):** Mohamed1637 / Shutterstock; **p114(r):** Pack-Shot / Shutterstock; **p115(a):** JeniFoto / Shutterstock; **p115(b):** Gilang Prihardono / Shutterstock; **p115(c):** Fotofermer / Shutterstock; **p115(d):** Bjorn Keith / Shutterstock; **p115(e):** Ina Meer Sommer / Shutterstock; **p115(f):** frosher / Shutterstock; **p116(t):** xbrchx / Shutterstock; **p116(b):** Sklo Studio / Shutterstock; **p118(a):** AYO Production / Shutterstock; **p118(b):** anton havelaar / Alamy Stock Photo; **p118(c):** Lizardflms / Shutterstock; **p118(d):** MJTH / Shutterstock; **p118(e):** SpeedKingz / Shutterstock; **p120:** JoeZ / Shutterstock; **p121:** Pressmaster / Shutterstock; **p122(a):** Kaspars Grinvalds / Shutterstock; **p122(b):** Denis Moskvinov / Shutterstock; **p122(c):** ArtRoms / Shutterstock; **p122(d):** FREEPIK2 / Shutterstock; **p122(e):** ViDI Studio / Shutterstock; **p123:** DavideAngelini / Shutterstock; **p124:** Khorzhevska / Shutterstock; **p126(a):** BAZA Production / Shutterstock; **p126(b):** wk1003mike / Shutterstock; **p126(e):** kizer13 / Shutterstock; **p126(f):** TR STOK / Shutterstock; **p127:** A. Aleksandravicius / Shutterstock; **p128(l):** emerald_media / Shutterstock; **p128(m):** Anna Puzatykh / Shutterstock; **p128(r):** hrui / Shutterstock; **p129(t):** xamnesiacx84 / Shutterstock; **p129(b):** RONEDYA / Shutterstock; **p132(t):** saranya33 / Shutterstock; **p132(b):** RogerMechan / Shutterstock; **p133:** Andrew Mayovskyy / Shutterstock; **p134(t), 135(t):** Romolo Tavani / Shutterstock; **p134(inset-t):** LMPC / Contributor / Getty Images; **p134(inset-m):** Michael Ochs Archives / Stringer / Getty Images; **p134(inset-b):** Miceking / Shutterstock; **p134(b), 135(b):** Alfio Finocchiaro / Shutterstock; **p135(m):** OFC Pictures / Shutterstock; **p147(t):** ColorMaker / Shutterstock; **p147(b):** Larina Marina / Shutterstock; **p148(b):** mentatdgt / Shutterstock; **p148(c):** Andrey Arkusha / Shutterstock; **p148(d):** narikan / Shutterstock; **p148(e):** Cookie Studio / Shutterstock; **p148(bkg):** Maria Zvonkova Shutterstock; **p150:** G-Stock Studio / Shutterstock; **p155(b):** Maridav / Shutterstock; **p156(m):** Cast Of Thousands / Shutterstock; **p156(b):** Blue Planet Studio / Shutterstock; **p157:** Torsten Pursche / Shutterstock; **p158:** adriaticfoto / Shutterstock; **Backgrounds used throughout:** Daria Kubrak / Shutterstock; Gorbash Varvara / Shutterstock; Lenka_X / Shutterstock; Sarunyu_foto / Shutterstock; Slanapotam / Shutterstock; **Icons used throughout:** alpha paperart / Shutterstock; Beatriz Gascon J / Shutterstock; Cosmic_Design / Shutterstock.

Artwork by Q2A Media.

Every effort has been made to contact copyright holders of material reproduced in this book. Any omissions will be rectified in subsequent printings if notice is given to the publisher.